False Prophets

The Firsthand Account of a Husband-Wife Team Working for the FBI and Living in Deepest Cover with the Montana Freemen

by DALE and CONNIE JAKES

with
Clint Richmond

DOVE
BOOKS

ISBN 0-7871-1374-3

Printed in the United States of America

DOVE BOOKS
8955 Beverly Boulevard
Los Angeles, CA 90048
(310) 786-1600

Interior photos courtesy of authors unless otherwise noted

Text design by Carolyn Wendt

Cover design by Rick Penn-Kraus

Cover photography courtesy of Uniphoto Picture Agency

Printed and bound by Royal Book

First Printing: May 1998

10 9 8 7 6 5 4 3 2 1

To all the good people of
Musselshell, Garfield, and Petroleum Counties

✶ ✶ ✶

To God, for being our Lord and for His divine
protection and guidance throughout this entire ordeal

A special thank-you to Clint and Judith,
for believing and supporting us when
the rest of the world didn't

For all the love and support:
Al, Bob, Brian, Bud, Buzz, Carl, Christa, Dalene,
Dick, Edna, Frank, Jean, Jesse, Jim, Judy, Kathy,
Kim, Kim, Lynn, Mary, Nancy, Sandy, Scott,
Steve, Tara, Tim, Tim, Tony, and Valarie

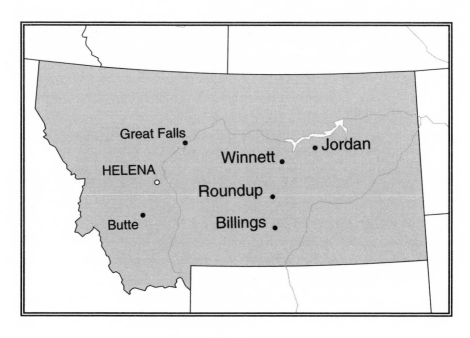

Montana

★ FOREWORD ★

On April 19, 1995, one hundred and sixty-eight men, women, and children were killed, and five hundred others injured, by a bomb blast at the federal building in Oklahoma City, Oklahoma. In numbers of dead and wounded, it was the worst terrorist attack against Americans in history.

Within a few days, a grieving nation was hit by a shock wave of another sort. The Federal Bureau of Investigation announced that these innocent victims—who had become, through television coverage, the neighbors, family, and friends of every American—had been slaughtered, not by some foreign enemy, but by our own.

A new term—*American terrorism*—was added to the world's lexicon.

The public at large should not have been shocked by the discovery of murderous American terrorists among the people. Victims of isolated smaller incidents of this kind have known for years they were present. American blacks, Jews, Hispanics, Asians, homosexuals, women's choice advocates, legal immigrants, and others have been increasingly victimized on an alarmingly regular basis since at least the early 1980s.

Local and federal government employees, including county clerks and attorneys, fish and game wardens, forest rangers, agriculture agents, lawmen, professors, judges, and even postal workers have been intimidated, been threatened with death, and had bogus liens placed on their personal property. Doctors, health workers, and ministers have been stalked in person and by phone, and occasionally killed or wounded.

More ominous, guerrillalike assaults have become commonplace. The Bureau of Alcohol, Tobacco and Firearms reports that
criminal bombings in the United States increased from 1,582 in 1990
to 2,577 in 1995. In 1995, there were 193 people killed and 744 injured
in bombings in the United States. A record number of bombing incidents—3,163—occurred in 1994, when three people were killed and
308 injured. In 1996, the Department of Justice had almost 250
church arsons on its list of investigations. In late 1996, the Federal
Bureau of Investigation was working a score of armed bank robberies in the Midwest that it classified as "political."

But most of the incidents come to attention only after such
high-profile events as the 1996 bombing at Centennial Olympic Park
in Atlanta. Even then, the terrorist attack is pronounced an "isolated
incident."

A few watch groups, such as the Southern Poverty Law Center in
Alabama and the B'nai B'rith, try, like voices crying in the wilderness,
to keep up a drumbeat of warnings about America's new terrorism.

Officially, the United States government seems to be in a state
of denial, perhaps because of its impotence in dealing with what
amounts to widespread lawlessness and even armed insurrection.

Referring to the spate of arson attacks against both white and
black churches, President Clinton almost apologetically said, "We
do not now have evidence of a national conspiracy, but it is clear
that racial hostility is the driving force behind a number of these
incidents."

After the October 1996 arrest of seven terrorists in a tristate
organization calling itself the West Virginia Mountaineer Militia,
U.S. Attorney William Wimoth said, "I don't want it to appear to be
some nationwide conspiracy or anything more grave than the
charging documents show. As far as we could tell, it was localized."
The Mountaineer militiamen allegedly planned to blow up the new
FBI Criminal Justice Information Services complex in West Virginia
and two other federal buildings.

A week earlier the FBI had arrested five white supremacists in
Washington state for a series of bank robberies and bombings,
including a Planned Parenthood clinic and a newspaper that was

carrying on a campaign against hate groups in the Spokane area. The FBI spokesperson was quick to say, "We are examining the possibility that the crimes were carried out by a small cell of right-wing terrorists." Later, a private citizen revealed that he had told the FBI he saw one of the Washington suspects at the Olympics bombing site minutes before the explosion. His tip had been ignored.

In July 1996, a dozen Arizona residents, billing their group as the Viper Militia, were arrested by the FBI; an arsenal of explosives sufficient to level at least eight buildings, along with machine guns, rifles, pistols, and shotguns, was seized. Elaborate plans to attack federal and state centers were revealed on a training videotape confiscated by the law enforcement officials. Authorities were quick to announce this operation an isolated incident. Janet Napolitano, U.S. attorney for Phoenix, Arizona, declared the investigation "basically completed." Earlier, a rail line had been sabotaged and a train had been deliberately derailed in Arizona. Most of the Arizona Viper suspects were allowed to plead guilty to minor charges.

But are these "isolated incidents," as the Justice Department and many members of Congress take such pains to pronounce?

In 1995, one American couple with anything but average capabilities reluctantly went deep under cover for the FBI into the shadow world of the new American terrorism, and emerged a year later with the shocking evidence that a nationwide conspiracy is indeed under way.

On the day the federal building was blown apart in Oklahoma City, Dale and Connie Jakes, who with their two children had fled a clandestine career as little-known "civilian investigators" seven years before, were called back into the dark world of professional informants.

This book is the first-person account of a dangerous year spent in deepest cover by a civilian husband-wife team working for the FBI in the armed strongholds of one of the most militant American terrorist organizations—the Montana Freemen.

The news media's depiction of the so-called patriot militia movement as a clownish Coxey's army of fat old men and hillbillies dressed up in surplus fatigues and puffing through the woods on weekends cannot stand up after the Jakes's revelations. Dale and Connie have firsthand knowledge that the more benign image of the patriot militia is a luxurious myth America cannot afford to believe.

The information surfaced by the Jakeses while under cover with the Freemen was so politically sensitive that the highest levels of federal law enforcement seemed to withdraw from reality. Bureaucratic delays turned what could have been a simple, bloodless arrest of a handful of criminal conspirators into an eighty-one-day, $50 million confrontation.

Time after time, the local FBI agent running the undercover team brought word back from Washington, "They [the militias] can't be that well organized. It's impossible."

The frustrations Dale and Connie Jakes encountered in warning of a larger nationwide conspiracy among the phantom right-wing militias is chillingly reminiscent of another American civilian's unheeded warnings in the late 1930s about the internal dangers posed by the pro-Nazi German American Bund. In 1938 and 1939, a civilian operative, John Roy Carlson, also risked his life to penetrate a radical, right-wing fringe group. Like the Jakes's experience, Carlson's intelligence was also doubted by a right-leaning Congress and a skeptical federal law enforcement establishment. And, like Dale and Connie Jakes with this book, Carlson finally took his information to the public by recounting his experiences in the bestseller *Under Cover*, published in 1943 by E.P. Dutton.

Dale and Connie Jakes's story describes their months in deep cover inside the Montana Freemen group, a criminal organization with connections throughout America. The story is told in the voice of Dale Jakes, but his wife was crucial to the success of the operation.

Before agreeing to help the Jakeses recount their incredible story, I talked to law enforcement officers who had worked with Dale, and later Connie, in numerous drug- and arms-smuggling undercover operations. They gave the Jakeses high praise and credibility for their tireless work as career civilian informants during the late 1970s and most of the 1980s.

The story of their coming out of retirement for one more operation follows actual events as closely as possible. Only a few names, dates, and locales have been changed to protect innocent citizens from being further victimized; or because not-so-innocent sympathizers have yet to be officially charged or indicted for their part in outrageous acts.

Several concerned citizen organizations have been tracking the new threat, primarily issuing reports on the Internet. A handful of journalists, writers, and academicians have published books and articles or televised reports warning of the resurgence of hate-based organizations on a scale not seen in this country since the heyday of the Klans during the civil rights era, or the days of the silver-and-black-shirted pro-Nazi bunds just prior to World War II.

Dale and Connie Jakes's saga as undercover citizen agents for the FBI inside the fortified headquarters of the Freemen offers a chilling eyewitness account of a nationwide criminal network, rooted like hate groups of the past in false and fanatical Christian ideology and misguided patriotic zeal.

Most importantly, Dale and Connie Jakes's story exposes a real and present danger that potentially imperils every community and family in the United States.

False Prophets is the first insider's look at the ugly face of our own homegrown, all-American terrorism.

—CLINT RICHMOND

★ CHAPTER 1 ★

And then shall many be offended, and shall
betray one another, and shall hate one another.
And many false prophets shall rise, and shall
deceive many.

Matthew 24:10–11

A dust plume marked the progress of a vehicle coming fast and straight at me across the Montana prairie. A rooster-tail cloud lingered behind it only a moment before whipping away on the brisk March wind.

Whoever was coming was either hopelessly lost—or looking for me. The dirt road ended on the banks of the Musselshell River two hundred yards below my hilltop perch in the pine thicket where I had been felling timber all morning. There was no one else up here but me and an assortment of hardy critters that for some insane reason chose to winter over in this inhospitable place where the Missouri Breaks begin. Hunting season had passed, so I was the only game in the vicinity.

The speeding vehicle would be forced to slow when it reached the broken terrain along the Musselshell River, where the trail would dip, turn, and roll. I had time to prepare. For what, I wasn't sure.

The Missouri Breaks is a desolate stretch of land that rambles all the way to the big Missouri River fifty miles north of where I was working that day. These badlands cover a good bit of eastern Montana, stretching from north of Billings across the Fort Peck Indian Reservation almost to Saskatchewan, Canada. The Musselshell River is a tributary flowing into the Missouri, which has watered much of the nation's westward growth since its earliest history. I didn't know it then, but another chapter in the history of this land was being written, and I would be a part of it.

As the vehicle came nearer, I dumped out the last dregs of coffee from my thermos cup, watching the steam rise from the still-frozen ground. The biting cold morning had given way to a noontime warmed only a little by bright sun in another cloudless, Montana big-sky day. I left the remaining crust of my sandwich, knowing some small critter would be tickled to find it.

From my backpack I pulled out the powerful, miniature folding binoculars I always kept close at hand to watch nature's creatures for pleasure, humans for self-preservation. As an extra precaution I rummaged deeper in the woods kit—pushing aside a rolled slicker, extra woolen socks, and assorted emergency items—to bring my Glock .45 within easy reach at the top of the pack.

The fast-moving vehicle was close enough now that I could identify it as a tan 4x4 with a topper of red, white, and blue lights. The roar of its powerful engine, gears straining to accommodate the rough terrain, broke the winter-crisp silence of the hills.

I was annoyed by this intrusion. Things were predictable up here in the clear wilderness air—not like the uncontrollable chaos that had sent me and my family running for our lives from a teeming, dirty West Coast megalopolis eight years earlier. We fled with a drug ring's contract of a million dollars on my head—Wanted: Dead or Dead.

A quick focus of the binoculars brought the brown logo—Musselshell County Sheriff—into clear view. I watched the lone occupant skid his powerful patrol car to a halt inches from my own 1990, F-250 Ford 4x4.

Something wasn't right. This deputy's jurisdiction ended way south. My logging job was on the Petroleum and Garfield Counties line. Eastern Montana lawmen knew the boundaries, not to mention being on a first-name basis with every mother's son who lived or roamed in the territory.

A large figure wearing a dark Stetson unfolded from the patrol car. His uniform was tailored tight across his broad shoulders and muscular chest. Khaki epaulets and pockets decorated his dark brown tunic and contrasted sharply with his faded-blue Levi's. He had the trim, lank build of the late 1800s frontier marshals portrayed in the movies, only this was the genuine article.

My binoculars brought his face into focus as his upturned head panned the hills where I sat. I was sure he couldn't see me in the shade of the pine trees and underbrush. But anyone could follow my morning's journey along a path of felled trees and fresh stumps. My wake looked as if an angry giant had marched straight across the hillside, knocking over all the trees in its path.

The man in the sheriff's uniform walked over to my pickup, poked around in the tool-strewn bed, then stopped to scan the hills again. I watched him for a few more minutes, enjoying my advantage of cover—until he returned to nosing around in my things.

He pulled out a sheaf of crumpled, oily paper from under the spare chain saw in my truck bed, unfolded a circular, and studied it.

The man was reading a Wanted poster—one of dozens that offered a reward for the arrest of a sheriff, judge, or attorney of Garfield, Petroleum, or Musselshell County. Deputies were also on the list, along with county clerks, utility managers, game wardens, all sorts of feds—and even a postmistress.

The rewards were offered by the Freemen of Montana.

The man flipped the papers back into the truck bed and yanked on a tarp covering my gas cans.

I bristled at his messing with my property and thought, just for a minute, I should pop a few .45 caps in the air. After all, he was out of his jurisdiction and dangerously close to trespassing.

But instead I stood up and yelled, "Hello down there! Get away from my truck!" My voice echoed, sending a grouse couple I'd hoped to entice for closer study skittering away in fright.

The shout also startled the lawman. As he jerked back from my pickup, his hand dropped to the holstered revolver strapped low on his hip.

"Come on down," he called back. "Let's talk."

I took my time before breaking cover, gathered my pack, and tossed it next to my chain saw. It was too early to call it a day; after checking out this lawman I planned on returning to finish off at least a couple dozen more trees. The logging crew would be up tomorrow with the Cat and skidder to haul off my cuttings. The job was about done; I'd already dropped most of the mature, harvestable pines, and I knew there wasn't another patch waiting to be cut.

Before I moved out of the trees and onto the road, I confirmed the identification of the familiar face I had been watching through the binoculars.

As I walked down the dusty road toward him, the deputy took off his hat to afford me a better look at his face. Despite the aviator-style sunglasses he now wore, I recognized his strong, dimpled chin and wide grin. I knew he was once a city detective and a highly trained professional law enforcement officer. He must have moved to the country by choice.

My unexpected visitor was Deputy Sheriff Orville "Buzz" Jones. I had worked with him a dozen or so years earlier when he served as a detective in Billings. That was at the peak of my career as a deep-cover civilian operative. Buzz and I were part of a multi-agency drug task force made up of local lawmen and feds. The Canadian Mounties were also on board for that one. The target was a large motorcycle gang running cocaine and marijuana between the United States and Canada.

"Well, I'll be . . . D.J. What are you doing out here?" he asked.

"Well, Buzz . . ." I stressed the *zzz*'s. "What are *you* doing out here?" I wasn't buying his surprised act at finding me here in the boonies. "You catch all the bad guys in Musselshell County and come over to help clean out Petroleum?"

The color rising in his cheeks gave him away. He would never make a good liar, blushing so easily.

"I couldn't help notice all those Freemen Wanted posters in your truck bed," he said, changing the subject without explaining why he was out of his territory. "You haven't joined up with that bunch, have you?"

"Not that it's any of your business, but I'm not a joiner."

I had always liked Buzz because he was a class-A cop. He was the kind of guy who made my early days under cover worthwhile.

He was like a solid rock behind your back when trouble came, as it almost always did in one form or another.

Our paths had crossed only once since we'd worked together all those years ago. That was months earlier, when he walked out of the woods in hunting togs, carrying a shotgun and game bag. It was quail season then. He came upon my logging crew working south of Winnett in the foothills of the Big Snowy Mountains. We recognized each other, but neither of us acknowledged it.

"Thanks for not speaking to me last winter," I said. "Wouldn't want to explain to the boys how I knew a *sworn* lawman."

"I figured you wouldn't." His grin broadened. "Still the old desperado, huh? Do they still call you 'Cowboy'?"

"Haven't been called that name in years—been out of the business since '87. Everyone just calls me plain old Dale now, which is fine since that's my name."

"Why'd you get out? You were pretty good. A little too ambitious for my taste, but pretty damn good."

"I'm married now, got kids, settled." I wasn't going to tell him too much, but figured he already knew all he wanted to know about me. This country was big, but there were very few people, almost no strangers, and practically no secrets, at least among the law-abiding folks.

"What ever happened to that good-looking blonde you worked with on that case in Billings? You two were an item during that sting. What was her name . . . Connie? You guys didn't stick around for the bust. Why was that?"

"Yeah, Connie . . . we moved west and got married. Still are. You know people in the CI trade don't hang around for the glory. We take our cash and leave the thunder to you boys in blue. Did you make the busts?"

"Naw, it got complicated after you left." He seemed uncomfortable with my questions. "We got into some interagency flap. The FBI accused the DEA of being too cozy with the perps, there were some young hookers . . . some kind of boating party or something."

"Are those bikers still operating out of Billings, then?"

"No. Definitely not! We compromised by running them all clean out of Montana."

I knew exactly what had happened. It wasn't pretty, and it wasn't fun and games. In fact, Connie had been exposed by either sloppy security or downright complicity by one or more local officers. She had almost been killed. We left Billings on a motorcycle with only the clothes on our backs, and didn't stop until we hit the Pacific Ocean.

We hid out during one of the most miserable but memorable years of our lives. But Buzz obviously didn't know that part of the story.

"Where ya living now?" he asked.

"We're renting a farmhouse out of Winnett. It's the ranch hand's place. Not much, but we're kind of in transition."

"You miss the business?"

I locked stares with his light brown eyes and lied.

"Are you kidding? A man would have to be a fool to stay in that business." I hesitated for a second before finishing. "I promised the better half I'd keep to some line of work where we could see the sunshine."

Buzz Jones just looked at me for a long minute without saying anything.

"Hey, Buzz, why don't you stop with the crap," I said. "What are you doing out here, out of your county, at the end of the last road on the way to nowhere?"

"Okay," he grinned. "Ya got me—I was looking for you."

The deputy admitted he'd gone to the logging company's office and found out where I was working.

"Oh, asking about me at the office. That's real cool. Helpful for me." I was getting irritated.

"Don't worry. I told your office lady that I was looking for you on some outstanding traffic warrants, and for driving without a license. You don't have a valid license to drive in Montana, do you? I checked. At least not in your name."

"Hell, I haven't had a license in my name in fifteen or twenty years. But if it's driver's licenses you want—uh—what state?"

We both laughed, and the tension was broken. But that lasted only a moment, until his grin snapped shut and his jaw stiffened.

"What about those Freemen posters in your truck?" he asked, very serious now.

"One of them is yours," I offered with a grin of my own. "What have you been up to, to warrant such a large bounty? You can have it for a souvenir if you'd like."

"Bullshit," he snapped. My former associate did not find the Freemen a joking matter.

"Buzz, I've been yanking those damn things off trees and fence posts all over this neck of the woods. As far I'm concerned, they're just littering up the landscape."

"You don't know the half of it," he said.

A cold wind began rising somewhere up the river channel, and the deputy went to his car for a parka.

"You want to sit in the car and talk?" he suggested.

"Naw, I gotta get back up there and tip over a few more trees. There's still hours of sunlight yet." I started to walk away.

"Wait, D.J. I need to talk to you about something."

"I didn't think you came out sightseeing—the tourist attractions are west of here, a couple of hundred miles." I waited for him to come to the point of his visit.

"Look, I didn't really believe those posters were yours," Buzz began cautiously. "But do you know anything about the people who are putting out the rewards?"

"Maybe." Many of the jobs I had taken in the past for various federal agencies or drug task forces started with just such a question. "And maybe not."

"I'm not asking for a freebie," Buzz said quickly. "Some people in Billings might be interested in talking to you. I know from the past that you'll level with us."

This was a proposition. Every instinct in my being signaled caution. After a few seconds of thought, I gave a noncommittal answer.

"Okay, for a cup of coffee next time we're in town, I'll give you my expert analysis."

Buzz waited for something more substantial, so I threw him a bone. "I think the ones I've met are some kind of religious wackos," I said.

"Do you hang with them?" he asked.

"I've been bumping into one form or another of tax protester, so-called patriot, or white supremacist ever since we came back to the Northwest. If you want to adopt one of your own, just kick any rock and something slimy will come crawling out. So what?"

"No, I mean, do you know any of the Freemen personally?" My old crime-busting comrade was getting a little impatient.

"Well, there's a skidder operator on this logging crew whose father-in-law is some kind of top dog with the Freemen," I said. "I've also hunted on a ranch at Cat Creek that's owned by one of them. He talks—or should I say, preaches—his gobbledygook all the time. I've taken to reading my Bible since the days we were chasing the bad guys, and for the life of me I can't find their stuff in mine. I think they must have written their own version."

"This isn't about the Bible," Buzz said. "I wish it was that simple."

A dark shadow passed over his face. There were no clouds in the sky. In a flat, matter-of-fact tone the officer recounted a tale that should have been set in 1895, not 1995.

"You know these people are terrorists, don't you?" he asked. "Domestic terrorists!" He almost spit the words, like a curse.

I looked closely at his face to see if he was kidding. He wasn't, and he did not wait for my answer.

His story came tumbling out.

For some time, the Freemen had been running roughshod over northeastern Montana, especially from their strongholds in Garfield, Petroleum, and Musselshell Counties.

The local reign of terror began in earnest in January 1994, when a score of Freemen marched into the Garfield County Courthouse at Jordan and declared they were taking over the county under the provisions of some obscure common law. A guy named Rodney Skurdal and his sidekick, Daniel Petersen, had driven up from Roundup in Musselshell County to empower a local farmer named Richard Clark to serve as the presiding judge of some sort of self-proclaimed common-law court.

The kangaroo court declared every elected official guilty of treason and abolished all the laws of the federal government, the state of Montana, and local ordinances. In a special ruling, Clark, newly appointed Supreme Court Justice of the Freeman Court, also wiped out the mortgage and federal and state tax liens on his family's 960-acre wheat farm.

The Freemen organization had been issuing bogus checks and money orders for more than a year. Since no one did anything much about the fraud, they became more confrontational, circulating Wanted posters for the arrest of county officials, including lawmen, judges, and clerks.

Every failed attempt to control the lawless Freemen resulted in an even more brazen flaunting of local authority. In June 1994, they upped the ante and issued their own forged subpoenas for the arrest of several state senators, appeals court justices, and district judges. Whenever a Freeman was arrested and brought to trial, prospective jurors received threatening letters.

Emboldened by the authorities' seeming inability to stop them, the Freemen expanded their terror tactics to surrounding counties during the rest of 1994. Their rampage came to a peak in an incident that had begun only a week before. Buzz Jones told about his role in a wild scene, which could only be described as deadly anarchy and lethal insurrection.

I had experienced many strange and increasingly violent things in the years before I left the criminal-hunting trade. But this was even more frightening. The average narcotics- or weapons-smuggling ring might be composed largely of scumbags, but most criminal gangs had the decency to operate in the dark. This gang of thugs Buzz described had the audacity to tromp around the small towns of Montana waving their guns and nooses under the noses of the authorities. They operated openly behind the cover of false religion and pseudo-patriotism. This bunch made me mad, not just for their flaunting of the law, but for their arrogance as well.

By the time the deputy had finished talking, the day was about done. The sun had become a hazy ball and cast long, dull shadows from the next ridge to the west. The prairie floor was already dark as he got into his 4x4, backed around, and spun loose rocks on his way out.

The wind picked up, blowing down the river channel from the north. I was well acclimated to the cold, but this wind seemed somehow more chilling. The sudden cold made me tired. I decided to leave the other chain saw and my backpack up on the ridge where I had been cutting.

Nobody was out here on the end of the road except me. And nobody would likely be coming here in the night to bother my things.

I was well on my way down the dirt road before I remembered leaving the Glock in my backpack in the pine thicket. I felt an old familiar dread, almost a warning from some deeply buried memory. I wished I had the pistol on the seat beside me.

★ CHAPTER 2 ★

Only a slice of sun setting behind Big Snowy in the distant southwest was visible by the time I reached a hardtop road and turned toward home. I was greatly troubled by what the deputy had told me.

For weeks I had been hearing rumors and stories of the intimidation of people in several surrounding communities. It now seemed the harassment of local lawmen had become intolerable.

The blatant defiance of law was not the least of the Freemen's bullying. In addition to filing bogus liens against the property of officials, Freemen ignored local taxes, court summonses, or court orders; jumped bail; openly flaunted traffic regulations; and defied arrest warrants. They confiscated their neighbors' cattle straying on open range land, seized hay bales, and wrote worthless checks for goods and services, forcing merchants to accept them. Anyone crossing a member of the Freemen could expect a gun to be pulled, or some other threat of physical retribution.

Montanans are a fairly tolerant bunch by virtue of their mind-your-own-business upbringing. But they have an addendum to their golden rule: Your fist ends where my nose begins. The Freemen were certainly putting their fists in other people's faces.

In response to the Freemen's peculiar crimes, local officials dusted off some rarely used Montana laws. Charges ranging from impersonating an officer to criminal syndicalism were filed against more than a dozen Freemen during late 1994 and early 1995. But outgunned local officials were having little success in making arrests or charges stick.

Less than a month before Deputy Jones's clandestine visit to me, Garfield County Attorney Nick Murnion did succeed in getting a conviction against William Stanton, a sixty-four-year-old rancher and acknowledged Freeman. He was convicted of criminal syndicalism in late February 1995.

Stanton, like many of the rank and file Freemen, had lost his property in the farm bankruptcies of the 1980s, but had held on for a long while. In a desperate effort to save the ranch, Stanton had tried to use some of the Freemen's bogus financial paper to pay off federal farm loans. In exchange, Stanton had joined up and served as a "constable" for the Freemen. One of his duties was the arrest of local officials for trial before an ad hoc Freemen court.

At that time the Freemen claimed a following of 150 members scattered around the small towns, farms, and ranches of eastern Montana.

Buzz Jones estimated their hard-core armed numbers at closer to fifty. But in the three counties most heavily occupied by Freemen, there were only three sheriffs and fewer than half a dozen deputies. Garfield County Sheriff Charles Phipps, for example, had one part-time deputy, and the two of them protected more than 5,000 square miles of territory. Sheriff Bob Busenbark at Winnett in Petroleum County had no deputies.

Headquarters for the Freemen reign of terror was a large log cabin four miles outside of Roundup in Musselshell County. Constructed from nearly foot-thick timbers, with small windows well spaced to give clear views in all directions, the cabin could easily double as a fortress. It was perched atop high terrain and surrounded by twenty acres of heavily forested mountainside. The headquarters was sanctuary for the highest-ranking official in the Freemen's self-proclaimed republic, a tough, former crop-duster pilot named LeRoy Schweitzer.

The property had long since been foreclosed by the Internal Revenue Service for the owner's failure to pay back taxes. The cabin had belonged to Rodney Skurdal, another top Freemen official. Skurdal was an ex-Marine who had once served in a presidential honor guard. Numerous warrants were outstanding against Schweitzer and Skurdal, so they rarely left the cabin. The Freemen had long dared anyone to try to take possession of the fortified property.

The big trouble Deputy Buzz Jones related to me began the day after Stanton was sentenced—March 3, 1995.

Outside Roundup, the deputy spotted a pickup heading into town without license plates. He stopped the truck in town, near the two-story brick courthouse.

Two men Jones quickly recognized as Freemen were told to get out of the pickup. When they did, he saw each was carrying a concealed weapon, and neither could produce a permit. Then he spotted a large cache of weapons in the vehicle. The deputy quickly summoned backup, and Deputy Sheriff Mitchell "Dutch" Van Syckel responded.

The two Freemen, Dale Jacobi and Frank Ellena, were marched across the town's main street to the small jail in the sheriff's office.

A search of the pickup yielded an astounding assortment of weapons and survivalist equipment. The deputies hauled semi-automatic assault rifles, shotguns, and handguns from the truck, along with hundreds of rounds of body-armor-piercing bullets. They found thousands of dollars in gold and silver, and almost $30,000 in U.S. currency. Even stranger paraphernalia was found. They also discovered more than two dozen plastic-strip handcuffs, duct tape, a Sony video camera, a 35mm Minolta camera, and several pieces of radio-communications equipment.

A further search of the two arrested men revealed a more chilling piece of evidence: a hand-drawn map of Jordan. Marked with X's on the map were the offices and homes of both the judge who had sentenced Stanton the day before and the county attorney, Nick Murnion, who had successfully conducted what amounted to the first felony prosecution of a Freeman.

Musselshell County Attorney John Bohlman agreed with the arresting officers that something other than routine motor vehicle and arms violations was involved, and began searching law books for his options. Meanwhile, the Musselshell officers warned their neighbors in Garfield County to be alert for some sort of assault on officials who had been involved in the Stanton case. Reserve deputies were named from the citizenry to guard the district judge, Roy C. Rodeghiero, and County Attorney Murnion.

Before the Musselshell attorney could decide on charges against the two arrested Freemen, three burly men stomped into the tiny jail office demanding that all the contraband—now spread out over a table—be returned, and the arrested men released immediately. All three men wore side arms partially concealed beneath bulky coats.

As a startled Deputy Van Syckel tried to reason with them, Deputy Jones slipped into the next office. He returned with a 12-gauge riot gun leveled on the three, and they were arrested, too. With five Freemen now locked up, Deputy Jones stepped outside the building to see what else might be confronting the beleaguered town of Roundup.

Two men were sitting in a parked vehicle talking over two-way radios with unseen Freemen somewhere in the vicinity. At that point the deputy had no idea how many more armed men were in or around the small town, or what their intentions might be.

Deputy Jones walked up to one of the cars and saw guns inside. He demanded the men get out, but they locked the car doors. Jones reacted quickly, smashed a window on the passenger side, and ordered the men out at gunpoint.

One of the people in the car, a distinguished-looking older man with a well-groomed silver beard, protested he was not a Freeman, even though he was in the company of those arrested. He was later identified as John Trochmann, the founder of the huge Militia of Montana. Trochmann's organization was headquartered at Noxon, Montana, on the other side of the Rocky Mountains in the western part of the state.

This discovery further unnerved local officials, who were already outgunned better than ten to one by Freemen in the area. Jones and other local lawmen reckoned that if the powerful Montana militia was teaming up with the Freemen in some unholy alliance, the game of the past year was over—good guys 6, bad guys 600.

Within hours, the local county attorney had to turn the seven arrested men loose. Only a couple of weapons charges could be made to stick. Bonds were set releasing Jacobi and Ellena, the two men charged with the minor offenses. Once more the Freemen boldly walked away after a brazen daylong incident that terrorized the town.

In broad daylight heavily armed outlaws had challenged the law, sent the citizens scurrying for the shelter of their homes and businesses, and virtually terrorized the eighteen hundred citizens of the small American city of Roundup, Montana.

This sort of anarchy could not happen in the USA in 1995. Yet it had—only a week before, and just forty-five miles from my home and family. I felt I had been time-warped back to Montana's lawless frontier days. The place I'd come to in an effort to escape big-city crime, to try to make a normal life for my family, was being taken over by something every bit as bad as what I'd left behind.

It was this incredible tale that crowded out every other thought in my mind as I drove into the gathering dark toward home and my family that night.

★ ★ ★

The only thing between eastern Montana and the North Pole is a barbed wire fence somewhere up around Lodgepole. And rumor has it that the fence blew down last winter and nobody put it back up. Every winter the towns between Winnett, Montana, and Duluth, Minnesota, feud over whose temperature is the coldest in America.

By the time I drove up to the porch of our rented ranch house, an arctic wind was promising us a shot at breaking the record.

But the two-bedroom frame house was toasty warm, and Connie had a hot beef roast waiting. She had loved being mother and wife these past years since our escape to Montana. I have to admit being a dad and regular breadwinner had its rewarding moments, too.

"Wash up and come on to dinner," Connie called from the eating area that also served as the kitchen, laundry, and daytime classroom where we home-schooled our two young children.

"Roast and all the fixin's," I said. "What's the occasion?"

Connie deftly dodged the sweep of my hand aimed at her behind without spilling a drop of the brown gravy she was carrying toward the table.

"No special occasion. We'll talk after dinner."

There was that faint edge to her voice I had come to recognize as indicating a minor problem.

The conversation at dinner that night was subdued. The north wind made more noise outside the old frame farmhouse than we made at the table. The four of us were an unusually close-knit family, a companionship imposed by the baggage of a past secret life we all carried with us. The children, young as they were, could sense the tension.

When they were quickly tucked in their beds and the dishes done, Connie broke the silence with a forced cheerful question. "Who goes first? Your bad news or mine?"

"Bad news? What bad news?" I challenged her intuitive reading of my telltale mood.

"Okay, I'll go first," she said. "Mike Taylor came by today and said we have to move. He needs the house for his new foreman's family."

"That's not bad news," I lied, rushing my own bad news out quickly. "We're running out of timber on this cut, and there's not another job in sight right now. I guess I'm about to get laid off."

"Oh?" The little worry lines appeared for an instant at the corners of her eyes.

"So you see, we won't be needing this house anyway. I doubt if there's another job within a day's drive of Winnett." I tried to put a cheerful spin on losing my job. Connie had brought the kids over from Kalispell in far northwestern Montana only four months earlier, because it looked like this logging job was going to last a long time.

"What do you think we're going to do next?" she asked. "Maybe we should move down to Billings." Her grandmother and brother still lived in her old hometown.

"Maybe we could. I heard today that the bad guys from our last job there have been run out of the country," I said, introducing in a casual way my conversation with the deputy earlier that day.

My little verbal ploy didn't work. As I always said, Connie was a better intelligence resource than anyone still in the trade. She didn't miss a thing.

"So who told you that? The chipmunks out where you're logging?"

"Naw, I ran into Buzz Jones. You remember Buzz. He was a detective on one of the drug task forces we contracted with out of Billings."

"So a Billings detective just happened to be strolling around in the woods two hours from town, ran into you, and told you a motorcycle gang that was hunting us from fifteen years ago had left town."

"Of course not. He's a deputy down at Musselshell County now."

The worry lines had turned to a dark scowl.

"They're not asking you to go back under, are they? How did they find you in the first place? You're not considering it, are you?"

"Well, some yeses and some nos. Which question do you want me to answer first?"

"Dale, why would you even consider going back under cover?" She pressed for an answer.

Instead of responding directly, I told her the details of the Freemen outrages that had been related to me that day by Buzz.

He had explained that so far the local authorities had not been able to make anything very serious stick to the Freemen leaders. He also said that despite repeated pleas, the FBI had not moved on federal fraud indictments it held against the leadership.

Now the deputy believed something far more serious—even deadly—was about to happen.

"The feds have Weaver fever," I told Connie. "Buzz says they have the charges, but after Ruby Ridge and Waco they're afraid to muck up their public image again with another shootout."

Weaver fever is the Northwesterners' politically correct description for the bureaucratic inertia ascribed to federal agents when they fail to take action against the fanatical hate groups rampaging over much of the Pacific Northwest and upper Midwest.

The August 1992 siege of the Ruby Ridge, Idaho, cabin of tax protester Randy Weaver ended in the deaths of U.S. Deputy Marshal William Degan, Weaver's wife, Vicki, and their fourteen-year-old son Samuel—all dead from gunshots.

Weaver's attorney, Gerry Spence, forced the government to settle $3.1 million on the Weaver family. Perhaps more damaging from the FBI's point of view than the monetary judgment, which was paid by the taxpayers, was the criticism leveled against the federal law enforcement agencies by the Senate Subcommittee on Terrorism, Technology and Government Information. The subcommittee had concluded that "a chain of mistakes led to three needless deaths."

And in the aftermath of Ruby Ridge and the Branch Davidian siege at Waco, senior officials from both bureaus faced various punishments from demotions to charges of obstruction of justice.

For years after those incidents, local community leaders throughout the Northwest, as well as federal workers on the vast public lands in the area, complained that the government's law enforcement agencies were paralyzed to enforce any laws.

And there were a good number of citizens, not just members of militias, who believed the law enforcement agencies had crossed the line of duty in the Weaver and Waco cases.

So it was in this Catch-22 environment of "damned if you do, damned if you don't" that local officials like Buzz Jones were trying to deal with the rapidly growing armed militia menace.

Connie listened intently, but I saw from the stubborn set of her jaw that the predicament the local lawmen faced was not melting her resolve to remain above the fray.

"So what does any of this have to do with us?" She had a way of cutting through the rind to the core of the matter. "You didn't agree to get involved, did you?"

"No, I just listened."

"I think our bigger question is where are we going to live and what are we going to do for a living."

Of course, she was right. But there was also a living to be made as an undercover operative. We needed a job now and, except for my promise to stay out of this line of work, I was sorely tempted.

"Dale, you know I hate that life," Connie said. She looked genuinely distressed, on the verge of tears. "The kids are older now. What about them?"

Finally, I assured her I was not going back under cover, and that all the deputy had said was, "It sure would be good to have someone like you inside that operation."

I understood her unwillingness to go under cover again. We had been twice burned by federal agencies on jobs we had worked together—twice too often.

During the next week I could hardly sleep for thinking about the conversation with the deputy. As I lay awake nights, the betrayals, the danger, the disappointments of my years in undercover operations were whispered in the moans of the north wind tearing at the old frame house that sheltered my family.

There was a sound of fury in those late winter winds, and I knew it was calling to me.

CHAPTER 3

I guess, no matter how uncertain the paydays or how dangerous the jobs, I probably would have stayed in the undercover business for the rest of my life.

I loved the adventure, the thrill of putting the pieces together, working my way inside a gang to the rotten core, and then seeing an evil operation destroyed. From the late 1970s, when a couple of government men recruited me from a drifting, meaningless existence that probably would have made a bad guy out of me too, it had been my war. I was a soldier, on the right side of the law. I moved from job to job, always in deep cover on dozens of large and small assignments for the Drug Enforcement Agency (DEA), the Bureau of Alcohol, Tobacco and Firearms (ATF), the FBI, U.S. military criminal intelligence units, state crime task forces, and even a gig or two for the Canadian Mounties.

My targets were every sort of criminal organization—mostly drug-related—but also involving arms smuggling, counterfeit name-brand merchandise, and stolen cars and heavy equipment.

In the early years it was almost a game. In most cases I didn't even have anything personal against the bad guys. They were just breaking the law to make a living. Back then most of the druggers weren't that mean—oh, they would have pulled my plug if they'd suspected I was a narc—but they were not nearly as deadly as the ones to follow in the 1980s.

Early on, the good guys, for the most part, were truly good guys. A handshake sealed a deal. The FBI, DEA agents, local narcs, and the Mounties were dedicated. When civilians like myself went under cover for any of the agencies, it was with the assurance that we could count on our backs being covered. When the operation was finished, we could count on the payday. One FBI agent even ordered up a triple bonus for one of the jobs I successfully completed for the Bureau.

But all that changed in the mid-1980s; and looking back, I can trace the change to one word—*crack*.

Not very long after crack cocaine began pouring onto the streets of cities in Southern California, it became hard to tell the good guys from the bad guys. It seemed that this new form of an old drug made everybody crazy, cops and robbers alike.

When I was a boy growing up in the wilderness of the Cascades in Oregon, my father and mother taught me and my sisters—and the dozen or so waifs who wandered in and out of my family's care in our rural home over the years—some simple rules about right and wrong.

We didn't pay a lot of attention to what might or might not be the law. If a deed hurt another person or damaged or took away someone's property, it was wrong. If it didn't, it shouldn't be against the law. Thus, there could be no such thing as a victimless crime.

My first introduction to illegal narcotics fell into the category of victimless crime. When I was eleven or so, a friend and I bicycled down to a mill pond to gather the leaves of some tall bushes that grew wild on its banks. We plucked the leaves, dried them on an abandoned railroad track, stuffed the crushed leaves into a pipe, and smoked it.

All we knew was that my grandpa had said some people smoked the damned stuff to get high. He preferred his liquor and suggested that smoking the weed was stupid, but not necessarily illegal. The stuff was marijuana, a plant imported by Chinese railroad laborers into the western United States in the 1800s.

My second notable encounter with marijuana came when I was about seventeen. I had dropped out of high school the year before because I could make as much money working on construction crews as most of the adults I knew. My father always augmented a meager farm income by working as a heavy-equipment operator. I was big and very strong for my age, so I learned to operate every piece of road-building and logging equipment there was before I was old enough to get a license to drive a car.

I also learned to handle construction explosives and worked as a powder monkey for blasters before most city kids get to light their first firecracker. On the farm I even learned to make my own explosives from fertilizer nitrates and made small charges to blast fence-post holes in the rocky soil of the Cascades.

My dad had said if I wasn't going to finish high school, he was going to emancipate me, and he got the necessary papers to cut me loose a few days after my sixteenth birthday. By then I had a pocketful of cash and wanted to see the world.

A friend and I decided to go to South America after my sixteenth birthday, and we headed out in an old panel truck. We got almost to Guatemala before the engine block cracked. We'd been trying to replace the leaking oil with cooking oil. The friend—I think his name was Roy—was bad news on the whole trip, drinking a lot and constantly getting us into jams.

So I left him somewhere down in southern Mexico and started hitching north. I worked my way back toward the States, taking odd jobs for food and lodging. I kept what cash I had left hidden in my boot. Anyone suspecting a lone gringo kid had cash would have relieved him of it, along with his head.

Outside Durango, in northern Mexico, I met two brothers whose family had a ranch, and they took me in for a few weeks' work. Part of the job was cutting and stacking marijuana, most of it to be sold locally, but some to be shipped north. The illegal crop was treated just like any other cash crop and nobody talked about whether it was legal or not.

After several weeks one of the brothers suggested I could do a big favor to the family and make myself some money at the same time. He said I should hitch back to Oregon, get a truckload of refrigerators and Levi's jeans, which were in great demand in Mexico, and come back down to trade it for a load of grass. He would supply the front money.

It sounded like a good idea to me at the time, so I went north and did just that. I drove a beat-up old bobtail truck down to

Durango with the fridges and jeans, and unloaded the trade goods. Then I filled the back of the truck to the roof with weed and drove it back to Medford, Oregon.

I had no idea what to do with a truckload of grass, so I rented a cabin in the woods on the edge of town and went around telling people at bars that I had a load of marijuana. A couple of days later two very large, very ugly guys came to the cabin and asked me to show them the load in the back of the truck. When I did they pulled out the biggest pistols I've ever seen.

The men announced they were buying my whole load, including the truck, for $8,000. It was an offer I could not refuse: The "take it or leave it" meant, "take the cash and live to enjoy it, or die." I took the offer, even though I barely broke even, and decided it would be my last venture into crime. I was just turning seventeen and had already been a mule for Mexican marijuana. I honestly did not realize that I was a teenage felon at that moment. One of my granddads, Red Carpenter, had been an infamous if somewhat petty outlaw, pulling all sorts of stunts around Southerland, Oregon. But my family were mostly hardworking, fistfighting woodsmen who had no time for criminals. I never even considered a life of crime as an option; in fact, my teenage dream was to become a Marine.

At eighteen, I fit the bill on the Marine recruiting posters. I was proud, strong as an ox, and patriotic as hell. The Marine recruiter, after making me get my high school equivalency diploma, accepted me as one of their "few good men." I was on my way to realizing my dream of a career as a member of the elite Marine Force Recon.

While waiting to report for duty, I partied with friends. One of our favorite pastimes had always been mountain motorcycle racing, and I was reputed to be the hottest daredevil in the Oregon mountains. Just days before reporting to the Marine recruiting office I was racing a hot bike down a mountain road when I missed a curve at over 100 mph, soared hundreds of feet into the air, and crashed, shoulder first, into a giant juniper tree.

My body was smashed beyond what local doctors thought could be repaired. The docs in a small-town clinic took one look and shot me full of dope to give me some relief from pain for the short time they thought I had left to live.

My dad told the medics their diagnosis of doom was unacceptable, and arranged for a flight-for-life helicopter to take me to a larger hospital. Thanks to God, my folks, and a body toughened by a life of ranching, construction work, and logging, I did not die from that accident. Days of surgery were followed by months of rehabilitation. I left the hospital a badly crippled but determined eighteen-year-old and went immediately back to the Marine recruiter.

The sympathetic Marine gunney took one look at me and announced there was no chance.

"We ain't taking one-armed Marines, son," the old gunney said. "I'm sorry, but there's no way, no matter how tough you might be."

After months on pain-relieving narcotics, I was lost and gradually becoming hooked. But I was determined to overcome the loss of my arm, and began a brutal body-building program. Raised working with chain saws and heavy equipment, trained as a powder monkey blasting tree stumps for mountain roads, I shifted all my strength to my one arm and built up my upper torso. But I also began heavy use of street drugs when my legitimate prescriptions were canceled. For a year I drifted between college courses, logging, and construction jobs. I perfected skills in handling all manner of heavy equipment. If anyone doubted my ability to drive big Cats or log skidders, I'd jump on the seat and roar off for a demonstration.

To compensate for my missing arm I even customized a chain saw, which is as essential to most of the trades I knew as paper is to a bureaucrat. I rigged a padded shoulder strap and connected the handlebar of the saw to the strap with a metal loop. This held the weight of the saw while in use. For safety purposes, I created a weak link between the shoulder strap and the metal loop, which enabled me to push back and break away from the saw if it jammed in a tree.

With this special rig I could outcut most loggers I met.

Still, my income was sporadic, and I started running with petty criminals on the fringes of the law, mostly motorcycle gangs. I hung with these bums to be close to a supply of pain-killing drugs, but I would not deal drugs myself.

It was in that tormented period of my life that I met a gang selling LSD to schoolchildren. No matter what I thought about using illicit drugs for my own phantom pain in the lost arm, I was incensed by seeing these guys selling stuff to kids. I saw some bad trips and I got mad. This was not a victimless crime.

I approached a local police narc with an offer to help put an end to the practice. There was a tacit agreement for me to work under cover, and I went along on a drug buy. When I returned with a small quantity of speed, the police busted the guy making the haul and took me as an accomplice for being in the car. Charges were filed despite my protest that I was working for the same police department. Since I had never actually formalized a deal, my earlier contact denied that I was working for him. When I confronted him, he told me that nothing much would happen to me. But the judge didn't see it that way and refused to believe my story. I was found guilty of felony drug-running and sentenced to a California prison-holding center at Vacaville. I languished there three months before being released.

After more drifting from job to job, I landed in Portland, Oregon, where I still gravitated to the rough edge of the underworld. A series of events unfolded that I've never felt free to discuss, even with Connie.

One night, as I walked home through a seedy neighborhood, two well-dressed men approached, flashed badges, ushered me into a car, and drove to a warehouse. The men, without ever identifying their agency, told me they had a new career in mind for me.

I still don't know who they worked for, but from the kind of work they wanted me to do, I was sure they were the good guys. I know why they selected me, but all I can really say is it had to do with some two-legged "vermin" eradication work I had done in a slum neighborhood where I lived at the time.

I seized the opportunity. I was young, and I still had this dream of serving my country.

The next thing I knew, I was hustled onto a private plane, flown to a warm and sunny climate somewhere in the United States, and put through a rigorous three-month training program. I learned a lot about nonconventional small arms and sophisticated explosives. I was trained in electronic devices I didn't even know existed. The food was great, the work was hard, and while I did not fulfill my dream of becoming a Marine, I came away prepared to be at least a good urban commando.

When I returned to Oregon, the assignments started coming in by phone or anonymous letter. Each little job I finished prompted cash payments. No fees were ever set, but the payoffs and expenses were generous. Each assignment was different, and there were no rules to follow. In fact, in most cases I was told to do specific things that would not have stood the light of courtrooms, but most of the work was simply intelligence-gathering. Other lawmen were using information I furnished to make the busts. Only occasionally was I required to testify.

My job was to slip into various drug operations, gun-smuggling rings, or other types of criminal endeavors, acquire the intelligence the contractors wanted, and get out. After each operation I moved to another city and affixed myself to another criminal element.

This was a good life for a single guy—thrills, adventure, good money, and the closest thing a one-armed warrior could find to fighting for God and country.

★ ★ ★

During those years I married a college coed I met while involved in a campus dope-ring investigation. It was a mistake for both of us from the very beginning, but we had a baby daughter anyway.

Life under cover is not for just anybody. One of the biggest hazards of the trade, next to getting discovered, of course, is living intimately close to the edge of the law, with drugs and other temptations constantly and literally being shoved under your nose.

A deep-cover operative has to appear to be a willing participant on the wild side. Drugs are always available and the temptations are sometimes overwhelming. My first wife, like myself, found some of these temptations too great.

While the marriage was coming unglued in Portland, I met Connie. She was a neighbor in the apartment where my on-again, off-again marriage was housed, and she had a daughter the same age as mine. We frequently met and talked about trivial things as we watched our little girls in the apartment play area or nearby parks.

I was posing as a shipyard equipment operator, but was actually under cover for a federal agency looking for a huge haul of heroin supposedly welded into the hull of a dry-docked freighter.

My neck was broken when a steel framework slid off a hoist, but that's a story for another time.

All Connie knew was that her neighbor was an injured dockworker and needed a friend. During my long recovery she often visited. Connie was married. Unbeknownst to her, some of her husband's associates were targets of my undercover operation.

After I recovered from the broken neck, I moved on to other assignments. Connie and her husband soon divorced, and she moved back to her family home in Billings, Montana, to work on a college degree in accounting.

Fate would bring us together again in Montana a few years later.

I was working a job for a combined Canadian-U.S. federal-state drug task force investigating a transborder drug ring operating throughout Washington state, Montana, and Canada.

Connie had returned home from Oregon to find a beloved younger brother involved in the lowest levels of the drug trade. Determined to save her brother, she volunteered to help local police bust a hometown gang she believed to be dragging her brother into crime. She had uncles who also dabbled in petty crime and vice in the Billings underworld and was herself well aware of the drug dealings in the area. She had experimented with drugs as a rebellious teenager and was not going to allow her immature young brother to be sucked into the drug world.

After not seeing Connie for a couple of years, I was thrown together with her on this new assignment for days at a time. She was working with the Billings cops and FBI trying to put the drug ring that was recruiting her younger brother out of business. I was under cover, working between Canada and Billings. Soon the two operations were combined. But I didn't know her role, and she did not know mine. For a time we each suspected the other might even be one of the bad guys.

After several weeks we were seriously, romantically involved. Then one day we both showed up for a meeting with a Canadian Mountie we each knew to be an undercover agent. The Mountie was chauffeuring us on a short trip out of Billings when it became clear to us that we were both actually working for the government.

But Connie was still surprised when I confessed that I had been a paid freelancer for years, even back when we'd known each other in Portland.

From that day forward we worked the case together, as a couple and as a team.

Just before the international gang was busted by U.S. and Canadian officials, we were at a meeting in a Montana bar with a group of drug dealers. I was wearing a body wire. After the suspects left, I shouted above the bar's loud jukebox, "Will you marry me?"

A thug came back into the bar, and Connie fell silent.

After he left, she answered, also in a voice louder than the music, "Yes, I'll marry you!"

A short while later we returned to the motel room where the DEA, FBI, local narcs, and Canadian Mounties were assembled for a debriefing. When we walked into the hotel room, corks popped and cheers went up. The team of agents had heard every word of the proposal over my wire—and recorded it.

The crime-hardened agents rushed out to get the makings for a celebration of the engagement. One of the grizzled DEA agents later said the greatest suspense on that whole case had been the necessary delay between my proposal, the business with the thug, and Connie's acceptance.

Connie and I, as an undercover team, became part of a tiny group of men and women—freelancers—who, unknown to the public, do a lot of the dirty work of intelligence-gathering for America's law enforcement agencies. Cops call us CIs: civilian intelligence or informants. CIs are a far cry from the turned snitch, called "rollovers," who inform on their associates rather than go to prison themselves.

It's a business for us—usually well paid, but with no fringe benefits. If we live long enough for retirement, we're on our own.

We're rarely called in unless the work is especially dirty and might require skirting some of the laws of evidentiary discovery. I've been told repeatedly by regular officers or agents who work the cases with professional CIs that they don't really like calling us in. Most CIs are so dedicated that they work night and day without time off. They don't hesitate to rouse their lawful contacts from their sleep or call them on their days off or vacation. When you are deep under cover, living the life of a mobster yourself, there is no such thing as a day off. Take a break and you're likely to get killed.

Soon after Connie and I teamed up, things in the undercover trade began deteriorating. I believe the invasion of the Colombian drug cartel, the rampant spread of crack cocaine, and replacement of small local gangs by networks of killer-dealers were to blame.

Connie began to really hate the life—I mean, really hate it. In one case we'd fled after her cover was blown and had to hide out in a cold-water, roach-infested flat in a West Coast city for several months. One of our babies was conceived during that miserable period of time.

It got so bad for freelance undercover operatives that the handful of American and foreign men and women working jobs for the various U.S. agencies formed a loose-knit union to protect ourselves from our bosses. The odd network, with seventy to a hundred freelance operatives, calls itself Nemesis. The defense system we set up to protect ourselves against grievances is quite unique, if slightly illegal. It involves keeping detailed records, hidden tapes, and other material that a lot of high-ranking officials would not like to have aired in public.

I continued to take jobs, but after the first baby came, Connie wanted to stop. The agencies began to demand more dangerous work of us.

Connie worried more and became disgusted, not only with the life, but also with the agency men. Promises for bonuses and percentages of busts began to be broken. Security and confidentiality—the very lifeline of the deep-cover freelance agent—became lax. We fought more and more over each job, but we stayed under, deep and dangerous. I was away on assignments for days, even weeks at a time. Connie was justifiably angry about my work. I kept doctor's hours without the pay and perks.

"I'm sick of sleeping with a Mossberg for a bed partner," she once warned me. Connie was referring to the short-barrel 12-gauge Mossberg Model 500 Persuader police shotgun we have kept under the bed for most of our married life.

Then came the case that proved to be the last straw. Even I couldn't argue with my wife's pleas to get out after this one. By then we had a toddler and a new baby in diapers. It was in the late 1980s in a California city that must remain unnamed for our own safety.

Four local and federal agencies were running a narcotics and cross-border drug and stolen-equipment operation. Connie and I set up a front business to launder money—bundles of millions were involved. When agents closed in for the bust, one large bundle of money simply vanished in the confusion. I never knew what happened to the money—whether it was taken by a good guy or a bad guy.

Some time later, one of the kingpins who had escaped the bust showed up at our supposedly safe apartment. Connie was alone with the babies. The drug lord left hinting that bad things happen to narcs. We knew someone in one of the four agencies had compromised us. We didn't wait to ask who or why. When Connie reached me by phone I told her to meet me at a shopping mall with the children. We bought suitcases, clothes, and plane tickets. We left everything we owned in that apartment, but kept the most important things—our lives and the lives of our children.

That's when we disappeared into the wilds of northwestern Montana, vowing never to go under cover for any government agency again.

★ CHAPTER 4 ★

We arrived in Montana in the middle of a beautiful summer in 1988. Mr. and Mrs. Dale Jakes and their two young children were just another small family, ostensibly on the move to escape the urban rat race by starting a new life in the Rocky Mountain country.

Our new friends and neighbors had no idea just how ratty our race had been, or that we had a million-dollar drug-gang bounty on our heads.

After looking over the state, we settled in Columbia Falls, a few miles from the Idaho border and just south of Canada. We chose it because it was beautiful, and because it was just about as far away from our previous life as we could get and still remain in the United States.

I was starting over at the age of thirty-seven. Connie was just turning thirty.

From that summer through the first winter, we managed a resort, with every intention of trying to buy it from its retiring owners. We would have closed the purchase but the owners' heirs decided to take it back.

After the resort deal fell through, I took odd jobs around logging operations until the crime task force I had worked with in California finally paid off for that last job. We were owed a six-figure payday, but we settled for $70,000 and said good-bye and good riddance to the bureaucrats who had wheedled us out of our promised pay.

I assembled some earth-moving equipment to set up our own small landscaping and logging company. I tinkered with inventions, bought and sold everything from cars to household appliances, and repaired lawn mowers and chain saws for extra cash.

When we started our own business, I lined up jobs at remote cabin-building sites, leading me to meet some strange and reclusive people.

It was working in these Rocky Mountain woods that I first encountered bearded, disheartened young men living solitary lives. These were the Vietnam veterans locally called "bush vets"—sad, suspicious wrecks of men who were more tragic than threatening. They just wanted to be left alone. They were dropouts from life. These broken vets had disappeared by the hundreds in the 1970s into the wilderness of the Pacific Northwest.

Most of these men were physically sound, some with lost limbs. But their scars were always just beneath the first layers of skin. One of the hermit soldiers I befriended finally loosened up to tell some of his harrowing tales. His stories, usually related over a few beers, would always end with this grown man reduced to a blubbering, broken mass of humanity. He would put his arms around me and squeeze so tight I thought my ribs would crack.

The true stories of betrayal by the U.S. government and rejection by the very American people they had fought for were far more horrific than my secret complaints. These bush vets, with all their tragic body-bag tales and legitimate grievances against their country, were still loyal Americans.

But as I worked deeper into the mountain woods, I began to encounter other reclusive men—for the most part much more suspicious and definitely hostile.

In most of the small towns in the Northwest where there have been large migrations of disillusioned city dwellers, the people are beginning to take control, working in their communities, working with local law enforcement and city government. But for some it is too late—things have been very hard for them. Their jobs have disappeared with the downsizing of corporate America, or they've lost their farms, or they've been wiped out by the debts from small-business failures. Their anger and frustration have caused them to take the law into their own hands. This decay of the American dream has given rise to the militias more than any ideological or religious revelations. Rightly or wrongly, many of the rank and file militiamen I've met believe their government is no longer effective—or worse, has become the enemy.

At this stage in their lives they are easy prey to a few fanatical, even criminal, leaders who are waiting to recruit them. These leaders, calling themselves prophets or patriots, have used this frustration to misguide their followers and make dupes of some otherwise average, middle-class American families.

In the woods of Montana around Columbia Falls, Whitefish, and Kalispell, I got to know a lot of them. These men, often with wives and children, were always armed and angry. They called themselves patriots of various stripes, and preached a fanatical, white-supremacist religion of intolerance and hatred for America's government. Connie and I had not encountered such hate before, even in the meanest motorcycle and drug gangs.

By 1990, these so-called Christian patriots, most of whom were white supremacists and tax protesters, were everywhere in the Northwestern mountain communities, trying to take over the institutions of the small towns—even in the church. One faction, headed by a fire-and-brimstone minister, turned the little church we had joined and regularly attended into a divided, intolerant congregation. The flagrant misquoting of Scriptures to justify violence against minorities and a democratic government was shocking to us. We later found this was the theology and ideology of the Christian Identity movement, currently being spewed by the Church of Jesus Christ Christian, the front organization for the Aryan Nations stronghold at Hayden Lake, Idaho.

Connie and I had determined when we left the undercover trade to build a new family life on faith, and these hate messages disturbed us greatly. They caused us to go into the study of our Bibles with more intensity than we normally would have done. We did not know it at the time, but these sermons and our own studies in response to them would serve as a necessary part of our training for challenges we would face in the not-so-distant future.

We had pretty much taken our patriotism and citizenship for granted until our exposure to the militants. I had always been a gung-ho Marine at heart, even though I didn't make it into the

Corps, and Connie and I always considered our undercover work for our government to be a thing of duty.

When the self-described patriots I encountered on my jobs found out that I was an explosives expert and good with all kinds of firearms, my stock went up. I began to receive invitations to participate in various militia meetings.

I had never heard of any militia, except the minutemen from Colonial times I had studied in my American history courses. I attended some of the meetings of these militiamen, but these guys didn't sound much like American patriots to me. In fact, they sounded like the opposite—like a bunch of fanatics from some Middle East country, substituting the name of Jesus for Allah. They didn't even believe in voting, just blowing away the government. No solutions, just destroy it and all the people of color they despised.

What I did see that concerned me was that these people had the capability of doing what they threatened. I had never seen any group of lawmen as well armed as the militiamen. They had state of the art military-class weaponry. Many of their semiautomatic rifles had been illegally converted to fully automatic weapons.

But Connie and I minded our own business. We were so happy to be breathing the free air of normal citizenship that, at first, we thought very little about these people.

I had frequent invitations to meetings all over the Montana-Idaho border area, and because I wanted to fit in to the community, I attended a number of them. Women weren't allowed—this was guy stuff—so Connie never went with me. She did get to know some of the wives and got a big dose of the propaganda the more militant among them were spouting.

In the small towns of the Northwest the members of the newly formed militias paraded around with their guns and combat fatigues, but nobody seemed to care. They claimed they were organizing to defend their families against some preposterous invasion by United Nations troops or invaders in black helicopters.

Connie and I often laughed about this. Of all the places in the world that anyone would not care to invade, it was northwest Montana. There was nothing here of strategic value that I could see, just a lot of trees and pretty scenery. The only invasion that I saw likely to occur here were city folks coming out for a vacation and deciding to stay. Sometimes the area seemed fairly overrun by this dangerous group of gawkers.

However, working far out in the woods, I had to take notice of the militias, if for no other reason than because they used live rounds on some of their training exercises. I thought about the irony of getting mowed down by automatic weapons out in the peaceful woods of Montana after all the years I'd spent toe-to-toe with criminals and drug dealers.

I frequently came upon large numbers of heavily armed men wearing full combat gear and obviously involved in professionally led assault training. I would often watch for hours from a distance as they drilled. Once, just for the fun of it, I stalked a militia combat team for an entire three-day weekend. They clearly were not training for defensive operations. They practiced storming imaginary positions, and simulated blowing things up and cutting communications lines.

But during our months in Columbia Falls, I still stayed on the good side of these people. Throughout this time I was filing away every scrap of information I could glean.

It was becoming alarmingly clear that these guys were serious—and dangerous. At one meeting I learned that one of the militia groups had an elaborate hit list. They had gathered the names and staked out the homes of at least a score of retired couples they identified as United Nations spies. I was astounded to learn that these older people were retired military officers, many of them Americans and Canadians, but some from European countries friendly to the United States. Like Connie and me, they had come to the Northwest for the beauty of the wilderness. But so paranoid were the patriotic zealots that they had pegged these people for spies.

I was fascinated to learn that members of this particular militia squad—which was comprised of men I knew from small communities throughout the area—were assigned surveillance duties to watch these old people. They actually had set up watch positions on the suspects' property or in nearby hills, and used night scopes and electronic listening devices to spy on them.

It chilled me to think that such practices could be possible. By day, these night stalkers were salesmen, bankers, grocers—a cross section of any typical American community.

When I told Connie about this, she first expressed anger, then concern, and then fear.

She knew me too well and suspected I was burrowing inside for a reason. I still remember the spat. It was our first big argument over the possibility of my going back under cover.

"Dale, why are you doing this?" Connie was angry.

"I'm just curious about them, that's all." I bristled at her accusing question.

"Until I joined up with you, I never knew life could be so horrible. Have you forgotten the cockroaches? The rotten apartments over the bars? The stinking border towns? Have you forgotten it's been only two years since we barely got out with our children— with our lives? There's still a million bucks' reward on your head. Do you want to go back to that?

"I don't like what these people are doing any better than you," she said. "But we've done our share. It's time for us to build our lives."

My wife's litany of ills about our old trade was accurate. She reminded me of my unspoken pledge to stay out from the cold, and I fully intended to honor it—in spite of the fact that I was still angry about those so-called patriots led by fanatical Bible-quoting false prophets stalking the old retired military couples.

But shortly after our argument, a violent incident occurred that was to send us running again from our adopted haven in the mountains.

★ CHAPTER 5 ★

Satchel Paige could have written my credo with his famous statement, Don't look back; something may be gaining on you. In order for me to survive as a career undercover operative, I had to forget about all the bad guys who would like to do me in for busting them.

So I boasted to Connie and anyone else in my small circle of confidants—mostly lawmen and agents I had worked with over the years—that I never looked over my shoulder.

That bravado just about got me killed in our presumed safe haven at Columbia Falls. This was a little resort town, snuggled securely on the edge of the Waterton-Glacier International Peace Park in the Rocky Mountains. People who live in places like Pleasant Valley, Lakeside, Evergreen, Whitefish, or Hungry Horse never think to lock their doors—so they certainly don't look over their shoulders when they walk down the streets of their towns.

It was 1993, and we had been living reasonably well in our little corner of Montana for five years. I guess I had grown complacent about my security. One evening, after working a day in the woods, I dropped by a neighborhood watering hole for a beer and conversation. When I left my friends in the pub to head home for supper it was already dark, but not that late. My pickup was parked on a side street around the corner from the bar.

The last thing I clearly remember before waking up in a hospital several weeks later was the black-clad arm of my assailant bringing a fish bat down on my skull. Connie had to tell me the rest.

Since I was not robbed, had no enemies in the local population, and had not been arguing politics or religion with my companions in the bar, we had to assume my past had suddenly gained on me. I should have been looking back. The blows to my head were expertly placed, and with such force that there could be no doubt the intent was to kill. I suffered severe multiple skull fractures and brain hemorrhages.

"You're talking in your sleep." The beautiful face of a blond angel was smiling at me. These were the first words I heard as I floated up out of weeks of coma. The angel was my wife. I wasn't in heaven, but in a hospital bed in Kalispell.

"Sleep talk is not a good idea for people in our trade," I cracked through dried lips. My head felt larger than the room. I reached for the top of my skull and felt a turban-sized bandage.

Even after learning that this attack could have been fatal, I was more concerned to hear that I was talking in my sleep. There were too many tales from my past that were best not told.

"We're not in the trade anymore. You can talk in your sleep all you want," Connie said.

"Did they catch the bum who did this to me?" I asked her.

"No, and I don't think they are trying too hard," she said. "They're treating it like a bar brawl."

"What? I don't brawl in bars."

"That's what I told them," Connie said. "Everyone else in the bar told them the same thing. The guys told the Columbia Falls constable that you and everyone else were in good spirits that night. No disagreements, nothing."

The alarm on her face was obvious. The possible implication of the attack merited more than her little worry lines. "Did you see who did it?" she asked.

I thought hard through a throbbing headache and could see only the swift fall of an arm coming in my general direction. At the end of the arm was a fish bat. I was sure it was a fish bat, a stubby miniature of a baseball bat used by fishermen to club big salmon. I had used such a wood tool myself, on several occasions when the steelhead were running. And I often thought that the ordinarily benign device, with its lead core, would be a deadly weapon if used against a human.

"I didn't see anything. Probably just someone who didn't like where I put their driveway," I lied.

"Dale, we're going to have to get out of Columbia Falls. It's too small. They know where you are. Next time they won't just injure you . . . and . . . what about us?"

By "us," I knew she meant the kids. Connie was dauntless where her own safety was concerned. But when it came to our children she was a lioness on the defensive.

"Besides, the doctors say you are going to be laid up for months." She hesitated. "Maybe forever. This wasn't just another bump on your thick head."

Connie didn't have to trouble me with the financial implications of our predicament at the time. I knew my forest landscaping and logging business was down the tubes. The heavy equipment was liened up to the hilt, and the notes could not be paid without my operating the equipment. Connie was a great improviser for her family, but she couldn't operate a dozer or a back hoe.

Shortly after I left the hospital we moved to Kalispell, where Connie could take part-time jobs while I went through a slow recovery. I had fought back from serious physical injuries before, and I would do it again. But recovering from a brain injury was more difficult than rebuilding my body after the motorcycle crash that cost me my arm, or the broken neck I suffered on the docks. I was alarmed by lapses of memory, sudden and unpredictable bouts of slurred speech, occasional vision loss, and seizures.

Slowly I did improve, got out of bed, and once again went back to a rigorous routine to rebuild my strength. We found a nice cabin with a little acreage outside Kalispell, and I worked around the property to fix it up. We decided to exercise an option to buy, with every intent to settle down—permanently this time.

I gradually cleared ten acres of rough land at the top of the property, brought in electricity, and dropped a well. The view from the A-frame cabin covered a panorama from the Mountain Gate in the Swan Range to north of the Flathead River. When the owner came out to collect the rent, he saw what we had done with the property and raised the sales price completely out of our reach.

Meanwhile, I was reduced to odd jobs, buying-fixing-selling equipment and appliances, anything to keep us going. Connie worked at whatever temporary and seasonal jobs a small town had to offer.

But it became clear there had to be real work with real paydays. I heard about a job for a logging company on the other side of the Rockies, near the small town of Winnett.

I jumped the hump, as locals describe crossing the Rockies, to work four hundred miles from my family in Kalispell, on the other side of the state. Like all the other jobs in my past, I had to prove myself to a skeptical employer. I demonstrated that, with my specially adapted chain saw, I could fell timber with one arm as well as most men with two, and I got the job. During the weeks that followed, I commuted the long eight hours one way between Winnett and Kalispell as often as possible. When Connie could find a baby sitter, she occasionally joined me.

Neither of us could stand the long periods of separation. The one thing we clung to was our children. So when it seemed the logging job was going to work out, Connie moved with the children into a small house on a farm eleven miles out of Winnett. It wasn't as pretty as our mountain property at Kalispell. But whatever our new surroundings lacked in scenic beauty was more than made up for by the warm generosity of the ranch families around Garfield, Petroleum, and Musselshell Counties.

I continued to work in the low mountain foothills, surrounded by prairies often miles from any inhabited area, and frequently alone. To get access to timber contracted for cuts by the logging company, I often had to cross a ranch or farm. It was in those isolated places that I first encountered men who called themselves Freemen.

At one point I struck up an uneasy acquaintance with a particularly well-placed Freeman named Lyle Chamberlain. He had a ranch near a crossroads service station and store in an area called Cat Creek, a few miles out of Winnett.

Chamberlain was a likable man, tall and lanky, with a giant graying red beard. He knew all about the teachings of the Freemen, and at every opportunity told me of their theories on government and religion. But he did not seem to participate in threats against others in the community, and as far as I could tell never tried to pass off their phony checks. Perhaps he didn't have to, because he was selling off twenty- and thirty-acre parcels of his family's once sizable ranch. Lyle would often comment that it was easier to sell the homestead off in bits and pieces than to pay taxes on it.

In his dusty jeans, flat-brimmed felt hat, and boots, Chamberlain was a living throwback to the old frontier. He also wore a six-shooter on his hip, strapped to his right leg, quick-draw style. And it wasn't just for show. Lyle had won several quick-draw competitions in Montana. He could pull the big revolver, fire off six shots with sharpshooter accuracy, and have the gun back in its holster before most people could blink twice. He was every bit as expert with a rifle. On a hunting trip, I once saw him bring down a deer at a thousand yards with his bolt-action 30.06 rifle.

Lyle Chamberlain, cautious and suspicious of strangers, gradually warmed to me and began introducing me to others he described as Freemen or men sympathetic to the cause. Several times he suggested I go with him to a mountain cabin near Roundup to meet the leaders, but I always declined with the excuse that, while I might be angry with the federal government for my own reasons, I did not join anything.

As far as I could determine, the men in the Freemen movement were few in number, and most of the people around these parts had as little to do with them as possible. In fact, a large number of the townspeople and area ranchers made it clear they despised the members of this group.

I would soon find out why.

At the same time I was making acquaintances with Freemen, Connie began to meet the people in the small community of Winnett. Gregarious and accepting, Connie makes friends easily, and unless given reasons to act to the contrary, keeps them for life.

Our main concern over being forced to leave the farm and move into Winnett was for the children. The kids loved living out on the prairie where they could roam at will, and Connie and I were getting settled in for a long stay when the double bad news about losing our rented house and my job hit at about the same time.

On top of that, the visit from Deputy Buzz Jones further complicated things for us.

★ CHAPTER 6 ★

We attended a community social at Winnett's favorite gathering place for such activities—the Kozy Korner Bar and Cafe—in mid-March 1995. When the good people of Winnett learned of our dilemma, it took them only about one hour to solve our twin problems. They suggested jobs for both of us and a temporary place to live.

Buck and Ellen Wood, the owners of the Kozy Korner and typical of the caring people of Winnett, were all ears when Connie mentioned that we needed a place to live and some work. The whole town assembled there said they didn't want to see us leave the area, and—*presto!*

The people of Winnett, mostly settled middle-agers or retired oldsters, did not like to see anyone forced to move from the community. They had seen too many younger people driven away by hard times, farm and ranch bankruptcies, and plain old lack of opportunity. Even as a crossroads town and agribusiness supply center, there were only about two hundred souls left in town when we moved into a trailer home situated across the street from the city hall, fire station, and general activity center.

Connie was offered a job fixing lunches at the Kozy Korner Cafe, and I took a job as part-time bartender at the bar adjoining the cafe. Lyle Chamberlain's wife, Jerri, was the regular bartender, but she had no one to spell her. It was a temporary arrangement, welcomed by us. But no matter how much we appreciated the help, we knew the part-time jobs were only a stop-gap measure. We could not live long on the few dollars these jobs paid.

I was beginning to have serious pain from the knee I had blown out dumping over a big Douglas fir at White Sulphur Springs, and I needed an operation. These jobs were not going to provide us the money for surgery, and I couldn't make the kind of bucks we needed unless I could get back into logging.

I thought, too, about the relatively good bonuses that going back under cover could provide—probably enough for my surgery and to get us a new start somewhere in the Northwest.

Buzz Jones had made it clear that the feds were interested in talking to me about going inside the Freemen operation; though at the time I had little knowledge of the extent of federal crimes this group was actually committing, or what the feds would want me to do about it.

Of course, I did not talk again with Connie about contacting the FBI in Billings.

As it turned out, I didn't have to bring the subject up.

We had not been living in town very long before the deeds of the Freemen came rudely crashing into our lives, affecting Connie even more than me.

In my job as bartender I discouraged talk about politics or religion when the rough-and-ready ranchers came in for beers. On a couple of occasions I had to separate a group of Freemen from a group of hostile ranchers, but I accomplished this by suggesting that the two groups sit at opposite ends of the bar.

I noticed the conversation would freeze up whenever Freemen were mentioned at our various social encounters with the sheriff, Bob Busenbark, and his wife, Pat, or some other Winnett citizen. There had been not-so-subtle questions about whether we were in sympathy with the Freemen or their families. We tried to be friendly with everyone, including the Freemen, so neither the Freemen nor the locals could make out our loyalties. The truth is, we had not taken sides.

One afternoon when the bar was empty and Connie had finished up with the lunch-hour crowd, she sat down for coffee with one of her new best friends, Louann Knudson, the postmistress. Louann was a sweet, gentle lady who covered her open-hearted friendliness with a touch of pioneering grit. But suddenly she broke down and told Connie that her life was a waking nightmare.

Freemen had put a bogus lien on her modest property simply because she had a government job. She had been harassed, threatened, and terrified for months.

She nervously spilled out stories about other people in the little town who had been systematically intimidated. As Louann shook with anger and anxiety relating her tales, Connie became incensed by the terrorism against her friend and other townswomen, particularly the older, retired people.

When word spread that Connie was a sympathetic ear, she heard dozens of stories about the silent terror in which the Freemen held the community.

Bonnie Allen, the county clerk, came in for lunch at the Kozy Korner and stayed to confide in Connie. The usually calm official was beside herself with worry. News of the arrest of the Freemen at Roundup had traveled around eastern Montana like a wild prairie fire. But our friends and associates did not know that Connie and I had been privy to an inside account of the incident through Deputy Jones. We kept silent when others talked about it.

Bonnie said she knew Connie had frequently driven alone across Montana on her visits to me, and that she carried a big canister of pepper spray instead of a gun. She wanted to know all about how the blinding spray worked.

The county clerk was in a state of panic.

"We don't know what else to do down at the county courthouse, except to arm ourselves," she said. "We know they [the Freemen] are going to try something. We live every day in fear that they will come busting through the door."

A still sadder story was told by Tilly Bon, who was in her late eighties or early nineties. Tilly said, "I came to this place right here in a covered wagon as a little girl. I've seen a lot of things happen when this was really the Wild West, but these Freemen people scare me. I don't feel safe here anymore. What do they want with us, anyway?"

Joey Hietz, the mayor's wife, had stories of the torment her husband, Ron, had endured for more than a year. Bonnie Allen's husband, Chuck, who managed the local water district, and their daughters also were victimized by threats.

Connie became increasingly troubled that she could not offer solutions but only solace to her new friends. "Why haven't you been to the sheriff?" she asked the postmistress at one point.

Louann chose her words carefully. "What can he do? Sheriff Busenbark and his wife sit up all night watching their front door."

Connie was stunned. Sheriff Busenbark was a tough combat veteran of Vietnam and Desert Storm. He looked as though he could easily handle himself in any situation that might arise in tiny Winnett.

I knew he had a million-dollar bounty on his head, posted along with scores of other officials over the three counties. But I figured he couldn't care less about it. He had even once scorned the reward poster, saying that nobody would take it seriously because locals knew the reward would be paid in worthless Freemen paper.

But Connie and I were both surprised to learn that Sheriff Busenbark took the threats seriously enough to sit up all night in his living room with a double-barreled shotgun lying across his lap.

Over the next days we learned that almost every family in town had been threatened with violence, physical or financial, by the Freemen. At first, everyone had been reluctant to talk about it. But as they got to know us, the answers to the mysterious quiet that hung over the little crossroads town began to emerge. There was good reason for the pall of fear.

We soon learned the Freemen's assaults were not limited to people with connections to government. A ranching couple came into the cafe one morning and over coffee told us the Freemen had filed a bogus lien against a neighboring family's ranch. Everyone in town became upset, because the lien had been placed against a personal homestead of people who had nothing to do with any government function. If such a family could have liens against their property for no reason, then anyone's life's work could be legally entangled by the Freemen.

The phony property liens, one of the favorite weapons of financial terrorism used against government employees by the Freemen, were more than a nuisance. When a lien is filed, that property becomes tied up. A lien prevents the property owner from selling or borrowing against the property. It is particularly devastating to a farmer or rancher who might want to leverage his property to buy equipment or even seed and fertilizer for next year's planting. A property owner must go to great expense, often having to hire an attorney, to have the liens removed. The legal delays could literally wreck a farmer's or businessman's chances to make a living off his property.

None of the locals knew if the liens were legal or not, and the county attorney rarely came to town. He lived over a hundred miles away, and had already made it clear he wanted nothing to do with the Freemen.

Connie and I grew steadily more saddened and enraged as we learned what was happening to the people who had been so kind to us.

It seems the majority of the people in Winnett wanted to do something about the reign of terror, but didn't know how to stop the Freemen. The more aggressive the thugs became, the more irate the citizens were with law enforcement, at both the state and federal levels, for not doing their jobs.

Over the weeks we heard more stories of people in the area, many of them just ranch families working their land and minding their own business, who were systematically threatened with physical violence or financial ruin. Their only offenses were usually just expressing their disgust for the Freemen ideology, or crossing paths with a sympathizer in the course of normal business or social dealings.

Connie, because of her seemingly worldly experience, had become the unofficial counselor for half the wives in the area. Nearly every day she came home drained from sharing the women's grief and fears about the terror gripping Winnett. The men would never admit they were afraid of these gun-toting thugs, but their wives told of the indignities their menfolk endured. The situation amounted to a virtual occupation of Winnett and the other small communities flung across the adjoining prairie.

This was like something out of an old Western movie, only it was real and growing more dangerous the more brazen these Freemen and their visiting allies became.

The more Connie learned, and the more I heard in bar conversations from bragging, swaggering Freemen, the uglier this bunch looked to us.

The Freemen leaders were extremely radical and aggressively bent on attacking the government. They had already begun their financial assaults on the institutions of local, state, and federal government. They now appeared to be preparing for physical assaults on the people they had selected as their enemies—anyone with anything to do with government at any level or anyone who dared challenge a Freeman, a member of their families, or their sympathizers.

As bad-talking and -acting as the militias we'd met in western Montana were, these Freemen and their extended families were putting feet to their proclamations of mayhem. Most importantly, they were attacking a bunch of decent people who had in no way threatened them.

The problem was, everyone seemed paralyzed to do anything about the worsening situation. This lack of counteraction only emboldened the Freemen to become more brazen in their daily activities.

Since nothing was done about the Freemen encounter with lawmen at Roundup, local members came into town swaggering around and boasting that they would soon be running things in eastern Montana. They were always armed to the teeth.

Odd as it seems, Connie was the one to finally suggest the solution. One evening we were verbally wrestling with the whole dilemma, going back and forth over my actually getting involved as an agent. I reminded her that the deputy had suggested the FBI in Billings was interested in talking to me. She still hoped there could be another way to deal with the situation, but her heart and her head were at war.

"How could these grown men turn on their neighbors?" Connie asked. She had been holding hands again that afternoon, trying to comfort her friends at the cafe. "They're just hardworking average people and old couples trying to live their lives."

These victimized neighbors even recounted stories of helping a number of the Freemen families in the past when they had gotten into financial troubles.

I argued that the Freemen were not your typical neighbors.

"These Freemen are not like most of the militia people we knew over on the western slope," I said. "They aren't just a bunch of dropouts with bunker mentalities, stocking up weapons, ammunition, and provisions for some imagined coming invasion by the United Nations. These people are terrorists."

"Why won't the authorities stop this?" Connie's frustration was complete and she was snapping out her questions with growing anger.

"The local cops are outnumbered at least ten to one," I reminded her. "They need help, and the feds don't seem to be able or willing to do anything, either.

"They have to be stopped," I said. "Somebody is going to get killed. Probably somebody we really care about. Somebody has to stop them."

We talked well into the night. We prayed. We even looked up references to false prophets in the Old Testament. Since the Freemen and other hate groups we had encountered justified so much of their deadly doctrine with Bible passages, we had marked our own Bible with some of their references and searched out our own counterpoints.

Finally, we had exhausted all our arguments and Connie had cried out the last of her tears of frustration and fear. It was almost dawn.

"If nobody else can stop this madness, then we can," she said in a low, calm voice. "You have more experience with busting up gangs than all the cops in eastern Montana. Why can't it work with fanatics like these people, too?"

She had come to the same conclusion I had reached weeks before when I drove home from my meeting with Buzz Jones. The time was right—the place, the circumstances. Without knowing it, I had been gathering intelligence on people like these for all the years I had been back in Montana. I knew the lingo, the hot buttons that would get me inside. I had been invited dozens of times to join one group or another. I had specifically been invited to go down to the cabin fortress at Roundup and meet the leaders.

It was as if I had a special calling to do this one last job. When I thought about my children sleeping in the back of the trailer house, I was ambivalent about returning to the dark underworld. But

I felt that rush of excitement, that tiny voice daring me to risk everything, that little swell of pride my self-claimed patriotism allowed me. And I needed the money I knew a job like this for the FBI would bring. I needed it to give my family another new start.

Connie was mostly concerned about the children. What would their lives be like if anarchy like this was allowed to become commonplace?

"I don't know what's going to happen," Connie sighed. "But this cannot go on any longer. It has to be done. Maybe nobody else can do what has to be done to stop this insanity. Maybe you—we—are the only ones who can do it."

Then, with the first ray of late winter sun streaming through the frayed curtains of the little trailer house, I saw the worry disappear from my wife's eyes, replaced by a steely glint of anger and the determined set of her jaw.

I knew the enemy could now be engaged.

I placed a call and woke a sleepy-voiced Buzz Jones over in Musselshell County. Early that morning we drove to Roundup and waited around a service station near the weathered building that housed the sheriff's office. Connie went shopping for a few grocery items.

In no time at all Deputy Jones pulled his patrol car up to the pump for gasoline. I pretended to be interested in the car's big engine and chatted amiably with him at the pump.

When our chat was over he nodded good-bye, got into his car, and drove rapidly out of sight down the main street.

I knew that in a short time Buzz would be on some secure telephone calling the Federal Bureau of Investigation at Billings, Montana.

★ CHAPTER 7 ★

The following day Connie drove me to a prearranged meeting with the FBI at the Western Federal Savings Building in Billings. It was April 12, 1995.

The FBI offices took up the entire second floor of the bank building. I was ushered into an office after a brief wait in the lobby. A big shield covered the wall behind the reception desk. It read, "Fidelity, Bravery, Integrity"—the motto of the Federal Bureau of Investigation.

A tall, slender man in dress slacks and a jacket entered the office. He was in his fifties, graying, and could have passed for a professor on any college campus.

He introduced himself as Tommie Canady and said he was the special agent assigned to work the Freemen of Montana. He chatted about trivialities for only a few minutes before coming to the point of the visit.

"So what makes you think you can penetrate the Freemen?" The question was brusque and edged with doubt. "You aren't one of them, are you?"

I spent about fifteen minutes sketching for him my background as an undercover civilian intelligence operative. But I never mentioned any specific cases I had worked for the FBI, the DEA, or ATF, figuring he probably had a complete dossier on me, anyway. In the distant past some of my assignments had included working with task forces that actually involved former Bureau agents from the Billings office, although I doubted any of them were still around.

Then I told Canady that I had left the field seven years before and was still pretty sore about the treatment my wife and I had received on the last job. When I told him we had had trouble getting the promised pay, he quickly became defensive.

"Was the FBI involved?" he snapped. "If we were, I'll look into it. We pay our bills!"

I assured him the FBI had not been involved in that caper.

Back on the subject of my going under cover on the Freemen case, I told the agent I had since spent a lot of time mingling with the members of various radical racist groups in western Montana.

And I also told him about the numerous contacts I now had with the Freemen in the counties north of Billings—some casual, a few personal.

"Why haven't you joined them by now?" He still sounded skeptical.

I was surprised that he seemed to want me to say that I was a white supremacist.

"I've been invited to join them on several occasions," I said, a little angry at being cross-examined.

Agent Canady briefly told me about his extensive experience in working organized crime, including some long stints in the Chicago area. His implication was clear. In working organized crime, the agency frequently uses mobsters who have turned on their organizations. He was treating me like a rollover instead of a professional CI, and I was about to tell him to shove the job.

"I'm no stoolie. When I was in the trade I was as professional as any sworn cop. You can check me out six ways from Sunday—if you haven't already," I said.

Canady seemed to ignore my protestations about being a rollover. "So I take it you've worked for people like me before."

I knew the agent was toying with me, but I played along through the lengthy first interview. Finally, he said he would like to use me for about two months to go in and gather intelligence on the Freemen stronghold at Roundup. I assumed, from the type of information the FBI wanted, it was a simple assignment to set up the men inside the fortresslike cabin for a quick, bloodless arrest.

It sounded easy enough. Look things over, size up the targets, help make a plan for an arrest of the leaders. In and out, slam bam, thank you, ma'am. Take my money and go home.

"Why do you want to do this?" he asked. "It could be a little dangerous."

Having met at least a dozen of the heavily armed Freemen since tending bar at Winnett, and from my previous contacts in the woods on the logging job, I agreed there was some danger. But I did not comment on the agent's assessment that going under cover might be risky.

"I took a vow to defend my country, and I consider these people to be domestic terrorists," I told him. "But I have to have money, too. I need the job."

The veteran agent agreed the Freemen were domestic terrorists, but of a sort the world had never known.

"We already have cases on them, we just need to arrest them," Canady said, immediately adding a strong caution. "But I can't begin to tell you how politically sensitive this is."

"What have you got?" I asked.

"Federal fraud on three of the leaders. They're white-collar crimes, sealed indictments," Canady answered. "Nothing violent. And I don't want there to be any violence."

I tried to tell the FBI man about the reign of terror I had encountered in the town of Winnett, and assumed he already knew more than I could tell him about the recent incident at Roundup. Deputy Jones, after all, had been our contact. Agent Canady impatiently waved me to be silent when I talked about the living hell of the elderly people in Winnett.

"We already have enough on the Freemen to put them away for thirty years," he snapped. "Let's just leave it at that. Let's just arrest them."

"How do you want them?" I asked, probing for a reaction.

"I know what you mean." At that moment our eyes locked and I saw the same ice-cold gaze I had seen on some of the hardest combat and drug-war veterans in my previous career. His lips were saying one thing, but I knew this agent would have just as happily settled for these criminals to be brought in feet first.

Nevertheless, Canady took some pains to make it clear he did not want any shooting, at least nothing involving the FBI.

I asked if he was talking about the ramifications of the Waco standoff and the siege at Ruby Ridge. The agent nodded.

We talked about money and he asked, "What's an operation like this worth?" When I hesitated, the agent suggested $10,000 and added, "No more than sixty days."

I was surprised he came to a figure so quickly. Before I could think through what he was asking, I responded, "You pay all expenses—every red cent. I want $2,500 start-up, and $25,000 for two months' work, free and clear."

Canady got out of his chair, very animated, very excited. He waved his arms and said, "I'm passing this upstairs immediately. There's no way they'll turn this down—$25,000 is far less than even one day of a siege would cost."

I had no idea what "one day of a siege would cost," and by the agent's eager acceptance I thought I must have sold my services cheap. But the job didn't sound that rough—or that dangerous, if the Bureau didn't get reckless and there came a shootout. Both Connie and I wanted these characters to be stopped from terrorizing our neighbors. So I felt okay about the $25,000 fee and expenses, even if it was a little cheap for an undercover operation.

But I had this nagging feeling that something was not right. From all the Freemen's conversations I had overheard, I believed they were capable of committing murder. I knew the Bureau had information on how dangerous these men could be, so their assurances that this was a white-collar case just didn't hold water.

I was already thinking about shipping Connie and the kids back to the western slope and out of harm's way for the short two months of my assignment.

Agent Canady accompanied me from the building, ostensibly to get a cup of coffee and chat further about what he needed.

We ran into Connie at a drugstore next door. The agent had a look of recognition on his face before I even saw my wife. Canady really had been toying with me; he knew who we were—at least who we had been. He clearly had photographs of Connie, because he spotted her all the way across the drugstore coffee shop.

My queasy feelings were justified. At that point I was sure the

Bureau was not telling me everything it knew about me, and was probably not being up-front with other information. I wondered what the FBI man wasn't telling me about the Bureau's real agenda and what other details were left out about this assignment. It was an uncomfortable situation for a guy about to go under cover inside the Freemen stronghold.

I still don't know the answers to those questions, but whatever the Bureau's real goal was concerning the Freemen on that April day in 1995, it was about to be blown off the drawing boards.

★ CHAPTER 8 ★

The phone began ringing at midmorning on April 19 in our trailer house in downtown Winnett. It continued ringing off the wall until midafternoon. Connie answered the calls, but no one spoke at the other end of the line. She went across the street to the Kozy Korner Cafe, cooked for the luncheon guests, and returned to a still-ringing phone after the noon crowd had been served.

I had been out for a stomp during the morning and returned to open the Kozy Korner bar at noon. Everyone who dropped by the bar was talking about the big bomb blast at the Alfred P. Murrah Federal Building in Oklahoma City. Although the bombing was twelve hundred miles southwest of our little town, the shock waves were felt by the people in Winnett, just as the blast reverberated in the hearts of Americans everywhere.

At 1:30 P.M., Connie finished her luncheon chores and returned to our residence. The phone was ringing again. This time when she angrily answered "Who's calling?" there was a response.

The caller was Special Agent Canady, but he wasn't in Billings. He was calling from a Department of Justice conference, which had been under way for several days in Yellowstone National Park.

"Where's Dale?" The agent sounded agitated.

He didn't answer when Connie asked if he had made the half-dozen anonymous calls earlier in the day.

Connie walked over to the bar, intending to tell me to return the FBI man's call at the Yellowstone number. I saw her look in and then leave. A few minutes later she looked in again, and again she left.

Seated at a table watching the unfolding saga of Oklahoma City on the TV were a handful of Freemen.

It had been a week since our initial contact with the FBI in Billings. We had not heard a word from Canady, and guessed the bureaucracy was grinding away somewhere between Billings and Washington, D.C., on his request to insert an undercover civilian operative inside the Freemen organization.

Assuming the operation would get the blessing of Washington, I had already moved closer to the Freemen leaders. It turned out my part-time job at the bar was an ideal place for me to start. Not only was the wife of one of the most trusted Freemen followers the regular bartender, but Freemen and their sympathizers frequented the place. After a few beers, these hardscrabble ranchers- and farmers-turned-zealots felt comfortable talking freely about their leaders' preachings and teachings.

By quietly listening, I had picked up enough of the baloney to sound like one of them. After it became clear that I would be going inside, I stopped challenging their more outrageous Bible and common-law claims. I became genuinely interested in their blather and assumed the starry-eyed posture of an acolyte. I stopped saying I wasn't a joiner and began to suggest, finally, that I was seeing the light.

Some of the bar patrons—ranchers who were bitterly anti-Freemen and townspeople who were their victims—expressed disappointment in my changing attitude.

One friend, the bar owner, Buck Wood, lamented that he thought I was at least neutral on the Freemen, as he and his wife tried to be. They wanted to refrain from taking sides because their little cafe and bar served everyone in the area. But I could tell from comments dropped by the couple that they would just as soon see the Freemen movement get out of Montana. Buck told me he hoped I was not falling for their radical spiel. I had to bite my tongue to keep from assuring him otherwise.

As the afternoon progressed, the full extent of the horror in Oklahoma City became clear. Casualties were mounting, and the televised scenes of the bodies of the dead and wounded evoked gasps from some of the patrons in the bar.

Word came over the tube that a Middle Eastern suspect, a businessman, had fled the country via a Washington, D.C., or New

York City airport, and that a Muslim organization in the Dallas area was being investigated.

The table of Freemen in the Kozy Korner bar laughed at this news media leak, loudly boasting that the attack was American to the core. They noted with a high degree of pride that this day was the second anniversary of the fiery end of the fifty-one-day siege at Waco.

"It's payback time," one Freeman snarled. His fellows cheered.

I felt the same horror and revulsion I had when, several years earlier, I had been forced to watch in silence as the Montana militia showed a film of the Waco disaster. The widely circulated Waco film purported to prove that the feds had deliberately started the fire that immolated eighty children, women, and men at the Branch Davidian compound.

In the screening of that obviously doctored film, the speaker pointed to a glint of light that the radicals claimed was a flame spewing from an armored vehicle battering the walls of the compound. Anyone viewing the film objectively could easily see it was only light reflecting off a piece of building material. But the radicals claimed this was proof that the government had used a flame-thrower to set the final blaze that burned the compound. Likewise, the militia version never mentioned that the whole mess at Waco had been sparked when four ATF agents were also gunned down.

And now again, on this terrible day of the bombing in Oklahoma City, the facts, horrible as they were in reality, were already being twisted to fit the radical logic of a hate group.

When pictures of the carnage in Oklahoma City revealed that many of the victims were children, another Freemen supporter noted loudly and with general approval from his cohorts, "This is a holy war. Women and children die in war. It's too bad, but that's the way it has always been."

This callous half-apology, half-explanation drove two non-Freemen patrons from the bar with jaws locked and fists clenched. There would have been a serious brawl that day if more of the non-Freemen ranchers and townsmen had been at the bar.

The vast majority of Montanans were every bit as stricken and heartsick by the catastrophe in America's heartland as the rest of the nation. Only a hateful, cynical few celebrated this violation of the national trust, joined by the tiny but deadly minorities of their like-minded ilk, festering in dark corners of communities across the land.

My own near-confrontation with this hate came later that afternoon, when the Twitchel brothers entered the bar. The Twitchel farm up near Jordan, Montana, bordered the Clark family ranch, which was already a stronghold for Freemen activities. The brothers had recently been involved in a confrontation with the Freemen over the grazing of valuable cattle. Apparently, if the Twitchels's cattle strayed over onto the Clark spread they would turn up missing. When confronted, the Freemen justified taking the livestock with their odd brand of common law. Something about possession being nine-tenths of the law.

One of the Twitchels was sitting at the far end of the bar watching the horrible news from Oklahoma City and sipping his beer. I saw his face glaze with anger, and he seemed about to stand up and head for the cluster of Freemen seated at a table loudly spouting their holy war rhetoric.

Every time I moved near the Twitchel brothers I could hear them mumbling, "Those dirty bastards!" Their epithets grew louder as the Freemen became more boisterous.

Even though I was sickened by the Freemen's conduct, I did not want to see a fight break out. There were four or five Freemen with their sympathizers and only two of the Twitchels.

I finally decided the better part of wisdom was to ask the good guys to leave the bar, which personally and publicly placed me on the wrong side of the issue. Finally, the Twitchels and a few other good citizens just threw their hands up and left in disgust.

This one act on my part reminded me how painful my role as an undercover agent and feigned Freeman was going to be. The Twitchel family, like most of our friends in Winnett, were longtime pioneering stock in the community. They were clean-cut, hard-working, and honest as the day is long. They were as patriotic and supportive of this country as any Americans ever to salute the Stars and Stripes. The Twitchels are typical of the community of ranchers and farmers throughout eastern Montana.

It hurt me a lot to have to assume the role of the fanatical, anti-government white supremacist. That day, as babies were being pulled from the bombed-out ruins of the Murrah building, it was hard to swallow that I would soon be identifying myself as one of the traitor-patriots. Every nerve in my body cried out to join the Twitchel boys in mopping up the barroom floor with these loud-mouthed anarchists.

Of course, at the time, no officials knew who had committed the atrocity in Oklahoma City. But there was never the slightest doubt at the Freemen's table that the Oklahoma City bombing was the work of domestic bombers, and never any reluctance to proclaim the perpetrators true patriotic heroes. The mood of these sympathizers was of a victory celebration for the good work done by some of their own kind.

For once, I found myself in agreement with one small claim of the Freemen. I was certain the Oklahoma City bombing was the work of an American terrorist. But that was where my agreement ended. My stomach churned with nausea at the sights pouring out of the TV tube. My resolve to avenge this atrocity became overwhelming.

Finally, the beered-up Freemen ran out of money and they swaggered out of the bar, boisterously declaring that the long-awaited revolution was at last at hand. It was nearly three in the afternoon.

A short time later, Connie slipped into the bar with the message that Agent Canady was urgently trying to reach me from a phone number in Yellowstone. I had to wait for the regular bartender to relieve me, so it was after four when I returned to our trailer to place the call.

Agent Canady came on the line after a long delay.

"Where the hell have you been? I've been trying to get you all day." He almost shouted the question into the phone. My attempt to explain the delay was abruptly cut off by his breathless chatter.

"The Bureau wants you to go in immediately. When can you start?"

I waited for the agent to stop talking and replied, "I've already begun."

★ CHAPTER 9 ★

A person doesn't just walk in and join the Freemen. There's no initiation fee, membership card, decoder ring, or secret handshake. Becoming a member of the Freemen is not like joining a labor union or a country club. Its membership lists are not widely circulated and its organizational structure is deliberately vague—more akin to the secretive cells of the Irish Republican Army than to a typical club or society in America.

Because of the clandestine nature of the Freemen and other groups like it, would-be investigators have had a difficult time penetrating even the front organizations.

Two days after my first meeting with Agent Canady, I accepted longstanding invitations from Freemen members to meet the leaders at the cabin headquarters on Johnny's Coal Road, three miles south of Roundup.

I called Lyle Chamberlain, the self-proclaimed Freeman rancher from Cat Creek, and announced I was now ready to join up. A meeting at the Freemen headquarters was arranged. I had no idea what to expect.

Lyle and I drove down from Winnett to Roundup, where I was escorted directly to the cabin, which sat fifty yards off a graveled road on a wooded hillside. The place reminded me of a log fortress. When we stepped out of the vehicle, Chamberlain made a great show of announcing our arrival, waving and shouting our identification toward the brooding cabin. I imagined—and later learned my guess was accurate—that guns were pointed at us on every step toward the structure.

Once inside the large main room of the cabin, I was confronted by four armed men. Each one was staring at me suspiciously. These men were the heart of the Freemen movement, the sovereigns, the justices. I was quickly introduced to LeRoy M. Schweitzer, Rodney O. Skurdal, and Daniel E. Petersen. The FBI had told me a little about these three men. A fourth leader, Dale M. Jacobi, stood back from the rest after being introduced. The FBI knew he was staying up in the cabin with the Freemen leadership, but did not know, or at least had not provided me with, any information about Jacobi. At the time he was wanted only for bond-jumping on a minor firearms violation.

Schweitzer, a clean-shaven man in his mid-fifties with salt-and-pepper blondish hair, was introduced by Chamberlain with some deference as the chief justice of the Freemen court. He didn't look much like a chief justice of anything, with his beer gut and T-shirt and jeans. Schweitzer was just a click under six feet tall and carried a .357 Magnum revolver. I would soon learn his side arm was loaded with body-armor-piercing ammunition. Schweitzer fashioned his bullets with case-hardened masonry nails imbedded in 157-grain hollow point ammunition. His facial expression was a sour scowl, except for the rare broad grin.

Skurdal, over six feet, wore a bushy, bowl-shaped haircut. He was bearded and walked with a limp from two badly injured knees. A man in his mid-forties, he carried a Glock .45 caliber automatic in a black web belt. He usually wore jeans and a plaid flannel shirt. I came to learn he was a tremendously powerful man who frequently demonstrated his strength—and a dangerously erratic personality.

In the coming weeks and months Skurdal's temperament would grow more volatile, to the point that the least disagreement would send him into a rage. The log house had been his since early 1990, and was now lost to the IRS over tax delinquency. He kept a bedroom upstairs for his son, who would never visit him. Skurdal would prove even more dangerous after Connie was brought into the undercover operation.

If any of the Freemen leaders was less than I had expected, it was Daniel Petersen. Standing five feet, eight inches, in his early fifties, he should have been, and in fact was, somebody's kindly grandfather. But some real or imagined injustice or insult had sent

Petersen spinning right down the path of hate and into the arms of the Freemen leaders. His piercing brown eyes belied his otherwise grandfatherly demeanor, making his graying brown hair and partially paralyzed right arm almost a disguise. He wore desert boots with white socks showing through holes, and heavy flannel shirts, even in the hottest weather. Petersen's weapon of choice was a Western-style .357 revolver. He, like the others, slept with his side arm. From the first moment, Petersen proved to be the most suspicious and, thus, to us, the most dangerous of the leaders. He walked slowly, deliberately, constantly studying what others in the room said and did.

From my briefing I knew these three were all under sealed indictment for issuing various types of fraudulent money orders or checks. I was told their schemes involved millions, but the indictments mentioned only $1.8 million. Skurdal and Schweitzer had not been seen off the property in nearly two years. Theoretically, they would have been arrested the minute they left the mountain sanctuary. At least they believed there were agents lurking everywhere waiting to capture them. I knew they could probably have gone into Billings on a shopping spree without much chance of arrest.

I had quickly learned from my briefing that the FBI had little information about what went on inside the cabin or what the leaders were involved in since taking to ground.

The fourth, Dale Jacobi, over six feet tall and two hundred pounds, was a further enigma for law enforcement. He was a former Canadian police officer, suave and always immaculately groomed, even within the rustic confines of this isolated cabin life. Jacobi stood erect at all times with an almost military bearing, and was clearly the best educated of the leaders. He wore crisply pressed dress shirts, which he ironed himself each day, and dress slacks. In his late forties and slightly balding, he slicked his hair straight back. In the months to follow, I would see him display just a hint of emotion on only two occasions.

Jacobi carried a .357 Magnum, the same revolver he had worn as a policeman, but his ammunition was manufactured with armor-piercing rounds. He would boast on several occasions that his ammunition could penetrate the body armor worn by any police officer or fed attempting to storm the cabin.

My first observation of the men in the cabin was that, in appearance, they had only one thing in common—their eyes. Hard, cold eyes revealed a smoldering rage that lent credibility to the threats of terror against their imagined enemy. I had no question that these men would do what they threatened.

Lyle Chamberlain did not stick around for the interview and left the cabin to rove around outside. During the coming months I would see very little of Lyle, and never saw him directly involved in any of the schemes originating in the cabin. If anything, he was only a foot soldier and probably more representative of the rank and file of the so-called Freemen and their sympathizers. Supporters like Chamberlain spouted the religious and legal mumbo-jumbo of the Freemen, but did not seem interested in the criminal financial schemes practiced by their leaders.

After my interrogation began, another Freeman who was equally out of character with the leaders came into the cabin. He was Richard E. Clark, a fortyish farmer from Brusett in the Jordan area, whose family farm had long since been foreclosed on by a bank holding a government-insured farm loan. Richard, along with his father, Emmett B. Clark, and uncle Ralph, had held the foreclosed farm by threat of violence since 1994. They, too, were devoted Freemen and had participated in the takeover of Jordan and the posting of bounties on their fellow citizens in Garfield County.

The younger Clark—unlike Emmett and Ralph, who looked like weather-weary farmers, more grandfatherly than militant—was a cross between a thick-bodied prizefighter and an 1800s gunslinger. He was well groomed in typical Western garb, including cowboy boots, Stetson, and a Colt six-shooter slung low on his right hip. Richard's usual dress sharply contrasted with the worn-out, ankle-top work shoes, bib overalls, and faded flannel shirt of his father. When Richard spoke, the same venom spewed from him as from the other radicals. It would be at the Clark farm where the ultimate FBI siege would occur, but that was to be another year in coming.

The Freemen leaders directed me to sit at a large table, and the inquisition began. As the four launched immediately into a cross-examination of me, Richard Clark walked around the big room, apparently not interested in the proceedings. I had met Clark some months earlier, but he either didn't remember me or didn't think it important enough to tell his associates.

The foremost question my inquisitors had was about the reasons I wanted to join the movement.

Ironically, Jacobi's questions, like a police interrogation, paralleled the questions the FBI agent Canady had asked about why I wanted to go under cover against the Freemen in the first place.

My answers were the mirror image of those I had given the FBI during my recruitment interview.

I had given the FBI three reasons, so I gave the Freemen three reasons.

"I took a vow to defend my country," I had told the FBI.

"My country is in trouble and needs people like you to defend the true ideals," I told the Freemen.

"I consider these people [the Freemen] to be domestic terrorists," I told the FBI.

"I want to be a part of defending this country from the invasions of foreigners and the United Nations," I told the Freemen.

"I need the job," I told the FBI.

"The system has financially ruined my family," I told the Freemen.

My initial meeting with the Freemen leaders was not well structured. All four fired questions at me simultaneously. Schweitzer was particularly interested in my willingness to take up arms against the government and to take orders from the Freemen leadership.

The interrogation went on for quite some time, and I could tell from the questioning that these men already knew a little about me. At least they were aware of what I had been doing lately—certainly not about my past as an undercover operative for the feds. I definitely would not have walked out of the cabin that afternoon had that information been available to them.

On this first visit inside the cabin I was able to draw a mental picture of the big structure's ground floor. The main room contained a large oval table, which served a triple purpose as a dining

table, conference table, and ultimately the center of judicial proceedings for the justice court. It was at this table that my interrogation was conducted.

The room that got my attention was located just off the main
room. It was a well-equipped communications center, complete
with radio telecommunications sets, several computers linked with
modems, and a large computer printer.

As the afternoon wore on, I was intensively grilled about my
religious and political beliefs. Jacobi, who led the questioning about
my religious beliefs, was soon convinced I knew my Bible well.
They all kept haranguing me about my interest in becoming a "Freeman of character," which they call their true members. My sincerity
was constantly examined from different angles by each of the four
men. It seems they all had different roles.

At one point Skurdal, who I would learn was himself severely
injured in an oil-field accident some years before, asked me a
pointed personal question.

"What happened to your arm?"

"It was bitten off," I responded with a broad grin. Nobody at the
table laughed, but nobody pursued Skurdal's crude question, either.
These were not humorous fellows, and I sensed that this assignment, even for sixty days, was not going to be a visit to Disneyland.

They continued to pepper me with questions, but my years of
associating on the fringes of militias and other racist and antigovernment groups had well prepared me with the right answers.
I only had to embellish them with my own feigned hatreds and an
exaggeration of my real anger at Uncle Sam.

But my final acceptance by the leaders came down to a more
practical issue—my credentials. The Freemen were keenly interested in my reputation as a good black-powder and plastic explosives man.

My assignment for the FBI was supposedly only to get inside
the Freemen stronghold and bring out intelligence. The Bureau said
it wanted to know the strengths and weaknesses within the protec-
tive shell surrounding the militants, so an arrest could be effected
without bloodshed.

That soon changed. On the drive back from this initial meeting I had the first inkling that the job was going to get a lot more complicated than a simple arrest.

As Chamberlain drove toward Winnett, he also took up the grilling, but his techniques were less obvious. In a calm, almost disinterested manner, he probed for my reaction to the meeting with the leadership.

I told him I was impressed with their sincere commitment to their mission.

"Schweitzer is very charismatic," I said. In that regard I only had to partially embellish my assessment of the top man, because he was a real charmer in his own rough way.

"He's clearly the backbone," I said. "A true revolutionary leader."

I asked if Jacobi was the chaplain and Chamberlain said he did not know.

"Well, if he isn't, he should be," I schmoozed, knowing that every word I said to Chamberlain would be relayed back to the cabin at Roundup as soon as I was dropped off in Winnett.

"Are you going to join?" Chamberlain asked.

I responded that I had heard every crackpot and nut case from white supremacists to fanatical militiamen, and that most of them "couldn't find their own ass in broad daylight" with both hands.

"But these Freemen of character seem to finally be well grounded and dedicated," I said. "They are the kind of men I would be willing to work for and with to get this country straightened out."

The lanky rancher then asked me how far I was willing to go for the cause, and casually pointed out a microwave communications tower just off U.S. Highway 87.

"See that tower?" He pointed a fist at the tall steel structure jutting above the horizon. "It's the telephone relay for most of eastern Montana."

I grunted acknowledgment.

"Is that the sort of thing you can take out?" The Freeman rancher's question was matter-of-fact. "When the day comes it might have to go."

"If I had the right stuff, I could have it down in two minutes," I said. "It would fall like a big ol' tree."

"What would you need?" he asked.

"My first choice would be C4 or C6, with radio detonators. But it could just as easily be done with stick powder or nitrates—or, if need be, we could mix our own concoction and use a fuse."

That seemed to satisfy him. I tried to probe for an explanation of "when the day comes," but he just drove on in silence.

"You wouldn't want to blow up a facility like that if you planned to occupy this area. There would be a need for telephone and radio communications."

He mulled my answer and agreed I might be right.

So my initial meeting with the Freemen went okay. The leaders appeared eager for me to become one of their members. But I had an uneasy feeling deep in my gut that I would be asked to prove my loyalty to this unholy cause in the not-so-distant future.

This operation was not going to be like any I had undertaken in the past. These suspects seemed radically different from the common criminals I had worked with before. The assignment had already taxed my considerable abilities as a consummate con man, a trait demanded of the successful and "live" civilian undercover operative. It would not be a simple matter of pretending to be a drug addict or participating in a smuggling operation.

I had the nauseating feeling I might be asked to participate in something far more murderous.

CHAPTER 10

One week after the bombing in Oklahoma City, Special Agent Canady, who was to be my sole handler during the Freemen operation, arranged for a planning session. He expressed surprise that I had already been inside the cabin stronghold at Roundup and apparently been accepted into the Freemen ranks. When I called to set up the debriefing, he told me he had expected it would take a month to get invited to the cabin.

Since I had already entered the lion's lair, we agreed for security reasons we would not meet at the FBI offices in the future. An unlikely location was selected for this second meeting and most future informal debriefings. The clandestine face-offs would be in a latter-day hippie coffee shop called Artspace at Second Avenue and 29th Street, a block and a half from the FBI offices in downtown Billings.

It was reasoned that no racist types would patronize this establishment and chance on one of our sessions. In fact, most of the regular patrons tended to wear weird clothing, tattoos, and strange hairdos, and further embellish their looks with body-piercing art. This clientele was definitely not one to attract the boots-and-jeans-clad militiamen types.

The Artspace coffee shop specialized in light lunches as well as espresso. Loud music from a jukebox, offering pop renditions from the '60s, assured that no eavesdropper was likely to overhear our conversations.

I have no idea what the regulars thought of frequently seeing a somewhat distinguished middle-aged suit and a one-armed woodsman huddled at a back table near the rear door. Management didn't seem to mind, as long as we paid for our coffee and meals.

In our first debriefing, Agent Canady wanted only to discuss a simple plan for the bloodless arrest of a handful of Freemen charged with white-collar crimes. And that was all I wanted to be involved with, too. The bombing in Oklahoma City was hardly mentioned and, at the time, there appeared to be no connection with other far-right activities roiling in the background.

Powerful militias, some with links to a reinvigorated Aryan Nations, had only recently formed in Montana and other areas of the Pacific Northwest and the Midwest and were spreading across the United States.

The Freemen's emerging role in this unholy alliance of insurrection apparently was completely unknown to the FBI. I had already learned from my conversations with members and in my first meeting with the leaders inside the cabin that the Freemen organization combined a jumbled mix of white-supremacist and neo-Nazi teachings. They primarily drew their inspiration from the anarchist Posse Comitatus. The Posse, which had its heyday in the 1980s in the Midwest, drew its membership from disenfranchised and disillusioned farmers who had been driven off their family lands by government programs that encouraged them to mortgage everything to the hilt.

The Freemen's far-right ideology seemed to come straight from the unholy teachings pouring out of the Aryan Nations at Hayden Lake, Idaho. A direct link with the Aryan Nations via the Militia of Montana became obvious when John Trochmann, one of the founders of the militia, was arrested with the Freemen by Deputy Buzz Jones in the Roundup incident.

Even though Trochmann denied his connection with the Freemen, claiming he was just in town trying to negotiate a peace treaty between the Freemen and local authorities, I had learned that one of Trochmann's former lieutenants, Dale Jacobi, was not only at the cabin but had apparently assumed a leadership role in the Freemen organization.

Agent Canady seemed surprised by this bit of intelligence and furiously took notes. But he kept bringing the subject back around to the federal fraud cases already pending against the Freemen leaders. He reminded me that a federal grand jury had already handed up indictments against Schweitzer, Skurdal, and Petersen.

In this initial debriefing, I warned the FBI agent that there might be more going on than was first suspected, especially since it appeared the Freemen might not be an isolated group. I recounted the casual reference to blowing up a microwave tower as part of an actual territorial takeover of property in the Roundup-Winnett area.

In my past dealings with the radical militia groups on the western slope, I had frequently heard of the Aryan Nations' ultimate goal for the establishment of a Christian Identity Kingdom in the Pacific Northwest. This was to be a white nation covering much of the western area of Montana, northern Idaho, and eastern Washington. All people of color—the so-called Mud People—were to be expelled or slaughtered and a Nazi-type, pure-blood, white government created.

The brief conversation I had with the Freeman Chamberlain when he drove me back from Roundup to Winnett seemed to be an echo of some of the plans for the creation of this whites-only nation. The difference was, now the Freemen seemed to be planning to actually launch such an insurrection and the targeted area was clearly defined.

Tommie Canady could hardly conceal his pleasure that I was already inside the Roundup cabin and providing what amounted to fresh intelligence. He assured me the highest levels of the Bureau had approved my deal. He implied the approval had come from higher authority, hinting that the Justice Department and even the White House might be aware of the Bureau's insertion of an undercover operative inside the Freemen organization.

As in my past experience with this type of operation for federal agencies, there was no written contract discussed. A handshake was usually good enough. For the sake of security, the less detail reduced to writing, the better.

At this first session in Billings, I made Canady fully aware that because of my training and previous experience, I had been mentally gathering data on the militants from the day I set foot in Montana, years before. So, I assured him, the Bureau was actually getting a lot of intelligence for its money. I told the agent that I had also carefully nurtured my false persona with the various hate groups on the other side of the Rockies, and was on an easy first-name basis with many of the members of tax-protesting hate groups in the western part of the state. I had even met and visited with groups from the infamous Hayden Lake compound of the Aryan Nations, the Order, and Christian Identity. I thought it was important to the Bureau to understand that, while my assignment was specifically to provide information for an arrest, I was capable of giving them a deeper look inside the shadowy underworld of these groups.

Agent Canady seemed interested. I suspected his appetite might have been whetted by the Oklahoma City bombing and the vague suspicions now emerging of a connection between the bombing and certain militia groups.

Despite his general interest in militias and other hate groups, Canady repeatedly made it clear that my primary assignment was to learn the Freemen's time schedules, habits, and movements, in preparation for sending in the Bureau's elite HRT to make the arrests. HRT stands for Hostage Rescue Team, the public relations name for the military-style tactical-assault teams.

During the session I gave the agent a thumbnail sketch of the Freemen leaders from my observations gained during my grueling, extended interview at the cabin.

They were all Bible-quoting zealots, but each seemed to have a specialty. Schweitzer was clearly the top dog in the pack. He obviously believed in the fanatical religious and common-law ideology he was spouting. Everyone I had seen at the cabin seemed to hang on his every word like adoring disciples. Skurdal left the impression that he was just along for the ride and appeared to be mouthing the spiel more by rote than conviction. Petersen had said he was sure the Freemen philosophy was right, but qualified his boast with, "If we were wrong, someone would have busted us a long time ago."

The mystery man was Dale Jacobi. I had learned of his former connection with the more radical Idaho-Montana groups during our first conversation. The ex-cop was a cold, calculating man, and I had been unable to form an opinion about his leadership position. Jacobi's questions of me during that first meeting were primarily of a religious nature. He obviously was expert in the Christian Identity teachings, and I had been exposed to enough of this nonsensical interpretation of the Bible in my own Bible studies to pass the quick test on that score.

Canady told me the FBI had very little on Jacobi's recent activities and that the ex–law enforcement officer was not among the Freemen leaders under indictment. The agent instructed me to pay special attention to Jacobi to determine his role in the organization.

I told Canady that my first meeting with the Freemen had been congenial and that shortly after the introductions, the conversation had been open and candid. There was not a hint of suspicion of me by the time I had finished that first visit to the cabin. The leaders had talked freely about their criminal activities and I quickly let the Freemen know I had associated with militiamen in western Montana around the Kalispell, Eureka, Thompson Falls, and Libby area. I dropped as many names as I could remember. I figured they had already checked me out anyway, so name-dropping, even if I really didn't know some of the militia leaders all that well, seemed safe.

While Schweitzer had grilled me about my beliefs and my willingness to participate fully in all the Freemen's activities, he had not specified what my assignments would be. But it was clear they expected me to participate in activities that were probably considered to be illegal by outsiders.

This opened a line of discussion on my feelings about the federal government. I had given the Freemen what they wanted to hear in an animated diatribe against the FBI.

For the benefit of the debriefing fed, I laid on some of my more outrageous and negative descriptions of the Bureau. Canady turned red and stopped me at one point to inquire, "You don't really feel that way about the Bureau, do you?" I just grinned and continued to describe my first meeting with the Freemen.

I told the FBI agent that it was Skurdal who had first brought up my training as an explosives and weapons expert, but all four of the Freemen leaders were clearly interested. The Freemen leaders had wanted to talk about weapons in general, and we had launched into a technical description about the merits of different sophisticated explosives, including the new C5s and thin-sheet explosives. I described how to dismantle a LAW rocket—a hand-held, antitank weapon—and put it back together. I knew most of this was over their heads and an overkill to cement my position as a demolitions expert in the group.

Agent Canady seemed somewhat disturbed that I had given such detailed knowledge about bombs to potential terrorists. But I had not actually shared any secrets that the militiamen I met did not already have access to. Canady wanted to know if I was now an "official" member of the Freemen. I told him the organization didn't seem to work that way—membership cards, secret handshakes, and stuff like that. But I assured him I had both feet squarely in the cabin door, even if I was perhaps only an understudy for the time being.

Schweitzer had actually been the first to invite me to join them, and, with his endorsement, the others were pounding me on the back as a comrade before that meeting was ended. He said I would have to dedicate myself to a study of their law and the true faith.

I assured them I would not hesitate to follow instructions and would be an obedient student and follower. I had heard enough in the weeks and months before actually confronting the leaders to talk the talk and walk the walk. When they asked how I knew so much about them, I said I had learned a lot about their beliefs from my conversations with Lyle Chamberlain and was eager to learn more. Schweitzer beamed and said he would like to see me become a Freeman of character.

As I related the experience to Canady, he frequently reminded me that I was not authorized by the Bureau to participate in any illegal activities—at least until I got his advance clearance.

The Freemen leaders had invited me to come back and bring my family to the cabin at Roundup at any time.

Other than his occasional small fits when I hit a nerve, Agent Canady seemed delighted with this initial debriefing.

By the end of my work session with the Bureau man, it was clear I was now fully invested with a mission to gather the needed additional information that would lead to an arrest. Part of my assignment was to look for weaknesses in the Freemen's security and recommend various scenarios for the FBI's Hostage Rescue Team to make the arrest in the near future. No time frame was discussed, but I assumed it would be within the two months of my work agreement with the Bureau. I should have known better. An experienced undercover operative never assumes anything.

We discussed a code name for the project and I suggested it carry a code name I had used before: Cowboy.

The agent's eyes popped with surprise and alarm. The last thing the Bureau wanted was to have someone named Cowboy, with all its connotations of reckless bravado, running loose in this politically sensitive environment.

If anything should go wrong on this assignment, I might have to testify before a grand jury or—God forbid—a congressional committee hearing. The FBI was ever-conscious of its public relations image, which at that moment suffered considerable tarnish. The Bureau brass would be horrified to have an undercover operative named Cowboy. I liked seeing the agent squirm at the thought and pretended that I would insist on being known by that name.

When I saw his discomfort rising to anger, I said, "Okay, call me whatever you like, just so you don't miss my name on payday."

He gave me the code name Talon.

CHAPTER 11

O_kay. Here's what we've got: a gang of blue-jeans-clad, six-shooter-toting bad guys holed up in a log cabin, terrorizing a bunch of Montana settlers. The local sheriffs are outgunned. In rides the hero—me—to round 'em up. Everybody lives happily ever after, and the hero rides off into the sunset. A grade-B Western set in 1995.

The problem with this scenario is that once I got inside the Freemen's fortress at Roundup, I quickly discovered that the nerve center was a sophisticated nationwide telecommunications operation linked by computers, modems, laser printers, facsimile machines, and shortwave radio. These bad guys weren't your typical cattle rustlers. They were perpetrating a complex new form of financial terrorism aimed at wreaking havoc on the banking system of the United States, while at the same time financing the building of an army of insurrectionists.

Shane meets *Tron*. Nobody would believe such an incredible script, and the FBI had no idea what was really going on inside that rustic cabin.

On my next few visits to the cabin, the Freemen leaders—with only occasional assistance from spouses and supporters—were always buried in paperwork. Except for the bare log walls, the place could have been a mail-order business office, understaffed because some greedy corporate manager downsized to please profit-hungry shareholders.

In my early days of nosing around I found, to my surprise, that a large storage barn across from the cabin contained not an arsenal of automatic weapons and bomb-making goodies, but reams of photocopier paper. The daily routine inside the cabin was a hum of computers, clicking keyboards, and chattering modems—not cleaning guns and building bombs. Every available hand was called on to print, stuff, and mail newsletters, answer mail and phone inquiries, and compile mailing lists.

All the time the talk was about the urgency to recruit an army of guerrilla fighters, but obviously the most pressing manpower need was to recruit a steno pool.

I mentioned to Connie that the Freemen were hurting for human resources of the clerical persuasion. She pointed out that her college training and work experience before we married had been in accounting and office management. By this time, Connie had fully accepted our role in bringing this gang of terrorists to justice—the sooner the better. Once Connie had agreed that I should go back under cover, she was committed one hundred percent to the successful conclusion of the operation. But she was determined to see it concluded on schedule, within the sixty days we had signed on for with the FBI. When she learned of the paper frenzy at the Freemen cabin, she asked if it might not speed up our operation for her to join me.

Connie had worked with me before in technically demanding situations where money-laundering was involved, and I knew her experience could be valuable in this operation. Also, as my wife, she insisted she had a vested interest in covering my ass.

I was ambivalent about getting Connie more involved in the operation than she already would be, since I was concerned for her safety. The Freemen leaders clearly had a low opinion of females in general, and I had observed that the few women involved on the fringes of their domain were little more than servants.

But Connie argued that she was already in it because of my involvement, and that her direct participation might speed up the operation. She just wanted it over and done, so we could clear out.

"Dale, if I have a more active role in bringing these people in, we can get on with a real life," she said.

Now all I had to do was convince the Freemen and the FBI.

In my next meeting with Canady in Billings, I reported the huge amount of paperwork required to support the now nationwide scheme of financial fraud, bogus liens, and training materials. I dropped a hint that Connie, with her office-management background, could be a tremendous asset to the operation.

The agent was already aware of her previous work as an undercover operative. He agreed Connie's administrative skills could prove useful now.

Most of the charges in the sealed indictments on which the Freemen leaders would be arrested were for financially technical crimes, including charges of conspiracy to defraud the United States, bank and mail fraud, and various interstate swindles. But I do not think the Bureau had any idea of the massive extent of the operation.

Schweitzer was the mastermind of the fraud, and had spent years studying the U.S. Uniform Commercial Codes, various English common-law texts, and the Christian Identity's skewed interpretations of the King James Version of the Bible. From these studies Schweitzer had cobbled together a witch's-brew doctrine, which he and other separatists and white supremacists called common law, but which amounted to a bizarre, racist natural law. Schweitzer knew enough law to throw a monkey wrench into the works of the legal system, and was rapidly spreading this disinformation through seminars held at the Roundup cabin.

Basically, the fraud worked around the issuance of false financial instruments—bank checks or money orders produced on laser printers. The bogus checks, which looked exactly like authentic instruments and were drawn against an existing bank, were supposedly backed by bogus liens. The liens were arbitrarily placed against the property of local officials who had offended the Freemen in the course of performing their duties—or simply by the fact that they held public office.

As brazen as the scheme was, it had worked on many gullible people. The checks had actually been used to pay off loans, mortgages, and even taxes. Freemen and their sympathizers used the worthless paper to buy everything from pickup trucks to weapons. The swindle was literally in the millions of dollars and covered several states.

The Freemen's modus operandi also included direct attacks on the American legal system by filing scores of phony lawsuits.

Freemen Schweitzer and Skurdal filed numerous suits against all levels of government to halt enforcement of tax liens resulting from their refusal to pay taxes. Suits were filed against officials to have them removed from office over antiquated bonding provisions or other trumped-up infractions gleaned from old law books.

These lawsuits clogged the local and federal courts in all parts of Montana. The paperwork caused by the filing of false liens against state and federal lands and the property of private citizens drove more than one county clerk to resign.

Computers in financial institutions errantly picked up the false liens as assets. Once the liens were determined to be bogus, harried clerks had to clean up a morass of paperwork. During this lapse the Freemen would set up bank accounts with bogus checks or money orders. The Freemen not only used these bogus checks and money orders themselves, but also sold them to sympathizers, with the promise that the schemes would get them out of debt.

Another potential cash cow for the Freemen was their seminar program—at $300 a person—to train others in how to conduct the schemes. The seminars served another purpose, and that was to spread their system across the country and thus multiply the chaos.

The Freemen had already shown like-minded hate groups how to duplicate their illegal operation in Texas, Oklahoma, and California, and were now putting together a program to extend this new type of financial terrorism nationwide.

At the end of the seminars conducted by the Freemen leaders at Roundup, the attendees would receive a stack of official-looking checks, produced right there in the cabin on laser printers.

One seminar graduate claimed that more than fifty percent of the bogus instruments were accepted by banks or creditors. This Schweitzer pupil apparently far excelled her mentor in perfecting the scam. The student, M. Elizabeth Broderick of Palmdale, California, and a group she sponsored on the West Coast, were eventually indicted on fraudulent check charges, which federal prosecutors privately admitted amounted to as much as $100 million.

By the time I went under cover inside the Freemen cabin in April, reports were trickling in from all over the country of bogus checks successfully passed to pay taxes, back child support and alimony, mortgages, and all sorts of purchases. The training course was being advertised in mailers and on the Internet. The Freemen were in the process of accelerating the seminars to be held at the cabin later that spring.

But before they could expand the classes, the four leaders at the cabin desperately needed clerical and administrative help. I discussed this big hole in the Freemen operation with Schweitzer. On one of my subsequent trips from Winnett to Roundup for a session with the Freemen leaders, Connie accompanied me. During the course of the conversation she let it be known that she was a college-trained office manager and had worked as an administrative assistant in several offices. The Freemen were all ears, but we did not volunteer her services at that meeting.

Connie also went with me to the next debriefing with the FBI at Billings. We checked into a motel adjoining a Denny's restaurant. She and the kids went to eat breakfast while I delivered my routine report. After that, Connie was invited to come back to the motel, and I went over to the cafe to sit with the kids. She was gone a long while. When she came back she said, "I'm going in, too."

"What's the deal?" I asked.

Connie reviewed, in detail, her somewhat strange conversation with the agent.

"I asked Tommie Canady straight out, 'If I go in with Dale, will you people pay me?' He was surprised at my question," Connie began.

"What did he say about it?" I asked, amused at my wife's no-nonsense approach to such matters.

"He said, 'Well, yes, but we can't afford much.' So I said, 'I'm willing and want to go in so we can get this thing done and over.'"

The agent told her he would have to get the Bureau's approval for her to join the operation—it would take a couple of weeks.

"Did you talk about your pay?" I asked.

"Yes."

The agent had told Connie the Bureau would start with a check for $1,000. When she countered with $1,500, Canady agreed. "Then you'll have the same arrangement as Dale," the agent told her.

"Okay, what do you want me to do?" Connie asked him.

"Just be our eyes and ears," he replied.

Connie told the agent she could not go to work until her children were safely out of the way, and the Bureau man agreed to get extra expense money for us to take them to a safe haven in another part of the state.

"What else did you talk about?" I asked.

"Just the weather and how bizarre the Freemen are," she said. "Oh, we also talked about my health and safety. He told me not to compromise myself."

"In what way?" I asked.

"Canady said there were only men up there in the cabin, and they had been isolated for a long while. He suggested I might have trouble keeping my integrity intact," she said. "I told him, 'You don't have to worry about that. I can take care of myself.' He said if I felt the least bit uncomfortable, I was out of there."

With the FBI agreement, it was now only a matter of convincing the Freemen. She would be as much a part of the operation as I was, and would have the same payday from the Bureau. We assumed—once again I am reminded that making an assumption is not a good idea for an undercover agent—that this meant $25,000 each, for an operation not to exceed sixty days, plus expenses. The FBI was now committed to paying expenses and an advance of $2,000 per month.

With the agreement for Connie to go under cover, too, I began working on the Freemen. They were at first nervous about having a woman come into the cabin on a regular basis. Up to this point female family members usually just dropped in with groceries or to run errands. But the Freemen leaders were exhausted by the paperwork their burgeoning financial empire demanded. They were spending eighteen to twenty hours a day typing, shuffling tens of thousands of pieces of paper, and corresponding with other separatist groups wishing to learn more about the scheme.

This was hardly the work of macho revolutionaries bent on overthrowing the government of the United States. So the Freemen leaders finally agreed that they would accept the help of a female menial.

However, the new servant was a fully invested FBI undercover operative—code name B.H.

A week later Connie's approval came down from the Bureau, along with her first cash advance and $500 expense money to take the children to another location for their safety. We took the kids out of harm's way for what we thought and planned to be the duration of the operation. They were safely with friends several hundred miles away from the scene. From our point of view, working as a team, we could count on wrapping up within the sixty days the FBI had contracted us to work. We would draw the double fee of $50,000 for the two months' work, and drop by to pick up our children on our way to starting our lives over again.

On my next trip to the cabin, I took Connie along. She officially started her undercover role inside the operation on May 25, 1995.

★ CHAPTER 12 ★

Now officially on duty for the FBI, Connie assumed the role of the biblically subservient wife. She was an instant hit with the Freemen leaders.

They practically stumbled over themselves with invitations for her to help with the massive paperwork logjam. With our children safely miles away, we could devote every waking moment to the Bureau's assignment. We quit our part-time jobs at the Kozy Korner Bar and Cafe in Winnett. Of course, there was no way to tell our friends what we were up to with the Freemen. We did stay, for the time being, in the trailer house at Winnett and made daily trips to Roundup. We concentrated on making ourselves indispensable to the daily routine of the four leaders holed up in their Bull Mountains fortress.

The Freemen soon became used to our being around the place, and Schweitzer told me it was time to begin my formal instruction so I could become a full-fledged Freeman of character.

On the first day of my classes, Connie showed up at my side. She took a seat slightly behind me at the large conference table where the instruction was to be given. With her head always bowed as the modest and servile wife, she brazenly took a pen and legal pad from her large purse.

The Freemen leaders looked stunned as she began writing.

Her outrageous bravado even frightened me on occasion.

"What are you doing?" Jacobi asked in alarm.

"She takes notes for me all the time," I responded. "She's my helpmate in all things. I need the notes to recall everything."

I admitted that I had dizzy spells, sometimes lapses of memory or even minor seizures, ever since suffering severe head injuries in an attack two years earlier at Columbia Falls. I rose to address the four leaders seated around the table.

With head bowed and hands behind my back, I said, "I respectfully request of the court that my helpmate be permitted at these classes so she might take notes for my benefit to study later." I explained that she almost always took notes for me when I was involved in important Bible study or other significant matters.

Schweitzer beamed at my humility in addressing the Freemen court in such a candid and submissive manner.

"The court grants permission," the chief justice opined to the approving nods of the other wise men of the court. They did not know they were planting the next best thing to electronic ears inside their secret empire.

From that day forward, Connie took notes of every session conducted by the Freemen.

On the back pages of her legal pad she recorded names of visiting militiamen, license plate numbers, telephone numbers, and ultimately computer code numbers from the heart of the telecommunications operation center in the cabin.

Soon everyone was used to seeing her walking around busily scribbling, hanging on this or that leader's every word of enlightenment. The meek helpmate was a stenographer-at-large for the Federal Bureau of Investigation.

When one of the Freemen leaders was conducting a common-law seminar, preaching on particular points of Christian Identity gospel, or exhorting some armed visitors to overthrow the government, hang a judge, or lynch a member of a minority race, the comments were duly recorded.

During times when no one was saying anything of particular interest, Connie would walk around outside, noting the license plate numbers and state names on visitors' cars. Or, inside the cabin, she would take down the phone numbers of calls to be returned—one for the Freemen, one for the FBI.

Conversations between Freemen and visiting militia leaders were recorded. Computer numbers—models, makes, serial numbers, and E-mail addresses—all went into Connie's notes.

The FBI wanted to know all about the computers in the communications center, types of modems and faxes. As soon as we had hard intelligence that the computer equipment, as well as the telephones, were used to conduct illicit interstate business, this information was used to secure wiretaps.

We were so firmly inside the operation that Connie's activities were rarely questioned. She pitched in to help with the voluminous paperwork, which gave her better access to names, addresses, and phone numbers of persons the Freemen were corresponding with in other states.

If Connie fell behind in her note-taking, she would leave a meeting to go into the kitchen to catch up. At the end of every session she added her own impressions of what had transpired, paying special attention to who said what to whom, physical descriptions of the visitors, nicknames, or peculiar habits. She recorded details about anyone who seemed to be especially violent or any discussion of a plan that might involve criminal activity.

These notes were periodically turned over to an astounded Agent Canady in Billings. Undoubtedly, Connie's work became part of the American militias' growing file at FBI headquarters.

I had previously agreed to wear a wire inside the Freemen cabin, even though discovery would have endangered Connie and me, and the viability of the operation itself. But Canady was so pleased with the stream of information from Connie that he decided the risk of using a wire was unnecessary.

In one of our debriefings at the coffee shop Canady was especially effusive about Connie's contribution.

"This is incredible, fantastic," the agent said. "We knew nothing about what was going on up there. Now we even know how the screen door works."

In another intelligence-gathering feat, Connie asked Petersen about some of the common-law references used to justify the phony money-order scam. He went to the computers and began reviewing all the material the Freemen had gathered over the years to set up their scheme. While Connie was given a crash course in the so-called law, I struck up a conversation with Schweitzer and Skurdal.

I told them I was behind in my pickup-truck payments and the finance company was about to repossess my vehicle. After some time the two Freemen leaders whipped out a bogus check.

"How much do you owe?" Schweitzer asked.

"About $8,000," I answered.

He wrote out a check for $16,000, told me how to make the pay-off to the finance company and demand the title be released, with $8,000 cash back, to be split $4,000 for the Freemen and $4,000 for me.

"By the time the check makes its way through the banking system, you will be gone with a clear title and bonus," the Freemen leader said proudly.

In our next meeting with Canady I turned the bogus check over to the FBI. I told the Freemen the finance company would send me the difference after the check cleared.

It soon became apparent that we needed to get closer to the group leaders on an around-the-clock basis. Driving down from Winnett each day provided us the opportunity to gather intelligence on day-time activities at the cabin. But we had no idea what went on during the evening hours—who visited the Freemen stronghold, or what security precautions they took. An FBI raid might need to be conducted late at night.

There was no room for us to move into the cabin, even if the Freemen leaders would have allowed a woman to stay over in one of the four upstairs bedrooms, which was not likely.

Besides, Connie pointed out that I still had the bad habit—a potentially fatal habit for an undercover agent—of talking in my sleep.

A small trailer or motor home parked on the Freemen property seemed like the best solution.

Connie and I raised the issue of setting up twenty-four-hour surveillance with Agent Canady. He thought the idea of parking a mobile home on the Freemen property was great. But we were surprised to learn that he had another plan in mind as well.

While the Bureau continuously praised us for the information we were bringing out, it just wasn't the same as having their own agent inside. Our early success at penetrating the Freemen high command had seemed so flawless that Canady said headquarters thought it should put in its own.

Whether the decision had already been made to terminate us or whether the Bureau just wanted confirmation by one of its agents on the new intelligence, I'll never know. What I did know was that a regular FBI agent had about as much chance of penetrating the Freemen as I would have shinning up a greased flagpole.

I argued that it would take a rawboned, dispossessed farmer type with a broad knowledge of fundamentalist Bible training to pass the scrutiny required before the Freemen would accept a long-term resident acolyte inside the cabin. In its arrogance, the FBI ignored the characteristics I outlined for such an undercover candidate.

The agent they picked for this impossible task was introduced to us at one of our two-day debriefings at a motel in the west industrial area of Billings. The FBI rented a suite at the Quality Inn Homestead Park whenever our debriefing sessions were to be extensive or whenever visiting FBI honchos came to town to talk to us.

One look at the agent they planned to insert in the Freemen operation and my only thought was "dead man walking."

We met the somber young FBI agent, Jimmy K. Cassaria from Utah, at the motel. Canady said Jimmy had worked under cover before. I had no doubt he was qualified to do some types of undercover work. But the minute I saw him I began to argue with the agent in charge that Jimmy would not fit into this assignment.

After about an hour of interviewing him, Connie and I saw that Jimmy was becoming more and more nervous. Canady was getting angry at the grilling I was giving the young agent. Finally he motioned for me to follow him from the sitting room in the motel suite and walk outside.

"What are you trying to do? Scare the shit out of Jimmy?" Canady bitterly asked.

"This guy may be good, and could have worked under cover all his career," I said evenly. "But he is not going to pass muster with the Freemen. The Bureau is going to get us killed and your man, too."

"You'll just have to coach him," Canady said. "The Bureau wants our own man inside that cabin for a look-see."

I returned to the suite and the conversation became more congenial.

We spent the next several days coaching Cassaria on what to expect on a day-to-day, hour-to-hour basis. But it was clear to Connie and me that Cassaria was not going to learn to walk and talk like a white supremacist or religious zealot, no matter how many hours we coached him.

The young agent himself had sense enough to know from our description of what to expect inside the cabin that he would stick out like a sore thumb. The more we talked, the more nervous he became.

Finally, at the end of the fourth day, the two agents left and told us to meet them the next day at a supermarket parking lot. The Bureau had located a motor home and wanted us to look it over before they had it overhauled.

The next day we saw what was to become our new living quarters. It was a ten- or fifteen-year-old motor home with a Chevrolet chassis and cab. The vehicle had been used by a hunter and his son for camping trips and, to be charitable, it was a clunker. It had an Arizona license plate and was registered to an FBI cover corporation in Phoenix.

I drove the bulky house-on-wheels around the block and figured its top speed would probably be about fifty miles an hour—and that on the flats in Billings. The cabin site where we would be taking it was in the foothills of the Bull Mountains. I doubted the twenty-two-foot behemoth would make twenty-five up those hills.

But for living accommodations, it would do fine. The vehicle had two bedrooms, one with bunks just off a narrow hall. It had a shower, a tiny bathtub, and a living room connected to a kitchenette with a fold-down dining table.

"One thing for sure," I told the agents. "We might drive this to Roundup, park it, and live in it, but I'm keeping my wheels handy for backup. I can't see trying to make a getaway in this heap with angry Freemen in fast vehicles chasing us around the mountains."

Agent Canady was not in the best of moods that day, either. In fact, he was in a very strange mood.

We were sitting at the eating table in the motor home and Canady was fidgeting with a briefcase. I had never seen him with a briefcase before. Another agent from the Billings office, Al Robinson, was at this meeting in the motor home.

Canady kept nervously going in and out of the vehicle, ducking his tall frame through the narrow door, pacing outside, and returning.

Jimmy Cassaria chatted with us about going inside the Freemen operation.

"You guys really spooked me about this job," he admitted. "I think when we do this we need to keep it very simple. Just introduce me as a contact you have from Arizona."

I had told the Freemen I knew dozens of ex-combat veterans, some of whom now worked as soldiers of fortune and mercenaries. It had been my intention to use that story to cover any FBI tactical-team men I might introduce in the future. Such a recommendation was forming in my mind at the time.

Connie and I had been inside the Freemen operation for over a month now, and we were becoming eager to get on with the arrests. Our two months would be up at the end of June, and the meeting at the motor home was held on June 6.

We discussed the case with Robinson and Cassaria and they both reminded us that our job was just to be "the eyes and ears for the Bureau."

"These guys are already indicted," Robinson said. "The case is made, they're looking at thirty-year sentences. We just need to put Cassaria in for a little while, to get the lay of the land."

So Connie and I talked calmly with Cassaria about how we could work around the biblical thing and his lack of knowledge of the pet peeves of the Freemen. We would cover him as a novice who just wanted to learn—someone we were trying to bring to the Lord, to a biblical understanding of what is wrong with America.

This did not seem to soothe the young agent's nerves much, but he was macho and could not admit he still did not want to try to infiltrate the Freemen fortress.

I had spent an entire adult life living under cover, most of my life in the woods, born and raised by a logger-construction worker family. Connie came from a construction family, too—her father, uncles, cousins, and brothers were all in the construction trades. We had both lived on the rough edge of the underworld for years, and knew that a single mistake could blow you away.

This young agent was a city boy. Even if he had the muscles and military training of a SWAT officer, he would fit better going under cover as a yuppie in a drug operation. We could never pass him off as an ideological right-wing fanatic. I could not teach him a lifetime of tricks of the dirty trade in a few days. But we would do our best.

We concocted a story that he was an ex–Green Beret and now an Arizona horse breeder. He was up here in Montana looking for some acreage on which to build his own little fortress.

That story might get him in; I was dubious about how long it would keep him alive. I had already decided I was not going to let this Bureau vanity about having their own guy inside get me or my wife killed. If it came down to fish or cut bait, when it came to Agent Cassaria, I was prepared to cut bait.

★ CHAPTER 13 ★

Our mission was changing, and if there had ever been any doubt about it, the next surprise move by the FBI made it perfectly clear.

There was an air of tension as we sat in the motor home and made small talk with Cassaria. Agent Canady returned to the motor home after pacing around the parking lot. He pulled out his briefcase, opened it, and extracted several sheets of neatly typed paper. The agent announced the papers were our official agreement. We had already been under cover for the Bureau since late April, and technically our two-month agreement was nearing an end.

I asked Canady why an agreement at this stage of the game. He just shuffled the papers without an explanation and walked away to take a call on his cellular phone. I was surprised about a written agreement in the first place, because in my previous experience with federal agencies I had never seen anything like a signed contract. Agreements were usually concluded with a handshake. Times were changing, so I didn't object.

Canady came back from the phone call and read my contract. He said Connie's was identical.

The contracts—typed on plain paper, not Bureau letterhead—stated that we would be "cooperating witnesses" in an FBI investigation into illegal activities of Schweitzer, Skurdal, and Petersen.

They specifically directed us to "meet with and should the opportunity present itself, physically reside on the property of Rodney O. Skurdal."

Further, the documents cited our responsibility to "meet with designated individuals" and to "make or have made by the FBI, consensual visual, oral, and wire recordings of [such] meetings and related telephone calls. Further, Cooperating Witness will provide written authorization to the FBI to monitor and record such meetings and conversations prior to such monitoring/recording."

The contracts required that we both appear as witnesses at the direction of the Bureau.

Then they went into detailed instructions forbidding us to participate in any unlawful activities unless the FBI expressly authorized us to do so. They specifically forbade us to "initiate any plans to commit criminal acts" or "participate in any acts of violence."

There were other boilerplate provisions and, finally, the whole thing was made completely voidable with a clause stating, "It may be terminated at any time by either party by deliverance of a written notice to terminate."

The documents were clearly intended to be cover-your-ass memos for the Bureau.

If that's what they wanted, why not? Connie and I discussed signing the contracts and agreed they included nothing beyond our verbal agreements.

However, Connie noted they did omit the most significant part of our agreement from our point of view. There was no mention of our promised pay, beyond a reference to the Bureau paying "reasonable expenses."

Connie went straight at the issue.

"These look fine, but what about our financial arrangements?" She shot the question at the agent.

Canady winked at me and grinned. "That's fine, we know what our agreement is on the pay."

When we signed the contracts, the three agents—Canady, Cassaria, and Robinson—seemed to spring into action.

"The operation is officially under way," one of the agents said.

That was a confusing statement since to our minds it had been under way for almost six weeks.

We went back to our motel with instructions to return to the parking lot the following day and be prepared to take Agent Cassaria, along with the big motor home, into the Freemen fortress.

Connie and I could hardly eat our dinner that evening and we barely slept at all.

The next day we met the agents at the lot and boarded the big brown-and-tan motor home. Agent Cassaria was to drive the vehicle, and I was to ride shotgun. I insisted that Connie follow in our pickup truck.

Roundup is fifty-one miles north of Billings on Highway 87, but the entrance to the Skurdal cabin on Johnny's Coal Road is three miles closer, also just off Highway 87.

We had scarcely cleared the city limits of Billings and headed north when I had one of the shocks of my life. It was a relatively warm June day, but Cassaria was bundled up in a long-sleeved flannel shirt with a bulky down vest buttoned up the front. I had on a short-sleeved cotton shirt.

"Why the winter clothes—expecting a cold front?" I asked, trying to soothe the agent's obvious stress with a joke. In the brief exchange that followed, much to my dismay, the agent revealed he was wearing a bullet-proof vest under his heavy shirt. And that was not all.

Cassaria was grimly driving along the highway, pushing the old RV to its maximum effort—about forty miles an hour. I thought he was mumbling to himself.

"Are you nervous?" I asked.

"Not so much," he replied, but he kept on mumbling, only louder now.

"Well, why are you talking to yourself?" I asked, irritated by his seemingly erratic behavior.

"I'm not, I'm talking to them." The young agent jerked a thumb skyward.

I leaned forward and looked up in the direction the agent had pointed.

"Holy shit!" I rarely curse, but I was incredulous at the new knowledge. Not only was this guy wearing armor, he was wired. And not only was he wired, but the feds were escorting us toward the Freemen stronghold with air cover—either a plane or helicopter was somewhere overhead and out of sight. I soon learned there were also vehicles loaded with agents trailing along behind us and on the road ahead. In addition, there was a small army of agents already in place in the woods surrounding the Freemen cabin.

I was completely incredulous that the Bureau would pull this without telling me or Connie. I was tempted to reach over and turn off the ignition switch to stop the vehicle in the middle of the highway.

The Bureau had told Connie and me nothing about this maneuver, and I did not have the vaguest idea what they intended to do when we arrived at the cabin.

We turned up Johnny's Coal Road, drove the mile to the cabin, and pulled the big trailer up into the long, direct driveway.

My heart was racing a mile a minute. I stepped from the cab of the motor home as calmly as possible under the circumstances and walked back to Connie, now parked in the pickup behind us.

I thought seriously about just getting into the pickup and driving away, leaving the big mobile home, the young agent, and the whole FBI sitting like ducks out on Johnny's Coal Road. But I couldn't do that—I was committed to the operation's success. And by now my curiosity was killing me. I hoped it wouldn't also literally kill me.

I knew from experience inside the cabin that any number of automatic and scoped hunting rifles were trained by Freemen on the strange rig that had pulled into their perimeter unannounced. It had been decided back in Billings, and against our strong recommendation to the contrary, that we would not announce our arrival to the Freemen beforehand.

That decision now led me to suspect the FBI must actually be planning a frontal assault on the cabin on this very trip.

All I could think about was getting my wife out of the line of fire. I walked over to the driver's window of the pickup and in a low, calm voice warned Connie.

"Don't get out of the pickup. Keep the engine running. These dumb shits are planning something, and they didn't even bother to let us in on it."

Connie looked alarmed, but waited for further instruction.

"At the sound of the first shot, you back out the driveway and scoot like hell for the highway. I'll cut through the woods and you can pick me up along Johnny's Coal Road somewhere."

I knew if I could reach the edge of the woods surrounding the cabin, no foe—Freeman or fed—could keep up with me. There was a small river I would have to swim before I reached my wife waiting down the road. No problem.

I was still stunned by what the agency had pulled on us, half angry, but too alarmed at the potential bad outcome to think about it now.

Connie nodded that she understood clearly what she was to do, and I walked back to the motor home. The agent was sitting in the cab looking sheepish. I'm afraid I had called him and the Bureau a few less-than-complimentary names upon learning we were in some sort of potentially armed confrontation situation.

The evolving scenario was all too familiar to me from my darker days under cover. Some agency, usually a local police force, fails to communicate with its undercover agent. Someone screws up. Someone lets himself be seen, or a shot is fired prematurely.

All I could think about as I scanned the surrounding woods was whether there were black-clad snipers lurking in the shadows. At that moment I was more concerned about getting caught in the cross-fire of FBI sharpshooters than getting shot by the Freemen in the cabin.

I'm naked, I thought. Not even packing. At least Connie was clear of the fire zone, parked behind the mobile home. She could get the hell out of there.

It was then I noticed several additional vehicles parked beside the cabin. I walked back to the RV and within earshot of Agent Cassaria.

"Great," I said, "the Freemen have reinforcements."

I had no idea who the visitors were, how many, or how well armed they might be. The cars had Oklahoma license plates, and I knew the Freemen had close alliances with Freemen in that state and with other Oklahoma militia types.

About that time Rodney Skurdal came out on the porch, his hand on the Glock .45 holstered on his waist. The Freemen leader was visibly shaken. He stood on the porch and glared at me. I knew rifles were at the curtained windows backing him.

I waved and he recognized me. I went back to the would-be undercover FBI agent and warned him: "Come on out and meet the Freemen. Let me do the talking. Just don't get excited no matter what they say to you. Don't—and I mean, don't—make any sudden moves."

The guy had turned green.

I walked toward Skurdal, motioning Cassaria to follow. It was thirty seconds before Skurdal calmed down and I introduced him to the agent.

"You shouldn't just walk in here," Skurdal snarled. "We didn't recognize that big vehicle—and this guy." He pointed at the agent. "You gave us a real rush."

I looked at Cassaria, standing exposed to the rifles I knew were aimed at his heart just a few feet away behind the curtains.

He stood there in his winter garb, clean-cut, short dark curly hair, thirtyish, and city-slicker clean in his new jeans, red vest, and hiking boots. I still half expected to hear a rifle crack and see this young agent blown down the driveway.

But Skurdal broke the silence.

"You should have called," he said. "We can't see you today. There's a private meeting going on inside. You'll have to come back."

"Geez, I'm sorry. I wanted you to meet my friend from Arizona. He brought up the motor home so we could have a place to stay while I complete my studies. This driving back and forth from Winnett is getting to be a drag." I acted contrite, but it did not take much acting skill to show humility. I was genuinely apologetic, but not for showing up unannounced. I wanted to apologize for the FBI's bungling on this potentially deadly caper.

"Now you have to go." Skurdal was insistent.

"I'm really sorry, I should have called first. Okay, we'll bug out, but can I leave the motor home?" I asked

"We've got some more people coming in. There's no room for that thing in the driveway." Skurdal was still agitated.

I ventured that since the big vehicle was already here, maybe I could move it out of the way.

"Park it across the road next to the storage sheds," Skurdal relented, making it clear he just wanted us to leave.

I was glad to comply and we quickly moved the big RV, locked it, and got into the pickup with Connie. Making our exit, Connie sprayed gravel halfway down Johnny's Coal Road.

I was too numb to talk, but I had a thousand angry questions.

We made small talk, with Agent Cassaria mumbling into his vest to unseen aircraft and an unseen convoy.

Then Cassaria brought up Ruby Ridge.

"I was there, you know," he said, with an edge of pride in his voice.

"I didn't know," I responded bitterly.

We drove down the highway in silence and were soon overtaken by an unmarked car. The driver blinked his lights and we pulled over. Agent Cassaria got out of the pickup and was whisked into the FBI car by Special Agent Canady.

The Bureau never tried to get one of its own inside the Freemen fortress at Roundup again.

★ CHAPTER 14 ★

An internal feud between the Montana Freemen leaders and a powerful branch of like-minded white separatists from Oklahoma so overshadowed the incident at the cabin on June 7, 1995, that the FBI snafu passed almost unnoticed.

Connie and I took two days off before cautiously returning to the cabin at Roundup. The motor home sat where we had left it, and the four Freemen leaders greeted us with open arms.

The cars with the Oklahoma license plates were gone, but the remains of the bitter debate that had been going on inside the cabin when we arrived with Agent Cassaria and the RV lingered. Shortly after our return, Daniel Petersen informed us that Schweitzer was not in a good mood.

It seems our clumsy intrusion three days earlier had interrupted an internecine feud between Schweitzer, who held himself up to be the chief justice of the Freemen supreme court, and Dennis Smith, who billed himself to be the chief justice of Our One Supreme Court.

Smith and Gerald J. Henson, who headed the Oklahoma-based United Sovereigns of uSA [*sic*], had brought a delegation over from Oklahoma to argue about who had the authority to run the seminars and training sessions for future recruitment.

The Oklahoma group had the manpower, claiming more than three hundred trained and active members.

The Montana Freemen badly needed manpower assistance to carry out the next phase of its clandestine plan—the establishment of an independent nation of white sovereigns. Henson would later be convicted of fraud in a U.S. District Court in Austin, along with a dozen others from Oklahoma and Texas. Sentences in those cases, ranging from nineteen to thirty-five years in federal prison, were assessed in federal courts.

Some of the evidence presented in those trials included bogus money orders signed by LeRoy Schweitzer and notarized by Rodney Skurdal. The U.S. attorney trying these cases presented ample evidence linking the Texas and Oklahoma operations to the Montana Freemen. It was only one of many such cases across the nation to emanate from the cabin at Roundup.

Apparently, the Oklahomans were not all that interested in setting up a new republic out on the windswept high plains of Montana. They were doing just fine, thank you, in the very heartland of America.

Petersen told me that the Oklahoma leadership had reneged on promises to provide the warriors, just as the Militia of Montana had declined to provide the soldiers after the confrontation that got leader John Trochmann arrested at Roundup a few months earlier.

So the mood in the cabin upon our return was one of gloom. Connie and I noticed the Freemen leaders were squabbling among themselves, whether as a result of these minor defeats or from cabin fever we were not sure.

The Freemen were obsessed with recruiting armed and trained followers and were being frustrated at every turn. Connie and I would discover soon enough why they needed an army, but for now we just wanted to finish our assignment and get out. The FBI's bungled efforts to get one of its own agents inside had unnerved us, and we decided that we would make every effort to wrap up our intelligence assignment, turn it over to the feds, and clear out of Montana.

The Northwest would not be big enough to hide our family in after this operation was concluded, and we had already begun making arrangements to head out and start over again—one last time. This time Connie did not have to convince me there would be no more undercover jobs.

We set out with new resolve to complete our job as quickly as possible. I began working on a plan to document every minute of the Freemen leaders' activities.

The motor home was parked across Johnny's Coal Road, away

from the driveway leading up to the cabin, and I wanted to get closer for better surveillance.

I had noticed a concrete pad adjacent to the cabin, which had been used as a one-hoop basketball court. It was now covered with loose tree limbs and other debris. I complained that the motor home could not be leveled at its designated site and I finally secured permission to move it onto the concrete, closer to the cabin.

Skurdal helped me clean off the pad. I watched in amazement as the powerful Skurdal, a former oil-field roughneck, grabbed railroad ties and, single-handedly, tossed them into the bed of my pickup truck.

We moved the big vehicle right up to the cabin, and within a couple of days we were as much a part of the daily routine as the Freemen's furniture. I observed the day and night operations, while Connie took copious notes on everything that transpired, drew maps, and made schedules of the visitors delivering mail, groceries, and other necessities.

We quickly learned that the Freemen had a careful security routine. They posted round-the-clock guards—someone with a high-powered rifle was designated to stay close behind curtained windows at all times, watching the gravel-road approaches to the cabin.

At night I put on dark clothing and slipped out to spy through the cracks in the curtains inside the cabin. It was on such late-night trips that I discovered Skurdal regularly watched pornographic movies piped into the cabin by satellite. The men had now been holed up in the cabin for over two years, seldom, if ever, enjoying female companionship.

This was not Skurdal's only weird behavior. Skurdal, who had suffered injuries in an oil-field accident several years earlier when a drilling rig pipe fell on his head, had a bizarre fetish about his kitchen—particularly his electric stove. He did all the cooking for the main evening meal, which was usually some form of hamburger concoction or spaghetti. When he was in the kitchen he would never allow anyone else to come into the room.

On several occasions when visitors unwittingly approached, he threatened them if they did not leave immediately. Faced with his wild glare, few people questioned he was serious. He would allow others to help clean up dishes, but no one could wipe off his electric stove.

Interesting as these idiosyncrasies were, they were not what Connie and I had been sent in to discover. But we reported everything to the Bureau.

Early in June 1995, more and more strangers appeared at the cabin. Carloads of heavily armed men, with license plates from all over the Northwest and Texas, Georgia, Arizona, Colorado, New Mexico, California, Nevada, Michigan, Ohio, West Virginia, Utah, and other states, arrived on a regular basis. They identified themselves as members of various patriotic militias.

Three-day training sessions, led by the four Freemen leaders, were held for each group. I sat in on all these sessions, usually attended by a half-dozen to a score of militiamen. Each Freemen leader had a well-prepared role in the seminars. During June and July, I must have taken the class at least twenty times. Connie took notes until she had the course memorized, and we also secured copies of the prepared text used by Schweitzer and Skurdal in making their presentations.

The classes were conducted from a lectern or pulpit set up in the living room of the cabin. Small groups would sit around the large dining-cum-conference table. If the group was larger, students would spill out onto the sofa and folding chairs were brought in to augment the other living room furniture.

The only audiovisual or stage prop used in the seminars was a large rope, fashioned into a hangman's noose, mounted on the wall behind the lectern.

Rarely did any of the visitors stay at the cabin. One spare bedroom of the four bedrooms upstairs was occasionally offered to the highest-ranking militia officer from each group. The soldiers were billeted at one of the two motels in Roundup, or with individuals in the area who were sympathetic to the cause.

The seminars offered a strange mixture of basic hate courses, which I described to Connie as Holy War 101 (religion), Insurrection 101 (civics), and Economics Chaos 101 (fraud).

Dale Jacobi was the warm-up speaker. He was well grounded in the teachings of the Christian Identity theology, having served his tutelage under the masters in the Aryan Nations before moving on to the Militia of Montana, and finally arriving to serve as a sort of chaplain-in-charge at the Freemen's cabin.

The Christian Identity theology—a white-supremacist doctrine with roots in pre–World War II fascist interpretations of the Bible— holds that Anglo-Saxons are the true lost tribe of Israel and are besieged by all other races and mongrels of mixed races. Jews are the spawn of Satan, and all people of color are not human, but Mud People. This religion, under various names, has been used by practically every hate group in America from the early Ku Klux Klan or Silver Shirts to the modern Aryan Republican Army, neo-Nazi skinheads, warrior cells of the militias, and the Priests of Phineas. The ideology forms the basic authority to justify murder, armed robbery, and every other imaginable crime.

The Christian Identity theology holds that the real racial divide began with Cain and Abel. Adam sired Abel as the first white man. Eve's sin resulted in the spawning of the treacherous Cain, who was the first Jew. After murdering his brother, the first Jewish assault on the pure white race, Cain began fornicating with other nonwhite beings, thereby spawning more Jews, blacks, Asians, Arabs, and an unholy assortment of mixed races—the Mud People. Misusing chapter and verse from throughout the Old Testament, Christian Identity concludes that these Mud People are not human; thus, to kill them is not murder.

The theology, according to Freemen doctrine, was simple for anyone with eyes to see: White people were heirs of God through Adam. Most of the radical white supremacists refer to their supreme being as Yahweh. Jews were of Satan through Cain and the Canaanites. Everyone else descended from subhuman Ammonites and Moabites, and were not even worthy of consideration of a trial and hanging.

Jacobi, clean-shaven and well groomed, was an efficient minister of this distorted gospel. He was articulate and educated and his presentations had an air of authority that convinced many of the seminar attendees that he knew what he was talking about.

"It was the Jews who brought the blacks into this country to destroy us," he preached. "They knew it would eventually happen, and it is. God tells his children to kill, many, many times in the Scripture."

Jacobi could have been a pretty successful fire-and-brimstone evangelical preacher, but no legitimate fundamentalist congregation would have tolerated his brand of hate religion for five minutes. So he sought a flock that had already rejected their down-home Christian faith for a religious license to cover their murderous intentions.

Once the biblical authority had been established by Jacobi, Rodney Skurdal made his presentation.

"Thus, as you can see, our liberties come from God. It [sic] does not come from public servants nor from any of our public officials." Skurdal opened each of his sessions with an exhortation to disobey all laws including, or especially, the payment of taxes.

White males, he theorized, were sovereigns and not subject to any law. Only the others, nonwhites and women—who were granted limited, specific rights by the Fourteenth Amendment to the Constitution—were obliged to obtain certain government permits, including drivers' licenses. All these "others" were not true Freemen.

To cooperate even to the extent of paying taxes was to support the Zionist Occupation Government (ZOG), and was thus an act of treason. All acts of treason are punishable by death.

Skurdal referred to the noose on the wall behind him as the appropriate instrument of that decision to be used on all white traitors—especially the ZOG lackeys who held federal, state, or local government positions. Nonwhites, of course, did not warrant the privilege of a trial and hanging, and should be shot on sight for any interference with white-supremacy edicts.

"The Constitution applies only to whites . . . 'we the people' refers only to white males . . . white women are to be wives, and wives cannot vote . . . we the people of posterity are exercising our citizen rights to govern ourselves as free sovereigns . . . we are an independent state in law." The law, according to justice of the Freemen court Rodney O. Skurdal, was expounded in his diatribe for two to three hours, depending on how lucid he was on a given day.

Skurdal, with his huge pot belly, faded, patched jeans, and

shaggy hair and beard, would not have been granted tenure at any law school I can think of, and I doubted that anyone in the classes was overly influenced by his presentation. Most of the attendees were hard-core, antigovernment separatists long before they came to the Freemen seminar in Montana.

LeRoy Schweitzer's presentation, the pièce de résistance of the three-day program, was saved for last and took up the better part of two days. The monotony of the program was broken occasionally with general demonstrations in the hands-on use of fraudulent checks and money orders. How-to sessions were conducted on the methods for filing bogus liens against the property of private individuals and government officials.

Once in a while the visitors had to relieve their boredom by going into the woods to make sure their many and varied weapons still worked. It was not uncommon to hear the report of rapid-fire weapons echoing down the valleys of the Bull Mountains during one of Schweitzer's long-winded presentations.

No one paid much attention to the gunfire. It was only another militiaman truant slipping from class into the woods to entertain himself with his AK-47 assault rifle or 9mm automatic.

Chief justice Schweitzer, a former crop duster who had lost his planes and his business for failure to pay taxes, was the mastermind and founding father of the supreme court of the Republic of Roundup. His closest adherents in Montana, numbering at various times from fifty to one hundred, revered his every word.

Some of the more sophisticated visitors did not always share this adoration. A few of the visiting militiamen even expressed shock at the radical teachings concerning the murder of minorities. It was probably this murderous dialogue that prevented the Freemen from accomplishing their real goal—the recruitment of fighters from out-of-state militias to come to Montana for the Freemen uprising.

Schweitzer made it clear to all seminar attendees that the Roundup location, which encompassed only twenty acres, was just a temporary location of convenience. A far greater Freemen republic, the exact territory unspecified at the moment, was forming; all that was needed was a small army of about two hundred good men, and the new state-within-a-state would be launched.

Likewise, each group in attendance was instructed to return to their home states and prepare to take over similar chosen real estate. Once the armed insurrections and actual takeovers were completed, Schweitzer had a blueprint for Bible-based governance, and that is what he taught at the sessions.

"We have both the law and the power," Schweitzer began his part of the seminar. "You are the power. We are the power."

To accomplish its goals, each unit must first identify and mark its local territory carefully. The first phase, of course, would have to be war, or at least skirmishes, to drive out the illicit existing government. Fighting squads of twelve, broken down into assault teams of four men each, were recommended. Once the land area was secured, local authorities hanged, and Mud People purged or shot, then the new governmental units could be formed.

Twelve was the biblically correct number to govern a sovereign republic—whether that entity covered a township, a county, or a state.

"Elijah took twelve stones and with the twelve stones he built the altar." This was Schweitzer's explanation for the necessity to pick twelve men to govern each unit.

These dozen leaders or justices formed the supreme court. Each court was to have a chief justice. After the area was secured and pacified, each unit of government would then appoint the number of constables required to enforce the laws of the court. The only other position called for in the hierarchy was a chaplain, a sort of white-supremacist version of an ayatollah to monitor correct religious conduct. Each newly founded government body was to operate as a quasi-Christian theocracy.

Schweitzer likened the new autonomous nation to a biblical new Zion, where a Freeman of character could hold office or even vote.

There was a clearly defined chain of command for this government:

"Almighty God, pursuant to His Holy Scriptures.

"Adam, symbol of the white race, God's chosen people.

"We the People of Posterity, obedient to the Laws of Almighty God, also known as our Common Law."

The others, living in the United States under provisions of the Fourteenth Amendment, were so low down on the charts that they were defined in the small print on the back of the covenants.

"Jews, who currently manipulate all federal, state, and local government through the ZOG," Schweitzer yelled, "you are of your father, the devil, and your will is to do your father's desire. He was a murderer from the beginning, and has nothing to do with the truth, because there is no truth in him."

He, of course, had to shout because there were certainly never any Jewish people within earshot of the seminars and the cabin.

Americans of color were also lumped into this group with the Jews; being the descendants of Cain, like the Jews, "their father was the devil, Satan."

These heirs of Satan and Cain created Baal, which the Freemen used as an interchangeable description for the current government in America; thus, all who served as government employees were deemed to be prophets of Baal. There was clear direction on what to do about them in Schweitzer's course book.

"Seize the prophets of Baal; let not one of them escape . . . and kill them there!" On his better days he would fairly screech the command, often waking drowsers among the attendants. "Prophets of Baal represent our so-called congress and/or state legislators . . . Satans of today, creating and passing manmade laws, regulations, codes, rules, and policies, under color of law . . ."

So after getting rid of these modern-day Satans—the congressmen and state representatives—the next order was to set up a true government. I often mused during the tedious seminar sessions that some of the politicians I had met might indeed fit the Freemen description of devils—but, no . . .

"In essence, this is our command, to establish a de jure government pursuant to the Holy Scriptures," he admonished the pupils. This de jure government was ordered by God and, therefore, superior to state or federal governments, which were termed "foreign governments."

Once the local governments were established along the lines the Freemen advocated, the job of coordinating them on a national level had to be tackled. It was a messy job, but somebody had to do it and Schweitzer offered the formula. He, of course, would be happy to serve as the national head guy in any arbitration between the local republics—sort of a first among peers in the chief justice system.

The new governmental structure was designed as a theocracy, too, based on some fuzzy biblical interpretations of a "Trinity form of government." The structure included:

* National Government (God) headed by the supreme judiciary branch;
* State Government (Son) headed by the executive branch; and
* County Government (Holy Spirit) headed by the legislative branch.

According to one of Schweitzer's favorite examples, it made sense that only white males could serve in any post of the new government.

"If a citizen from China was placed into our offices in our state, he would, of course, impose his laws of China upon us, contrary to our common law, pursuant to the word of Almighty God," Schweitzer reasoned.

Each of these levels of government was to be managed by justices elected by Freemen of character and administered by judges, commissioners, and constables. But even though some national structure was required, the government as seen by the Freemen was a bottom-up organization, with the township remaining the final authority for governance in any given locale. The ideal local entity or township would have a population of about four hundred persons.

It was such a township republic that the Freemen had in mind for their part of Montana, and which they ultimately established at the Justus Township near Jordan. That township, however, was just an embryonic structure for a more ambitious plan to take over a whole town. The Freemen's real plan for Montana was gradually revealed as Connie and I continued our daily chores of intelligence-gathering.

Some of the more militant militiamen attending the seminars

clearly lost interest when the teaching turned from guerrilla warfare to twisted biblical civics.

Having sat through scores of these sessions, I could sympathize with the younger men's lack of patience. The seminar presentations were not straightforward talks; rather, they were built on hours of seemingly endless quotation from obscure legal and Constitutional documents, as well as Scripture.

The Freemen bibliography included everything from out-of-date Webster's dictionaries to the 1889 version of the Montana constitution. Also cited as authority for the teachings were select parts of Articles of the U.S. Constitution, the Declaration of Independence, and cases from scores of yellowing, ragged old law books amassed in the cabin library. Even the Magna Carta of 1215 was a frequently quoted source for Freemen authority.

One of the earlier groups attending the session was from Arizona. The militiamen from that state called their unit the Arizona Viper Cell. I learned it was an offshoot of one of the main Arizona militias. During a coffee break, two or three members of this group gathered outside the cabin and I joined them. They were not happy with the seminar's discourse on civics. The group members, who identified themselves by first names only as David, Randy, and Scott, said they had hoped there would be more information on military tactics.

After I told them of my extensive background in explosives and made up a great story about my own military training, a Viper spokesman confided that their dozen-man unit was prepared for war.

He said they were well versed in explosives, already testing their bombs in the desert outside Phoenix. The Vipers boasted that they had videotaped most of their targets, which included federal buildings and law enforcement facilities in Maricopa County, Arizona. They had also amassed an arsenal and identified the officials they planned to take out.

We relayed this bit of intelligence on the Arizona Vipers to the FBI in one of our next reports. A year later, in July 1996, federal and state lawmen raided the Viper Cell, after having successfully placed a local game warden inside the group.

When the Arizona Viper Cell was busted, authorities seized

enough explosives to level eight buildings, and enough guns and ammunition to arm hundreds of terrorists. Just as the men bragged to me, the arresting agents found videotapes of target facilities all over the Phoenix area.

But at the time, June 1995, intelligence-gathering on groups we encountered at the cabin, such as the Arizona Viper Cell, was frosting on the cake. We still believed our primary mission at this moment was to gather every bit of information possible to accomplish the arrest of the Freemen of Montana.

Over the weeks we attended the seminars, a troubling pattern began to emerge. The Freemen were teaching an elaborate scheme of financial fraud. They were using aberrant biblical and common law for the justification of white supremacy and ethnic cleansing. And they were urging the militia units to return to their own communities and set up new government cells for the day they took the country back from local authorities.

But their agenda went further.

We learned that the Freemen were waiving the $300 per person seminar fee for a select few. In fact, they were offering the course free of charge to the more radical militia groups because they were asking something of far more value in return. The Freemen were attempting to enlist these groups in a nationwide uprising against the local and state governments back home. The Freemen reasoned that in order to successfully establish their own republic in Montana, there had to be simultaneous chaos all across the country. This would serve to divert the attention of the nation's law enforcement agencies.

At first, the FBI office in Billings was eager to get this new insight into the true Freemen and militia agenda. Then, abruptly, Agent Canady ordered us to cease pursuing this line of intelligence and focus on our mission of helping stage the arrest of the four Freemen leaders.

Connie and I were delighted that the end of the assignment might now be in sight. Canady told us that high-level tactical and psychological teams would shortly be coming in from Washington for a major, multiday debriefing.

CHAPTER 15

Nerves were fraying at both ends of the string during the first two weeks of June. Connie and I were trapped in the middle, as the string was pulled tighter.

In Billings, the FBI office was abuzz with preparations for the arrival of the high-level Washington teams.

In the cabin at Roundup, bickering between Skurdal and the other three Freemen leaders created an electric atmosphere of constant tension.

The cabin was Skurdal's castle. Even though he technically no longer owned the property because of IRS tax liens against it, he literally guarded his property by force of arms.

His odd and possessive behavior, which was earlier displayed over his kitchen, manifested itself in other ways. Skurdal often snapped at Jacobi and Petersen for trivial misdeeds, like leaving a coffee cup on top of the TV. He seldom challenged Schweitzer.

Connie and I stayed clear of the spats and tried to make ourselves useful to the men. Whenever a chore needed doing we would volunteer. In order to establish a routine that allowed us to leave the premises without notice, we carried mail to town and picked up groceries and supplies. We volunteered to drive the fifty miles to Billings for office and computer supplies whenever possible. Of course, every trip out of the cabin provided opportunities to telephone or make personal visits to our FBI contact. We established a cover story about personal and family business obligations to permit us to make overnight trips away from the cabin.

Jacobi, the former policeman, was the only one of the leaders who seemed suspicious of our comings and goings. He would cross-examine our story each time we asked permission to be away from the cabin for more than a day. Petersen seemed especially wary of what I had to say on any topic. Skurdal began taking a special interest in Connie's activities, watching her constantly and making up little projects that required her to spend time with him.

We chalked up the tension to end-game jitters, but sometimes felt as if the hunters were being stalked by the prey.

One afternoon Connie had just finished taking a shower in the tiny water closet of the motor home when we learned that the Freemen were spying on us, too. She had toweled off and was dressing for dinner at the cabin. I was lying across the couch in the vehicle's small living-dining area. Connie and I had been talking about alternative plans for making the arrest. We had not quite figured out the mechanics of bringing in a sizable team to seize the Freemen leaders. We had discussed the possibility of introducing a dozen or more FBI tactical-assault men disguised as militiamen from some out-of-the-way cell in Alaska.

I heard, or sensed, a motion outside the shell of the vehicle and saw a shadow pass across one of the small windows.

I waved frantically to Connie in the next bay and made a shushing sign with my finger to my lips. We listened for a few minutes and then changed our conversation to a pretend argument over some obscure common-law point from one of Schweitzer's talks. Several more minutes passed before Petersen stepped through the door, unannounced. We had no idea how long he had been lurking outside or what he may have heard. Fortunately, we had several borrowed common-law books spread on the table.

"Oh, good, I'm glad you're here, Dan," I said. "Connie and I aren't clear on a point or two. Do you have time to help us with this?" I opened one of the books and asked the first question that came to mind. He seemed pleased that we were studying so hard.

It was clear to us that any small slip-up, even in the most private moment, could be terminal. Like all undercover jobs, this was a twenty-four-hour immersion.

Despite our heightened concern, the Freemen leaders seemed

to accept that we were dedicated pupils of their gospel. In the final analysis, they were glad to have the helping hands.

The Freemen's requests for the commitment of troops were rebuffed repeatedly by various militia leaders visiting the cabin. Schweitzer was growing more and more impatient to amass his own private army.

On one occasion after a visit to the cabin by Richard Butler, leader of the Aryan Nations at Hayden Lake, Idaho, the four Freemen leaders were complaining that they could not get on with their plans because of the manpower shortage. Butler apparently had told them that the Aryan Nations soldiers were needed for other missions. The radical minister was in a campaign to consolidate all militia, Klan, and other groups from across the nation under his own leadership. He was not about to dilute his power or authority by providing troops to the Montana Freemen.

I took the opportunity to join in the conversation around the conference table in the cabin.

"I may be able to help you with this," I said casually. I reminded them that over the years I had developed a sizable list of men—Vietnam vets unhappy with their treatment by the government and the public's rejection after the war. I told the Freemen I counted numerous mercenaries among my former associates.

"I know at least fifty, maybe even a hundred, men I could assemble in a minute for the right cause," I said.

"We have the right cause," Skurdal snapped. "You believe that by now, don't you?"

"Well, yes, the cause is good, but why do you need so many warriors?" I asked.

The four leaders looked at each other with broad grins.

"I think brother Dale is ready to hear this," Skurdal said to Schweitzer. Schweitzer nodded.

"We're ready to begin the final phase of the Lord's plan," Schweitzer said. "We're ready to claim our rightful land and set up our true republic."

A weird scheme of surreal proportions tumbled from the mouths of the Freemen leaders.

"We told you we were interested in your explosives experience. That talent is just one that is needed," Schweitzer said. "We are going to take over Winnett, by force of arms if necessary, and all the territory, the federal lands, the ranches, everything around it. It will be the headquarters of the Freemen Republic in Montana. We will rename it Justus Township."

I couldn't wait to hear the details of what amounted to an armed insurrection within the borders of the United States; but, as with most of the Freemen preachments, I had to sit through a Bible lesson first.

The name Justus was symbolic to the Freemen cause. Most newspeople would later assume and report that Justus Township, posted on signs during the Freemen standoff at Brusett, was a misspelling of *justice*. But it was not.

Justus was an obscure biblical character in the Book of Colossians 4:11. He was a follower of Christ. Because his name was also Jesus, he took the name Justus, which means "righteous" in Hebrew. The man was also a converted Jew. The Freemen misinterpreted the verse. By way of their misunderstanding, they thought this person was the Christ. A careful reading of this passage makes it clear that Justus was another biblical figure entirely. Thus, ironically, the anti-Semitic Freemen actually named their capital after a converted Jew. They also liked the sound of the name Justus and referred to the township designation as "just-us."

Once they had explained the reason for the name of the Freemen's proposed new capital city, the leaders went on to reveal their plan for Winnett.

"You may wonder why we need your explosives skills," Jacobi said. "You will be needed to mine the roads and bridges."

I talked explosives for a few minutes—everything from excavating pits, rock quarries, and coyote tunnels to dropping bridges, buildings, and towers. I wanted to cement my position as the only bomb maker the Freemen would ever need, so they would not recruit someone who might actually do their deeds for them. I talked about everything from homemade black powder to nitromon canisters, from rocket-propelled explosives with hardened tips—set off on tripods and dropped into rock for a directed explosion—to timed devices, radio detonation, and delay switches.

The Freemen leaders were impressed since they had little or no idea what I was talking about. I probably could have convinced them I could deliver a small nuclear device.

"So back to what you need the extra manpower for . . ." I urged them to reveal more of their diabolical plan for Winnett and its citizens.

The Freemen's ultimate aim was to take over the small town, which was located forty-six miles northeast of their present location at the Roundup cabin in the Bull Mountains.

This plan was the source of friction among the leaders, since Skurdal wanted the new republic located around his cabin and property. The others did not want a headquarters out in the boonies with no facilities.

Since a number of Freemen lived in or around Winnett, it had been selected.

I could now see why the Freemen had been harassing the people in Winnett, why they put liens on old people's land, why they targeted even the postmistress.

Their liens and bounties and threats were not idle mischief.

It was revealed at the conference table that, to their way of thinking, all the Freemen now had to do was foreclose on their bogus liens against the citizens, the government property, the federal lands. According to their own perverse logic and law, they had a legal claim on all the lands they were planning to seize.

Of course, they realized this legal claim would not satisfy the outside world, so they would have to enforce their takeover with armed troops.

"We'll need another hundred or so, in addition to the fifty local Freemen we can count on to fight," Schweitzer said.

I asked about the additional hundred or so Freemen members he claimed lived in the area, and he mumbled that they were "probably too wimpy to confront the feds directly."

I looked into the eyes of the four men seated around the table so casually talking about armed rebellion. I guess I wanted to see some hint that they were joshing me. In each set of eyes I saw a flame of fanaticism that convinced me they not only were serious, but fervently believed they could pull this off.

The plan that unfolded sent chills from my scalp down my spine, even though the June temperature made the big room in the cabin quite warm.

One or another of the four eagerly explained the details of the operation.

Winnett was on the edge of the sparsely populated prairie, a strategic crossroads gateway to vast open ranches, farms, and uninhabited federal preserves.

Inside the little town of Winnett, the Freemen were going to take whatever houses they wanted, arrest the occupants, and bring to trial and hang all the local officials. They would shoot anyone who opposed them.

Winnett straddles the intersection of U.S. Highway 87 from Billings and State Highway 200 to points east and west. It sits in the basin of Box Elder and Flat Willow Creeks. To the north are the huge reservoirs of the upper Missouri River and the vast federal lands dedicated to wildlife conservation. The rough surrounding country is downslope from the Judith Mountains, rising to 6,427 feet above sea level, and the Big Snowy Mountains, to 8,370-foot elevation.

There is little of commercial significance in the vicinity. The country might best be described as a long way between nothing and nothing. Thus, it was ideal for Justus Township and the headquarters for the new Freemen empire.

By Freemen reckoning and experience, no local authority had the strength to oppose the takeover. And nobody else was likely to care enough to fight over it. Once the town was captured, the feds, based on their recent history of lack of response to the outrages committed so far, would just posture and grumble. The government didn't want another confrontation, and even if the FBI or ATF did, right-wing congressmen would keep them too busy to intervene by holding endless committee hearings in Washington.

But just in case the feds moved against them, the Freemen wanted to cut or at least mine the bridges on the two intersecting highways over Box Elder Creek to the east and Flat Willow Creek coming in from the south. The road to the west ran between the Big Snowy and Judith Mountains, so the narrows would be easy to control with just a few well-armed militia troops.

All in all, Winnett would be a pretty easy place to defend against local and state law enforcement. Once the uprising started, the Freemen thought they could count on hate-patriot allies in Washington to neutralize the FBI and ATF. They took comfort in their misguided theory from the endless harangues against the federal government that spewed forth from talk radio and television.

The Freemen expected they could hold the place long enough to win any negotiation.

I pointed out that even if roads and bridges could be held, the feds had air power. The Freemen leaders didn't seem to worry about helicopter or aerial assault, reasoning that the feds wouldn't dare do anything after Waco and Ruby Ridge. They were totally counting on the paralysis of the federal government. Recent events—particularly the congressional attacks on the Bureau—actually encouraged them to proceed with their plan quickly, and convinced them they would succeed.

"We're talking about defending large areas of territory, not some shack or isolated compound," Schweitzer added.

"What about the people who live there now?" I asked.

"When the little old ladies come to the post office for their Social Security checks, that's too bad," Petersen said. " Nothing will move in the town without our okay."

I asked what the residents would live on.

He suggested that would be the people's problem. "We want them to leave anyway, so the sooner we starve them out the better. Nobody but Freemen of character can live in our republic."

"We already have enough manpower to take the town right now," Skurdal said, rattling off a list of names of local Freemen he could count on. "But to hold it we need about two hundred men, total."

"So what about these mercenaries you keep talking about?" Schweitzer asked. "How much money would we have to pay them to come in for a few months until we negotiate a permanent republic?"

I wanted to keep this line open, so I quickly came up with a solution.

"The men I know would not want any money," I said. "They are all Nam vets who have been crapped on for years. They just want a place, maybe twenty acres of land apiece, to build a cabin over a bunker and settle down."

I made up a tale of drifting, exhausted mercenaries, roving the world from rebellion to civil war, tired and ready to put down roots, marry, and raise families.

Jacobi was the only Freeman who questioned me closely about my ability to bring in the extra manpower.

I was on firm ground in convincing them I could actually produce as many trained military types equipped with the latest weapons that the Freemen could ask for. They badly wanted to believe my tale of a vast reserve of willing recruits. And I could actually deliver on my promise. However, the Freemen would find these splendid troops lacking in only one regard—they would be from the FBI's tactical-assault teams. And instead of coming to help in the takeover of Winnett, they would take over the cabin at Roundup. Instead of hanging local citizens, they would arrest these mad revolutionary Freemen leaders.

Finally, we had arrived upon a workable plan to get the FBI's Hostage Rescue Team inside the cabin. I could hardly wait for the next briefing to tell the Bureau the news.

⋆ ⋆ ⋆

Meanwhile, moving the motor home closer to the cabin had been a wise decision, even though it placed us right under the noses of the Freemen leaders. This close proximity to the cabin greatly enhanced my ability to check on the Freemen inside. We could peer through the curtains on the tiny windows and see almost any movement on the ground floor.

I picked different times of the night to slip from the trailer in dark clothing and snoop around the perimeter of the cabin. I watched the Freemen's late-evening activities until they drifted off upstairs to bed.

Skurdal usually volunteered to do overnight guard duty. I had earlier learned it was his only opportunity to watch dirty flicks on TV. Night after night he would sit in the same place on the couch, facing the TV, with a hunting rifle across his lap. One night peering into the dimly lit cabin, I noticed Skurdal was sound asleep, his head dropped on the back of the couch, his mouth wide open. I could hear his snores through the thick log walls and sealed windows.

Neither Connie nor I had ever been invited to look at the upstairs bedrooms. On several occasions the Bureau had asked us to get the upstairs layout. So I slipped through the front door and walked close to Skurdal to check on the depth of his sleep.

I carefully nudged his arm, keeping an eye on the rifle in his lap, and prepared to make an excuse about why I was in the cabin should my nudge wake him. He did not stir.

I walked upstairs and went from bedroom to bedroom. Schweitzer and Jacobi were both snoring deeply. When I opened the door to look into Petersen's room, I froze. The room was completely silent. Petersen apparently does not snore, or at least he wasn't that night. I finally heard his faint, even breathing and carefully pulled the door closed.

I could have arrested all four of the leaders then and there, with nothing more than a good hard bump on each of their heads. The Freemen kept plenty of duct tape and plastic handcuff strips in the storage room downstairs.

But my orders from Agent Canady were clear enough: Take no action without permission in advance. In hindsight, I have often thought that this was the first blunder of the Bureau's $50 million mistake.

When I returned to the motor home, Connie was awake—she never dozed off when I was out on one of my night reconnoiters. She was fit to be tied.

"What do you think you're doing going inside that cabin at three in the morning?" Connie was angry, having watched me through the small trailer-home window as I entered the house. "I expected to hear a blast at any time."

As I whispered an apology for my reckless prowling, my hand

touched cold steel on the bunk bed beside her. She had pulled one of our two Ruger .22s from a hiding place in the cupboard.

"What were you going to do with that?" I asked.

"I was thinking about shooting you when you came out of that cabin, you jerk."

We had repeatedly asked Agent Canady to let us carry weapons on this job, but he refused.

"I don't want you cowboys shooting any of my Freemen," he responded to one such request.

So I fudged a little and took in two of the small-caliber rapid-fire semiautomatics. The little carbine-type weapon normally holds a clip of ten .22 caliber, long-rifle ammunition. This comes from the factory as a semiautomatic weapon. To compensate for the small caliber—compared to the Freemen leaders' .357 Magnum and .45 caliber automatic pistols—I made a couple of minor modifications. My little carbines held thirty-round clips and were capable of being fired on full automatic.

I told Connie I had been in each of the rooms occupied by sleeping Freemen.

"So was it worth the risk?" she asked

"Yes," I said. "Now I know how easy it would be to capture them."

Shortly after my night trip inside the cabin, we were summoned to the mother of all FBI briefings at Billings.

★ CHAPTER 16 ★

Tommie Canady made arrangements to premiere his star under-cover agents at a full dog-and-pony show for the Bureau brass from Washington. He had bragged to me that he was scheduled to retire in December 1996, and he wanted this Freemen capture to be the crowning event of his career. He wanted nothing to go wrong and thus micromanaged every step in the process. I told him of the missed opportunity to make an arrest of the sleeping Freemen leaders, and he brushed the incident aside.

Connie and I packed an overnight bag and made excuses for an absence of a few days. We drove to Billings and checked into the Quality Inn at Homestead Park. Agent Canady had preregistered us in a ground-level suite at the far end of the parking lot. The bedroom and bath were separated from the sitting room by a glass-paneled door.

The sitting room was furnished with a round table, two stuffed chairs, and a low leatherette couch along one wall. Extra folding chairs had been propped against the television set in the sitting room.

Minutes after we checked in, at about three o'clock, the phone rang. It was Canady, nervously questioning our late arrival. We were informed that a team from Washington was already in town staying at another hotel, and that we would be debriefed in shifts, with teams specializing in different phases of an operation meeting us at different times.

There were two groups from the FBI's Hostage Rescue Team center at Quantico, Virginia, and a team from the FBI's Behavioral Science Unit out of Washington headquarters.

Although we were ensconced in a luxury suite at the motel, the sessions were anything but a vacation. We were subjected to two days of grueling questioning by FBI assault planners and psychologists. Every detail of the mountain stronghold and its inhabitants was painfully elicited, examined, and reviewed.

The big debriefing and planning session began on June 15. Connie and I were sure this was the D-day countdown, since our sixty-day agreement was scheduled to be completed about the end of the month. We would have been under cover inside the Freemen's stronghold for two months.

Connie and I tensely awaited the arrival of the Washington specialists, whom we believed to be the crème de la crème of the Bureau.

I spotted them driving into the motel parking lot. Anyone could have pegged them as FBI agents. In pairs, they climbed out of three unmarked sedans and stood looking around at building tops in the surrounding office park. They all wore blue, plaid-lined windbreakers, khaki slacks, and stern scowls. The only thing missing was big yellow letters spelling out FBI on the backs of their jackets. Had Connie and I been under surveillance by Freemen sympathizers, the gig would have been up that day.

A couple of minutes later Tommie Canady's car drove up. I was watching, hoping they would just drift in, but they were so obviously agents that even motel employees later commented that we must be part of the government.

Canady hung around for only a few minutes, but after making introductions and before departing, he took me and Connie aside and warned us, "Don't forget who you work for."

We gathered in the sitting room of our motel suite.

Seven interrogators were in the first team—from a Bureau tactical-assault unit.

They sat in a U-shaped panel, filling the couch and chairs. Connie and I were seated in chairs against a wall, removed from the agents and facing them. It felt as if we were on a stage performing to the men on the other side of the small room. Before long it felt like we were in a scene from an old cops and robbers movie, sitting in our straight-back chairs with the bare light bulb glaring on us during interrogation.

The two leading questioners were heavy-set, obviously desk types. Their build was in sharp contrast to the muscular bodies of the strike-team members. One of these two did all the talking at first.

They wanted to know every last detail about the physical layout of the cabin, the Freemen's arms supply, and their round-the-clock schedule. They grilled us on the comings and goings of other militia groups to the cabin. They wanted a full description of their clothing, and particularly their weapons. The Bureau men were especially interested in our opinions about whether the Freemen could actually summon up reinforcements from these militia units should there be a long standoff; and, if so, how long such help would take to arrive.

Early in the interview we were told that some members of this Hostage Rescue Team had been at Ruby Ridge. From the remarks of bravado that went around the room, I could tell that several of the agents were carrying a guilt complex like a 500-pound weight around their necks.

They asked a lot of questions about the children. Were any children hanging around the cabin? Did any children ever visit the cabin? How long did they stay? What kinds of vehicles did the parents of the children have?

I made the mistake of commenting, "Boy, the FBI really messed up at Ruby Ridge. I guess you guys don't want to blow it again with the Freemen."

An older agent in the strike team almost came out of his seat in anger over my comment.

"The FBI did nothing wrong!" The big agent's voice was a roar. "We did everything right!"

At another point early in the interview, Connie and I were explaining the $16,000 bogus check the Freemen had given us to pay off our pickup.

One of the agents said, "Don't you wish it was real? That's a lot of money compared to what we're paying you."

I thought the statement odd, because even though we were still getting our advance payments plus expense money, we had a Bureau commitment for $25,000 each when the two-month contract was completed. I just figured Tommie Canady had not shared the details with the assault-team members.

At another point, the most vocal of the agents pulled out release forms stating that we would not hold the Hostage Rescue Team liable for anything that happened to us during the arrest attempt. We were told to sign it with our code names, Talon and B.H. I thought that odd, too.

But for the most part, we spent the first briefing answering tactical questions about the cabin and the men inside.

This first afternoon and early evening session concluded about six o'clock, and Connie and I were already exhausted. Canady told us to have a nice dinner and get some rest. We badly needed a break, not only from the intensive grilling, but also from the tense days leading up to the debriefing. Canady said they would return early the next morning to resume the sessions. Our agent-in-charge was clearly agitated and almost surly with me.

A short time later the phone rang. It was Canady.

"Dale, this is serious business," he snapped. "You were trying to be the wise guy; these people don't have time for that."

I had done some kidding around with the big, tough HRT interviewers, but they pretty much gave back ribbing in kind. I guessed they were still upset over my comments about Ruby Ridge. I was too tired to argue, so I told Canady, "Fine, I'll be a gentleman tomorrow." He hung up.

At nine-thirty the following morning, only two cars showed up. It was Canady and three dignified older agents in suits. They looked more like college professors than agents, and were in sharp contrast to the burly, rock-jawed Marine types on the HRT.

We quickly learned these three were the Behavioral Science Unit's profilers. Two were identified to us as psychologists; they gave only their first names. The oldest of the three, a pinch-mouthed, humorless guy with dark brown hair and a moustache, seemed to be the leader.

I thought they were going to profile the Freemen leaders, but the shrink leader dug right into me first.

"Why are you doing this?" he asked, as if accusing me of some heinous act.

I was so taken aback that I thought he might be kidding, so I wisecracked some answer. Canady glared at me and said, "I told you to cut your crap."

The FBI psych, whose first name was Clint, then asked Agent Canady and Connie to go to the motel coffee shop so they could shrink me in private.

Clint carefully explained to me that it was especially important that I answer all his questions carefully, whether the questions seemed relevant or not. He said the FBI had experienced a lot of problems from recent incidents dealing with these radical groups, and that he and his team wanted to make sure this operation was a complete success. "A victimless success," he added.

He confided that he had been at Ruby Ridge, along with most of the members of the Hostage Rescue Team, and that the Bureau never wanted another "er . . . problematic occurrence like that one."

I nodded agreement.

My grilling lasted two hours. The first hour and more was spent examining me and my motives for going under cover. The three shrinks passed around the questions in a seemingly disjointed interview, but it was clear they did not trust me. No matter how I tried to explain why I was a volunteer civilian under cover inside the Freemen group, they were not satisfied with my answers.

"It makes me sad to see what the leaders of these hate groups have done to some otherwise average men and women," I told the psychologists. "A lot of the rank and file are confused. They're farmers who have been destroyed by the system. Some of the Freemen and the militiamen we've met are just pawns—they're being manipulated."

"So you are a sympathizer then," one of the shrinks charged. "When were you converted?"

"Look, Doc, I'm not a rollover!" It was all I could do to keep from walking out at that moment. But it would get much worse.

I was treated like a suspect. The more personal they got, the angrier I became.

"What kind of bullshit question is that?" I snapped back. "The Freemen leaders infuriate me! When I see the damage they are doing, the lives they are wrecking I want to track down the bastards personally, and either cage them or kill them. They are worse than the drug dealers I used to work—they're terrorists."

I tried to convince these FBI psychologists that they were not dealing with common criminals. I told them of my experiences with the hate groups, all the way back to my brush with the Aryans on the Idaho-Montana border six or seven years earlier.

"I've shed tears, blood, and nights of lost sleep over it. I've warned everyone in authority who would listen to me about these people. They are dangerous," I said. "What we've seen so far—Oklahoma City, Waco, Ruby Ridge—this is just the tip of the iceberg compared to what's coming. It's only going to get worse. It's as plain as the nose on your face. I've seen hundreds, maybe several thousand, people duped into preparations to destroy this country."

The chief shrink gave me a doubtful "harumph" and said something to the effect that I might be exaggerating slightly. It was like talking to stones. The three sat around the room with their legs crossed and continued their nonsensical questions.

Finally, one of the psychologists asked, "How does it feel to be a cripple?" It was a reference to my being one-armed.

"I suppose, technically, I am a physical cripple," I answered between gritted teeth. "But you should be able to answer that question yourself, seeing that you are obviously a mental cripple."

There was a moment of stunned silence.

I could see my response had really angered the three men and thought that these people were bureaucrats first and shrinks last. Such a retort from a patient would never have rattled a psychologist working out in the real world.

My impertinent answer did, however, put an end to their personal quizzing of me, and we finally moved on to the Freemen.

To break the icy demeanors my nasty retort had caused, I tried a bit of humor.

"Wow, so you do want to know about the Freemen," I lampooned. "For a while there I thought you were setting me up for a personal siege by the SWAT team."

Nobody laughed.

Even when the psychologists got down to the business of asking about the four Freemen leaders, I could make no sense of their line of questioning. They seemed far more interested in personality quirks than in which of the four leaders might actually fight back if confronted by an arresting officer. I tried to force them to consider my analysis of the relative danger Skurdal, Petersen, Schweitzer, or Jacobi might pose to an arresting officer: Which one would pull his gun and kill? Who would dive for cover? Who would meekly submit? Who would run?

I guess the shrinks thought I was getting into their business, because they did not seem to care what I thought.

Clint spent more time on Petersen's reasons for being in the leadership circle than on the far more menacing Schweitzer, Skurdal, and Jacobi. I had to repeat the story of Petersen's reasons for joining the Freemen several times.

Petersen, whom I always thought of as a grandfather type, was an outstanding mechanic prior to joining the movement. He had been reduced to selling water-purification systems after his mechanic's tools were confiscated to pay a debt run up by his son. The son had pledged Petersen's expensive tools, which were his only means of livelihood, as security for a personal loan.

It was in the course of selling a purification system that fate had brought him to Skurdal's cabin in the first place. Once inside, Skurdal and Schweitzer had learned of his plight, and used it to convince him he should drop out of the evil system and become a member of the organization.

The FBI psychs were engrossed by Petersen's life story and kept asking more questions.

"What does that have to do with arresting the Freemen?" I finally asked.

"We ask the questions," the younger shrink reminded me.

All in all, I thought the session with the FBI's venerable Behavioral Science Unit was a big waste of time.

Finally, I was excused and Connie was called in for a thirty-minute session with the shrinks. The psychologists asked her much the same questions about her motives for going under cover. She told them that from a woman's point of view, the one Freemen leader who seemed the most dangerous was Jacobi because, while he was very quiet most of the time, he never missed anything that was said or done in the cabin.

Just before completing their examination of Connie, one of the psychologists told her she was a very brave woman, and she responded that there was "a very thin line between bravery and stupidity."

We broke for lunch, and that afternoon several members of the tactical-assault team came back to our room. We finally got down to business in earnest.

The tactical team spread an excellent geophysical map on the small round table and we pinpointed every feature of the roads and terrain around the cabin in the Bull Mountains.

They drilled us on different scenarios for making an arrest— what time might prove best, which member of the team would be next to what Freeman, different ways they could just slap on cuffs. I told them in detail of the plan Connie and I had to introduce a number of agents into the cabin as members of an Alaska militia unit. They loved the idea.

Unlike the shrinks, these tactical-assault team members were vitally interested in our assessment of which of the Freemen leaders might give them trouble in an arrest attempt.

On taking each one of the four, I tried to tell them that most of the Freemen leaders, if you got the drop on them, would surrender without going for a weapon. I thought that Jacobi, being an ex-cop, and Petersen, not an aggressive personality, would just raise their hands. Skurdal might dive under a table. But Schweitzer, the Freemen leader—he would be a different matter. I was not sure he would give up, no matter how many guns were pointed at him.

The big HRT agent, the one I assumed to be the team leader, suddenly jumped up from the couch, slapped one hand into the other to simulate a drawn gun, crouched, and shouted, "Freeze! FBI!"

He got my attention all right. He was a block of a man, with a large head to match his broad shoulders. I suspected he could run the length of the motel from the inside, through the walls, if he wanted to.

"What would he do then?" the big agent said, smirking and returning to his seat on the couch.

"Me? I'd surrender. Schweitzer would probably say, 'Piss on you, Fed,' pull out his Magnum, and blow your ass off," I told the agent. To my surprise, the big man blushed when all his troops laughed.

Connie and I had another opportunity to pull a fast one on this big agent, whose name I never did get. The team members had given us phony first names like Bob and Bill and Joe. I had asked them if all their last names were Doe.

Agent Ox, I'll call him, was as mentally sharp as he was physically strong. He grilled us on every minute detail. He even wanted to know exactly what the Freemen's kitchenware was like. We couldn't answer. As good and thorough as our intelligence was, we had never thought to memorize the silverware patterns. Later at the cabin, Connie would filch a butter knife from Skurdal's kitchen and have Agent Canady send the eating utensil to Agent Ox via priority pouch.

These tactical-assault guys were pumped; they could have passed easily for elite militia members. They were all ex-combat military men, or had completed rigorous training by one or more of the elite branches of service—the SEALS, Green Berets, or even a more clandestine counterterrorism unit.

The Freemen leaders would have done back flips to have them come in as militiamen. The FBI's HRT was paramilitary all the way. I knew I could insert a score of them with one phone call, and was prepared to do just that. The arrest could easily be made around the conference table during dinner, when the Freemen were relaxed. It would take only one FBI agent-cum-militiaman seated on each side of a Freeman, and it would be over in two seconds—no fuss, no mess, no bother—and no gunshots.

Late into the afternoon the HRT had all the information we could give them. They told us they were going back to Quantico to build a mockup of the cabin to go through extensive trial runs.

"Good," the agent-in-charge said. "We'll be in touch soon." Agent Canady arrived to pick up the team.

"Oh, one more thing," the bulky team chief said just before leaving our motel room. "Is there any way you could get photos or video of the inside of the cabin?"

"Sure," I said, "the Freemen invite all their visitors to tape their seminars. But I don't have a camcorder."

One guy from the team, the youngest-looking of the agents, stayed behind, telling the others he would join them later.

Out of the blue the young agent asked, "Have you ever considered working for any other agency?" I was puzzled by his question, wondering if he meant that some other agency was interested in the Montana Freemen.

"What do you mean?" I asked. He stared into my eyes for a minute. "I *have* worked for other agencies." I tried to interpret his question with my answer.

"We appreciate what you are doing," he said. "For people to put their lives in jeopardy for the sake of their country is commendable. We get a lot of our people from the Midwest because they are still real Americans. So you've worked for other people, not just the FBI?"

I said yeah, just about all the federal agencies.

"Have you ever worked for the Agency?" the young man asked. I knew he meant the CIA. I said yeah, again.

"I've learned that, with the Agency, it's best to get in and get out young," he said, still talking in riddles.

A few minutes later the phone rang. It was a call from Canady, asking for the young agent. After a terse conversation the young agent left.

Connie and I were exhausted but pleased. We thought the end was now in sight.

CHAPTER 17

Shortly after the Hostage Rescue Team had left the motel, the phone rang.

Agent Tommie Canady tersely snapped over the line, "Do you really think you could videotape the place?"

I told him sure, and before we checked out of the motel the Billings FBI had a used camcorder delivered to us. I only had to figure out a good reason to introduce the camera at the cabin.

The next morning we went back to Roundup.

Connie and I had not been back at the cabin from our whirlwind briefing for more than a few hours when the opportunity to use the camcorder presented itself.

Skurdal, who was frequently complaining about finances, told me he was considering having the twenty acres of his property logged for cash. He was now aware that he had lost the debate with the other leaders to keep the cabin as the center of the new Freemen republic and he wanted to strip everything of value in and around the property. On several occasions he had even grumbled that he would blow up or burn down the cabin before he would turn it over to its legal owners, the Internal Revenue Service.

Skurdal knew I was an experienced logger and approached me to give him an estimate of how much money he might get from having the big timber clear-cut. Immediately the idea on how to get the terrain videotaped came to mind.

I told Skurdal, within earshot of the other leaders, that the timber was worth big bucks. Because of the government's intrusion through confiscatory environmental protection laws, I told him, there was always a shortage of raw timberland.

Skurdal was enthusiastic about the idea, even though I knew no legitimate logging company would touch the property without the required permits. Since the land belonged to the IRS, it would be timber piracy to cut even one tree for commercial purposes. But that little complication mattered not to the Freemen, who had been ensconced illegally on the property for nearly two years anyway.

With the Freemen leaders standing by listening, I called a timber man of somewhat questionable reputation and told him I had a friend with twenty acres of prime land to clear. As I had hoped, knowing the logger's reputation, he didn't bother to ask if such a cut would be licensed.

But the timber man said he would have to come out to the property to survey it first. I told him that would not be necessary, and quickly volunteered to provide him a complete videotape of the land. After only a brief argument the logger agreed that if the video was descriptive enough it would be just as good as a survey.

So I produced the FBI camera. Skurdal was intrigued and wanted to do some of the filming. I showed him how to operate the camcorder. Skurdal and I walked the entire twenty acres, recording every rock, tree, gully, and bush. With me serving as director, Skurdal happily shot the cabin perimeters from every angle. I told him this section was especially important so the logger would know which nearby trees he wanted to save. Skurdal mumbled he could cut down the whole place and pull the logs off the cabin walls, too. But I convinced him that some trees should be saved to cover the cabin for the duration of the Freemen stay.

Connie and I were greatly amused that a Freemen leader was enthusiastically providing the critical videotape for the FBI's tactical-assault units—and with an FBI-provided camcorder.

The tape was delivered a day or two later to some stunned FBI agents at the office in Billings. I assume it was sent by overnight dispatch to the HRT unit at Quantico to assist in building the mockup of the arrest site.

In the coming days, I would be able to augment the outside video of the mountain property by periodically taping the seminars inside the cabin during militiamen training sessions. Ostensibly shooting the lectures, I would fidget with the camcorder to take shots of walls, windows, doors, locks, and every other inside detail. During the next week these additional tapes were also deposited with the FBI office in Billings, until the Bureau had visual documentation of everything we had provided in the earlier hand-drawn maps.

★ ★ ★

Paradoxically, at about the same time that I was engaged in taping the cabin for the FBI, another videotaping incident was about to be played out with potentially deadly consequences.

Connie and I returned to the cabin from Billings after running some errands and, of course, the requisite debriefing at the Art-space coffee shop.

As we turned off highway 87 and stopped, we saw two dark utility vehicles and a white rental van parked at the entrance to Johnny's Coal Road.

Two men got out of the vehicles and walked towards our pick-up. I recognized one of the men as Chris Wallace, a correspondent from *PrimeTime Live.* He approached the passenger side window, introduced himself, and asked, "Are you a Freeman?" I was caught a little off guard and didn't respond immediately.

Then he asked, "Do you live around here?" The other man, who I didn't recognize, came closer and said, "Don't do that. Don't do that to him." He then politely introduced himself to me as Harry Phillips, an ABC news producer. The newsmen had come out to get a story on the Freemen and to attempt to interview Skurdal and Schweitzer.

With pistols on their hips and beer cans in their hands, the two Freemen leaders had charged out of the cabin at Wallace and his crew, screaming "Get off the property or be arrested." The two leaders had followed the newsmen down the long driveway. A gutsy cameraman walked backward down the rocky drive filming the retreat with the shouting, waving Freemen leaders in pursuit. The dramatic footage would air several weeks later.

Connie and I arrived a few minutes after the Freeman leaders had shown their true colors. We turned onto Johnny's Coal Road, and pulled over to the mailboxes lined up on poles at the intersection. We generally stopped to pick up the mail to take to the cabin, since the Freemen did not feel comfortable coming down the mile or so in exposed countryside. Picking up the mail was one of the chores that ingratiated us to the Freemen. It also gave Connie a chance to write down the return addresses on incoming letters.

The last thing in the world I wanted was my face broadcast on every TV set in America. I moved quickly back into the pickup and told Connie to cover the little sub-gun with its banana clip lying between us on the front seat.

We talked amiably with the ABC crew for a few minutes, and went on up to the cabin. The place was as quiet as a church on Monday morning. When it was quiet, I got nervous.

We entered the living room of the cabin and were greeted inside by high-powered rifles and automatic weapons. A panicky group of Freemen stood at the curtains peering down at the driveway and road.

Minutes later when the white ABC van cruised back in front of the cabin, with a cameraman hanging out the window filming the fortress with our pickup sitting out in front. Unknown to the film crew, four high-powered rifles, some with scopes, were trained on the driver and his passenger. In the cabin a debate raged among the Freemen leaders as to whether or not to shoot them.

Fortunately, the ABC crew drove off after a couple of passes, none the wiser that they were within a hair trigger of being blasted. Their calculated risk would have cost them their lives, if the Freemen had had the courage of their warped convictions.

The Freemen calmed down after finishing off a good number of beers. I told them that Connie and I had run into the news crew at the mailbox.

"They tried to interview us, too," I said. "Didn't get anything, of course. I told them my name was Fred Cannon."

"Yeah, loose cannon," Petersen guffawed.

I am a strong believer in the Constitutional freedom of the

press. But all I could think about that day was the old adage, "Fools rush in where angels fear to tread."

CHAPTER 18

Waiting is often the hardest part of being in deep cover.

After all the intelligence has been gathered, all the plans made and rehearsed, the wait to execute becomes excruciating. Each incident, whether serious or insignificant, is magnified. Every day of delay is an agony of possible discovery. Paranoia is the congenital disease of the undercover agent. At the cabin in Roundup, Connie and I waited, expecting a "go" order at any moment. The end of our sixty-day commitment, June 30, was at hand and we were keyed up for the Bureau's assault on the Freemen leaders.

I spent more and more time extolling the attributes of the mythical mercenaries I had promised to deliver. After all, the HRT squad had enthusiastically endorsed the idea of bringing the team into the cabin at Roundup in the full combat regalia of a mysterious militia cell. The Freemen leaders were so convinced that their cavalry was on the way that they boasted to visiting pseudo-seminarians of their imminent manpower prowess.

Then, like a thunderbolt from an angry god, word came down that the plan had been rejected by the "highest levels" in Washington. It was even hinted that the plan had been rejected at the White House. Connie and I got the bad news at the Artspace coffee shop during one of our overnight trips to Billings.

Stunned by the rejection from the Bureau—maybe even President Clinton himself—we told Agent Canady that our operational effectiveness was at an end. At the time, I was more disappointed than angry.

Agent Canady told us we were too well placed to just abandon the operation. He wanted us to stay in, to keep gathering intelligence.

I protested that the Freemen were starting to demand that I deliver all these men I had promised. Other irritated confrontations were beginning to occur within the cabin. I could not go back now and tell the four Freemen my army of mercenaries had suddenly vanished.

I argued that we might as well pull out at the end of June, only a few days away, collect our pay, and get out of the neighborhood. Canady was concerned that our sudden disappearance would alert the Freemen to the fact that their organization had been penetrated by agents. I complained that was too bad, because our situation inside the cabin had been rendered barely tenable by the cancellation of the arrest plan. Our conversation with Agent Canady was like talking of a death in the family, not accusatory. He was clearly disappointed, too, and we shared the feeling of loss with him.

We talked to him about our desire to move our family and disappear into the Alaskan wilderness. In an unusually personal exchange for a Bureau man and his operatives, he shared his own feelings about the heavy toll this line of work took on everyone involved. Canady said he, too, had long wanted to retire from the rat race and settle in Alaska. He spoke wistfully of his coming retirement scheduled at the end of 1996.

But after a time talking of personal and family affairs, we stopped fantasizing and came back around to the problem at hand.

"Just go on back up there and string them along," Canady urged. "The information you're bringing out on the other people coming to the cabin is invaluable. It's new raw data."

The veteran agent stroked us about the importance of the secondary information on other militia groups.

"That stuff is just a bonus for the Bureau," I said, reminding Canady that we had been hired to gather intelligence to be used for the arrest of Skurdal, Schweitzer, and Petersen. "The job we agreed to is finished. Our time is up. If the Bureau chooses not to make the arrest, that's your business. Our business is done."

"Look, everybody wants you two to stay in for a while," he argued. "The information you're bringing us is checking out all over the country. The Bureau is matching license plates and names to organizations we didn't even know existed."

He hinted that federal bogus check and fraud cases were being developed against Freemen seminar graduates all over the country; he specifically mentioned Texas, Missouri, and California.

"Okay, if we can cover our story about the firepower we promised, and if we agree to stay in past the end of the month . . ." I paused to see if Canady was anticipating my next question. He was, and he finished my sentence.

" . . . our financial arrangement with you will simply be extended," he said.

"So what about just paying us off for the sixty days and starting the same deal on a month-by-month basis?" I suggested.

"I'll have a problem getting a lump-sum payment until we actually make the arrest," Canady said, suddenly finding that his third cup of espresso needed stirring. "But your monthly expense checks will continue."

Connie had been sitting silently across the table, facing us.

"What about my kids?" she asked flatly. "We have them with friends only until the end of June. I have to go over and pick them up. They can't live in the trailer at the cabin. No way are we getting them involved in this crap."

Canady mumbled, "Of course not," and said something would be worked out within a week. "Go have a big dinner on the Bureau, get a good night's sleep, and get back in there, team."

The agent's attempt at a pep talk was a little lame. I saw worry returning to Connie's face. I could almost hear the gears in her brain clicking out the message, "Here we go again."

We left Billings the next morning somewhat dispirited, and the drive to Roundup was accomplished in silence.

We arrived back at the cabin to confront a dozen unfamiliar late-model utility vehicles and stretch-cab pickup trucks. We counted eight utilities and pickups with Ohio license plates, along with local license plates on cars we did not recognize.

"What the hell?" I asked myself aloud. Connie eyed the line of cars winding up the long dirt drive to the cabin. One was parked next to our motor home in the space where we usually parked. It had a small Confederate flag on the CB antenna, but it also bore

Ohio plates. I noticed that all the pickups had empty rifle racks across the back windows.

A cluster of men dressed in combat fatigues stood outside the cabin boasting they had scared the hell out of residents in small towns across the Midwest. Later we learned these eight Ohio vehicles had been driven in a convoy all the way to Montana. Apparently, this group had made the trip waving their guns out the windows. But for now, just the sight of this many cars at the cabin was frightening enough.

A Freemen seminar was in progress. We haltingly entered the cabin to be confronted by a score of men in combat attire, armed to the teeth with every sort of automatic weapon imaginable. Every uniformed man wore at least one pistol. Some had two. And every man had a long gun, either a semiautomatic hunting-type rifle or a military-type assault rifle converted to full automatic. Several had tactical 12-gauge shotguns; two or three of the militiamen were wearing live fragmentation grenades clipped on web harnesses. The men were spread around the room, some seated, some pacing.

On first appearance these men were mostly clean-shaven, young to middle-aged. They were clearly a cut above the usual visitors to the cabin, with their spit-and-polish military bearing and manner. From their conversation, they were intelligent and motivated for extreme action. These were middle-class American males—from the look of their expensive, well-oiled new weapons. Their crisp uniforms and gear identified them as an affluent, well-financed unit, not some ragtag army.

Skurdal joined Connie and me and proudly announced this group as the Ohio militia; but, as with most militia cells attending seminars, we were seldom able to find out exactly which unit. They could have been from the northern, southern, or central Ohio militia, or a mixed force from several units. We had learned early in the operation that most states usually had several loose-knit militias of varying degrees of fanaticism.

Connie hung around for a few minutes, the only woman in an all-male congregation. I settled in for another Freemen hate session, but soon realized these Ohioans had very little interest in the teachings of the Freemen. The seminar speaker was constantly interrupted, as one militiaman after another pointed a weapon or noisily snapped magazines into or out of the weapons. The careless playing with loaded guns unnerved me, and I knew Connie expected some horrific accident at any moment. Having lived with firearms most of our adult lives, we were always extremely respectful of the deadly potential of a gun.

"These guys would flunk the most basic gun-safety course," I whispered to her, and she soon quietly slipped from the room to return to our motor home.

I watched the Ohioans in silence. These men loved their guns, and shared one common bond—each and every one hated the United States government. They rowdily spewed a ceaseless stream of venom against all government officials; many expressed the same hatred for people of color.

They showed little respect for the current speaker, Jacobi, and chatted loudly over his presentation. Jacobi did get their attention when he began expounding his theory about the biblical basis for the difference between the Mud People, which included all racial groups of any color, and white Anglo-Saxons.

However, not all the Ohioans bought into this bigotry. One of them began brazenly arguing with Jacobi. The Freemen's religion specialist was flustered by the challenge. Usually the leader's gospel was swallowed, whole hog, and none of the visiting supplicants dared to challenge the orthodoxy.

The challenger was Mike Hill, who seemed to be a group spokesman, if not the leader. He told Jacobi that he also served the Ohio unit as chaplain and was himself well versed in the biblical authority of Christian Patriots. Jacobi, who had received Christian Identity training from the very horse's mouth at Hayden Lake, did not like to be challenged.

"It has been proven that there is not just a biblical difference between humans"—by which he meant whites—"and manlike animals"—by which he meant all the rest of the two-legged *Homo sapiens* stock on earth—Jacobi argued, his voice becoming louder. The argument piqued the interest of the roomful of men and they stopped fiddling with their guns to listen to the debate.

"It has been proven that the white man, heir to Adam and God's chosen, has one less rib than the black," Jacobi announced with satisfaction, prepared to move on to his next topic.

"I've talked to doctors about that, and it's bullshit," the Ohio militia leader shot back.

"I'm sorry, Commander Hill, but it is not bullshit," Jacobi said in a shrill voice. "We have X rays to prove it."

"I'd like to see them," another Ohio militiaman spoke up, emboldened by his leader's argument.

Jacobi was stumped. I knew the Freemen didn't have any such X rays, at least not around the cabin. Connie and I had, by now, poked into every nook and cranny of the cabin, at least in the downstairs area.

A general din broke out in the large room as various members of the militia began arguing among themselves and with the handful of local Freemen mixed in the room. Someone called for a coffee break, and the argument continued as these paramilitary men tumbled, back-slapping each other, out of the cabin and into the warm summer air of the Bull Mountains.

I joined them outside, trying to pick up any information that might identify their organization. I approached one group of men standing against our motor home smoking. Skurdal came up as we chatted and introduced me as the Freemen's explosives expert. I saw Connie leave the motor home and walk up to another group to begin an animated conversation.

After I had been around the group, shaking hands and trying to remember as many names as possible, I joined another half-dozen of the Ohioans. They were still arguing the merits of the missing rib theory.

"Shit, we could settle this once and for all," a swaggering young militiaman said. "Let's just drive back into town and yank a nigger off the street, bring him out here, and cut him open. Count the ribs. That settles it." The other men laughed.

He turned to me and fairly snarled, "Any niggers around here, Dale?"

"I doubt it," I said, sickened by the thought they might actually try to kidnap someone. "There could be one or two hiding some-where, but we've already run most of them off. We'd have to go all the way to Billings to catch one."

These guys were aggressive, swaggering around with their arms. During the break several went off into the woods behind the cabin and began shooting at anything in sight. I heard the rapid fire of fully automatic weapons mingled with whoops of joy. I walked around the corner of the cabin to see three of the militiamen firing military-style assault rifles into the trunks of pine trees. The high-powered weapons were literally eating the bark right off the trees, leaving raw, splintered gashes in the wood.

Skurdal joined me and shouted at the gunmen to stop killing his trees. He told them he was having them logged in a few days, and didn't want the chain saws ruined by steel-jacket slugs. The men groused about having their play interrupted, but slouched off to the cabin.

When the session resumed, the young man who had suggested snatching a black man in nearby Roundup to prove the Adam's rib theory reopened the discussion. It went from a sick joke to a seri-ous, bizarre discussion about white man's God-given right to kill people of color in order to keep Aryan bloodlines pure.

I finally had all I could stomach and spoke up.

"Okay, say you were able to get your black to cut up," I posited. "That will prove only half the equation. Which one of you is going to volunteer to have your gut cut open so we can count the white man's ribs for comparison?"

Everyone laughed, and the ugly conversation ended, to return to the equally ugly garbage that was being served up as regular fare at the Freemen seminar.

I noticed Jacobi staring at me with a funny, almost malevolent grin on his face. I could not tell if he was pleased that I had saved his butt from ridicule, since he couldn't produce the X rays he'd promised, or was doubting my willingness to murder a black person to prove his outrageous hypothesis.

Of all the Freemen leaders, I believed Jacobi had the intellect to catch me and Connie at our undercover game. I felt a little foolish that I had revealed even a tiny part of my feelings in the presence of this dangerous ex–Canadian police officer.

The seminar was resumed, with Skurdal making his pitch before the afternoon session ended. The Ohio commander, Hill, was invited to stay at the cabin while the rest of his troops were sent to the two motels in Roundup. I could not imagine what terror awaited the good citizens of that peaceful town that evening.

Over the course of the three-day visit by the Ohio militia unit, I spent hours talking to individual members of the organization. I was especially intrigued by the paradoxical thoughts of one of the group's leaders.

The thirty-eight-year-old Mike Hill was, in more ways than one, not a typical middle-class American. He talked a fervent antigovernment, Christian patriot line most of the time, but drew the line on racism. His argument against Jacobi's white-supremacist diatribe came from a deep conviction. He seemed to be a real Christian— perhaps an ardent fundamentalist—but when he spoke about religion, about God, it was a loving and compassionate Jesus Christ. He even told me that in God's eyes all men were created equal, and that this white hate philosophy was Nazi or Klan talk. Yet he was extremely angry at all forms of government.

Mike Hill's days were numbered. We could not know it then, but he would be dead in a very short time.

It seems that Hill was returning from a militia meeting to his home when an Ohio state trooper stopped the car for a broken taillight. In a confrontation with the officer, Hill pulled out a pistol and the patrolman shot him dead. Another Ohio militiaman, named Joe, who was following Hill's vehicle, witnessed the whole event. I later heard the full story from one of the Ohio militia leaders with whom I maintained close contact long after the operation at Roundup had ended.

"Mike was pumped up by the meeting," my source said. "He was willing and eager to take on anyone who messed with him. When the patrolman pulled him over, it was virtually instinct that made him pull a gun.

"Unfortunately, the patrolman's instincts were quicker than Mike's," my confidant related. "The cop shot Mike three times."

After the funeral, the Ohio militias raised hell, and got the family to dig up the body for a second autopsy. While that autopsy revealed that one of the three fatal shots entered at an unusual angle, it did not give the militias the proof they wanted that the killing had been a government conspiracy.

But that fatal incident occurred some months later, and at the moment the Ohio militia was ushered into the cabin at Roundup for a second day of the seminar. Many of them were bleary-eyed from the previous night of heavy drinking in the tiny town of Roundup, and more than one nodded off during the seminar.

The lead-off speaker for the morning session was Schweitzer, and the chief justice solemnly took the lectern. I had never seen the four Freemen leaders so excited. Their talks were absolutely animated when they appeared before such a well-armed and disciplined—if a bit rowdy—group of warriors as the Ohio militiamen seemed to be.

As much as the polished Ohio militia inspired the Freemen, the organization frightened me. Seeing an organized, cohesive paramilitary unit sitting in one room together sent a chill down my spine. This was not just another group of weather-hardened, sad, and broken High Plains farmers who had lost their land and their hope.

These people were Main Street Americans, and could blend easily into any community in the country. In my conversations during the break I learned that a good number of them were ex-soldiers or Marines. Some were combat veterans from the Korean War, Vietnam, Panama and Grenada, or the Persian Gulf War. Several boasted of their current membership in the National Guard or reserves and their access to heavy military weapons stored in armories or quartermaster depots.

Perhaps they would be no match for the highly trained FBI tactical-assault team I had just spent time with. But given the element of surprise and better knowledge of the terrain in their own backyards and buildings in their respective communities, they would be a formidable force. As I surveyed the room, I had images of this unit, multiplied hundreds of times, rising up in cities and towns across the nation.

It would take the United States military to deal with such an uprising—and I had already heard horror stories about the rank and file of our armed forces being sympathetic to the radical cause.

The main difference between this group and many of the others I had seen at the cabin to date was that its members were interested in talking military operations, not ideology. The Ohioans wanted a firefight with the government so bad their trigger fingers were literally twitching. I studied the faces of the Ohio militiamen. The youngest were still in their teens, the oldest in their sixties.

I think it was then that the enormity of the whole hate movement, the so-called Christian patriot separatist movement, finally hit me. As I watched these otherwise clean-cut, typical American men absorbing the hate propaganda and talking about seizing their communities by force of arms, I realized more than ever in my life that my country was in great and imminent peril.

CHAPTER 19

I have lived on the edge of crime since my teens. This Ohio organization and dozens of groups like it who visited the cabin to perfect hate and learn how to turn this hate into insurrection, was something entirely new. Raised a rebel in a rough-and-tumble family with our own share of petty felons, I always had some perverse empathy for the criminals I encountered during my early days as an undercover agent. Perhaps it was this understanding of the criminal mind and my long association with criminals that made me so effective.

Criminals I had known intimately were lazy or greedy, nuts, or just plain mean. But these militia and viper-cell members, with their false prophets, were and are the most venal of criminals. They are traitor patriots who have bought a bill of hateful goods to salve their wounded egos at losing out on the American dream.

Many of these Ohioans, and most of the other militiamen I came to know so well, had fought for their country in various wars. Now their frustrations with government were over senseless things like whether they could carry guns on the streets of their hometowns or their right to buy and use military-type weapons. They irrationally demand individual rights to do anything they want, but have no interest in assuming responsibility for their acts.

A typical complaint was uttered by one young militiamen in one of our conversations. "That black bitch at the drivers' license bureau expected me to stand in line for an hour to get my license renewed. Well, I just tore my application up and threw it in her face."

They blamed government for the shrinking middle class, which included their blue-collar jobs, but never thought for a minute to blame greedy corporate executives and even more greedy stockholders.

They blamed blacks and Asians and Hispanics for the loss of their jobs. Blacks, because they dared ask for affirmative action. Immigrant Asians and Latinos, because they dared come to this country seeking liberty and prosperity, just as their own white European ancestors had done when they arrived from Britain, Germany, Scandinavia, and Eastern and Southern Europe a few generations earlier.

Most had never actually had a bad encounter with the government, other than perhaps an uncomfortable audit by the IRS. But a few demagogic radicals had easily preyed on their general dissatisfaction with the changing American society to turn them into armed insurrectionists.

Instead of organizing into voting blocs, they turned from the traditional politics of the grassroots movement to the politics of armed rebellion. Now the same men who might have gathered a short time ago to watch a Sunday afternoon playoff between the Minnesota Vikings and the Green Bay Packers sit discussing the justification for killing their neighbors because they work for the county tax office or drive a fire truck. To them, the innocent men, women, and children who were killed in Oklahoma City are nothing more than the unfortunate but necessary casualties of war.

How could this happen in America? I kept asking myself. Connie and I talked about it for hours into the night as we lay in the motor home, only feet away from the hate leaders propounding this false doctrine.

These typical middle-America white males, who had skills and professions and educational privileges, had been duped into believing that God had called them to do this evil work. They adamantly argue that the country has already been taken over by some mysterious foreign cartels, such as the Trilateral Commission or the Illuminati or the New World Order or International Jewry.

They see themselves as holy warriors ordained by God in a struggle against a satanic evil. Many of the militia members told me in conversation after conversation that they could see the mark of Cain on the faces of their imagined enemies, including government workers and members of minority races.

And most frightening to Connie and me was that we were seeing only a few hundred of these militia members. Watch groups say there are 10,000 to 20,000 active armed militia members in the hard-core groups. The leaders of various groups we met at the Freemen cabin in Roundup bragged that they had members and sympathizers back home numbering nearer to a quarter of a million.

Regardless of the numbers, more chilling still is the fact that, since the horrors of the Oklahoma City bombing, membership in these militias has grown rapidly. I would have thought that outrage and shame would have produced the opposite effect. That is why Connie and I were so stunned by the almost tidal increase in numbers of militia groups flowing into the Freemen seminars after the horrifying bombing.

Even if the real numbers are only in the low tens of thousands, if this Ohio group was typical, our law enforcement agencies and every citizen in this country are in deep trouble.

It isn't scary enough that two hundred million Americans own personal guns, but these militiamen boasted of much wider access to every sort of military ordnance from machine guns to rockets— even armored vehicles and handheld missiles.

And they talked of complicity by whole units within the military, in the event the fighting really gets started. When I heard these stories, as told by the Ohioans and other militia visitors to the cabin, I had to lend their bragging some credibility because of the known military backgrounds of Timothy McVeigh and Terry Nichols. The accused—and, in McVeigh's case, convicted—Oklahoma City bombers met in the U.S. Army.

Militiamen would often boast that they or friends in active National Guard and reserve units, networking through military commands and firming up their plans at summer training sessions, are prepared to rebel against the top brass if the U.S. military is ever called upon to put down internal rebellion. These men harbor a strong belief that the federal government is out of control. They often speak of the possibility, even a probability, that the perceived government suppression will lead to general rebellion.

Several militia leaders who visited the cabin over the course of that summer said that if the military is called upon to quell civilian unrest, they and their comrades in the military have agreed to mutiny against their officers. They plan to open armories to the general public—at least to carefully selected citizens. Proven militiamen would retain control, but would arm and train what they consider to be soldier material from the citizenry. No doubt the largest percentage of the recruits coming under their definition of an able-bodied and trainable populace would be screened for proper ideological beliefs.

According to this militia rhetoric, their members and supporters within the National Guard and reserves have already formed the necessary networks. Bizarre plans have been made and are discussed constantly during training sessions, by mail, telephone, and the Internet.

I asked one boasting militiaman, who also claimed to be a noncommissioned officer in the Army reserves, about the sizable number of minority troops in the active military. He told me many of the enlisted men, including blacks and Hispanics, are on board. "It's all part of our green machine," he said. "It's not a racial thing. It's not a radical movement. We feel we have a responsibility to America. This will not be an armed insurrection unless the government orders us to turn on our own people."

Oddly, this reservist also suggested that many black and Hispanic soldiers readily agree with the separatists' doctrine of the white supremacists and want their own segregated communities, too.

From mid-June onward, when militiamen and leaders began arriving at the cabin in larger numbers, we heard more and more talk of linkage between the paramilitary units and the active military. We were told stories of recruitment of militiamen from military bases in Kansas, the Carolinas, Oklahoma, Texas, and other states where large military complexes are located. We were also told of a clandestine black market in military arms, either stolen or sold off as surplus at various bases.

There is a network of civilian gun clubs using military training and firing ranges. In some cases laws still on the books allow sympathetic quartermasters to provide ammunition for such training. Gun lobbyists representing the National Rifle Association and military surplus dealers, allied with militia factions, made sure supportive congress-men blocked any attempts to delete these obsolete laws.

And there have been published reports of militia or neo-Nazi groups operating within some of the most elite units of the U.S. Army and Marine Corps. Defense Secretary William Perry ordered strict new regulations that would limit active duty personnel's participa-tion in hate groups. These directives only further angered the militia-men, and proved to them that the federal government had been taken over by mysterious foreign powers—or the United Nations.

I would not hazard a guess as to how widespread this phenom-enon in our military may be. But from my personal conversations during my months under cover inside the Freemen organization, I had ample proof that the regular military, along with the Guard and reserves, have been heavily infiltrated by members of active mili-tias. They secure training in sophisticated weaponry, establish cells within regular military units, and set up lines of supplies for arms and ammunition.

This military-militia connection made the discourse at the cabin all the more frightening, because much of the discussion during the last of the three-day meeting with the Ohio militia was devoted to confrontation and tactics.

LeRoy Schweitzer pointed me out as the Freemen's explosives man. "Every militia cell must have such an experienced person," he urged from the pulpit. "If you don't already have a demolitions man, you should scour your local Guard unit or penetrate your local mil-itary base to find such a person." Schweitzer volunteered me to conduct private sessions on explosives. Outside the seminar, I was deluged with questioners during every break in the regular meeting. The most frequently asked question was how to use easily available material to make ANFOs, a crude but deadly bomb made from ammonium nitrate and fuel oil.

The big question these would-be terrorists had was what pro-portions to mix to get the biggest bang, and what sorts of detonators would give the bomber the most time to escape.

I had been using such blasting mixtures to clear farmland and roadbeds since my early teens. But I dodged becoming a lethal-arts instructor by telling these eager students, "That crap is kid's stuff," and launching into long litanies about sophisticated rockets, C-group explosives, and other exotic materials they were not likely to get their hands on easily. With a sinking feeling in my stomach I knew, however, that the recipe for ANFOs was readily available at any good library or on the Internet. And I was aware that many of these potential bombers already knew it, too.

To conclude the final day of the seminar, the Freemen leaders, who by now were ecstatic over the success of the three-day session, made a recruitment pitch. They told the group that their fee for the seminar was waived, but that they expected the warriors to return the favor at a time in the near future when a takeover of a large territory in eastern Montana would begin.

I heard a chorus of "Sure, sure we will." But I did not get the impression that these men had any more intention than did the Montana militia to join their forces with the raggedy-assed Freemen leaders. They had their own leaders, and their own towns to take over. Post offices, police stations, federal buildings, communications facilities, newspapers in a dozen towns represented here had to be dealt with. I heard no solid promises to send the requested troops out to the Montana prairie to help take over bare expanses of farmland.

Before they departed, I struck up a close relationship with the subcommander of the Ohio militia, a man I'll call Joel Steelwill. He had diligently videotaped every minute of the seminars and the tactical-training sessions, and I wanted a copy of those tapes. He had made a point to get close-ups of all the faces of the participants. If I had tried that with the Bureau's video camera I am sure my undercover operation would have been brought to a speedy and unhappy end.

But I knew the Bureau would love copies of the Ohioan's four tapes, six hours each. Nothing could be more descriptive of the true agenda of the people the Freemen were training for that certain day sometime in the future.

I was wrong. When I told Agent Canady about the astounding session and the tapes, he just blew it off.

"We've got all we need on the Freemen," he reminded me again.

"These militiamen are just a bunch of weekend wanna-be's. Nobody takes their shit seriously at the Bureau."

"Then what the hell are you keeping us inside for?" I asked.

The agent did not answer.

★ ★ ★

The last few days of June, Connie and I were sort of in limbo, moving back and forth between Billings and spending several days each week in the motor home outside the Freemen headquarters.

The Freemen's paperwork increased in the cabin. After word of the success of the seminar with the Ohio militia spread on the hate network, demands for the training course were so great that the Freemen put out a bulletin stating that in the future they could no longer take large groups composed of the rank and file members of the militia. Only top leaders would be accommodated.

Calls for reservations came from Georgia, North and South Carolina, Oklahoma, Louisiana, Michigan, and several points in the Midwest. Three very tough and sinister militiamen from New York state showed up without reservations for one of the programs.

Through the end of June and into early July, militiamen kept coming, with Connie dutifully taking note of names, nicknames, license plates, and other details about the visitors.

The FBI had secured major wiretap authorization early in the operation. Affidavits supporting the wiretap authorization had been prepared and signed by me and Connie, after we signed sworn statements that much of the illegal activity was conducted interstate and by phone, fax, and computer modem. Months later these signed affidavits would become life-threatening documents for my little Jakes clan.

Eavesdropping by the Bureau was probably even more sophisticated than we imagined. Canady had been especially interested in our moving the motor home closer to the log cabin. I asked him if it was wired and he denied it. I never did check it out to see, but I suspect the Bureau was listening to more than our regular reports at the debriefing sessions in the Artspace coffee shop.

Dale Jakes in 1984 while working on an undercover assignment in the southwestern United States.

While visiting her family on college break, Connie, age 19, play-acts at being a gun-slinging cowgirl.

Dale and Connie in a tender moment.

Dale and Connie take a break from their civilian intelligence duties to attend the wedding of a friend in the late 1980s.

Dale out logging in northwestern Montana in 1995. To compensate for the loss of his right arm, Dale created a special harness for his logging equipment.

*Undated booking photo of
Rodney Owen Skurdal from
the Yellowstone County jail
in Billings, Montana.*

*LeRoy Schweitzer in a 1994
file photo.*

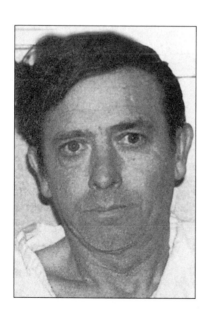

*Daniel Petersen in a March
25, 1996, booking photo from
the Yellowstone County jail
in Billings, Montana.*

*Undated booking photo of
Dale Martin Jacobi.*

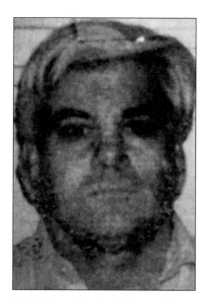

Booking photo of Lavon T. Hanson, dated March 1996.

Richard E. Clark in an undated booking photo.

Undated booking photo of Emmett Clark.

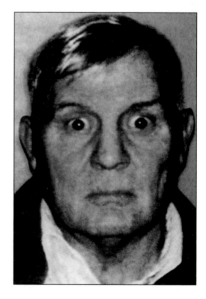

Ralph Edwin Clark in an undated booking photo.

Gene, a member of the Gadsden Minutemen militia group, instructs a ten-year-old boy named Scott in the use of a rifle during the group's campout in Glencoe, Alabama, on June 17, 1995.

One of the most organized paramilitary groups, the Michigan Militia, assembled at the Decker United Methodist Church in Decker, Michigan, on April 26, 1995, to participate on a segment of ABC's Nightline. *Left to right, front row: Doug Hall, Norman Olson, Ray Southwell, and Norman Price.*

In July 1996, Dale and Connie Jakes returned to the Freemen fortress near Roundup, Montana, where they spent months as undercover operatives. Rodney Skurdal's cabin can be seen in the background.

Freemen leaders participated in other seminars sponsored by right-wing separatist groups, such as the huge gathering in eastern Oklahoma advertised in this flyer.

Unidentified members of the Freemen (right) approach FBI negotiators for talks under a tent on May 18, 1996, at the Freemen complex in Jordan, Montana.

CHAPTER 20

During July 1995, our mission had subtly been changed from intelligence-gathering for a bloodless arrest of four men to wholesale information-gathering on militias throughout the United States. The only problem was that the FBI failed to tell us about the change.

Our contact agent in Billings kept us in the dark and manifested mixed reactions to our questions about the changing, more dangerous, aspect of the mission. At one debriefing he would praise our enterprise for the volumes of information on visiting militia members, and at the next he would assure us that the Bureau's primary interest was in arresting the Freemen leaders—that other information was of little interest to the FBI.

Since our original sixty-day verbal agreement had expired at the end of June, Connie and I became more and more frustrated. Up to that time, the goal of the assignment—to arrest the Freemen leaders—had been clear. Now we weren't sure what we were supposed to be doing.

We weren't the only ones frustrated. A steady stream of warrior types was flowing through the cabin at Roundup, but the Freemen leaders were unsuccessful in their ambition to secure a dedicated army to get on with their program to take over Winnett and establish the Freemen Republic of Montana.

The Freemen leaders were increasingly angered by what they viewed as Trochmann's double-cross, accusing him of reneging on promises to provide manpower. They blamed the commander of the Militia of Montana for all their woes. All the Freemen visiting the cabin began calling Trochmann a traitor.

Jacobi, who had been close to the distinguished, gray-bearded Trochmann before moving in with the Freemen, defended his former mentor less and less. From the time he was arrested with other Freemen by the Roundup deputies, Trochmann, along with the Montana militia, issued press releases denying any connection with the Freemen movement. Since Trochmann's Montana group was one of the largest and best-trained militia organizations in the country, his word carried a lot of weight with the others.

Those militias coming to the cabin were only too happy to receive the free seminars, which seemed to promise them a method for financing their operations and provided instruction on how to set up clandestine governments. But when asked for a commitment of manpower to help the Freemen launch their small war, they politely declined.

So the Freemen began to step up the pressure on me to actually produce the boogeymen I had boasted I could summon up at a minute's notice. It was getting more and more uncomfortable for Connie and me at the cabin, so we kept pushing the FBI to let us introduce a group of HRT members as militiamen. In answer to our pleas, Agent Canady kept telling us how politically sensitive this operation was, and that we should just be patient.

It's a little hard to be patient when you're sitting on a powder keg with the fuse lit.

I became so frustrated by the inaction of the feds that I told Canady I would just make the arrests myself. He told me in no uncertain terms not to even think about it.

Connie was visibly alarmed by my insistence that I could single-handedly capture the four armed Freemen. One afternoon she thought I had made just such a rash move. She was taking a shower in the motor home, when I noticed that Skurdal was stacking brush across the road. I had convinced him he needed to clean things up for the logger, who, I assured him, would be coming anytime to clear his timber.

I had seen Schweitzer take off for one of his strolls in the woods behind the cabin, and Petersen had left the cabin for a trip to Brusett, 125 miles north in Garfield County. He said he was going up there to "straighten the Clarks out." I knew Jacobi was inside the cabin studying the Scriptures.

I told Connie this would be a great chance to take each one of the Freemen alone, and left the motor home.

All of a sudden, gunfire rang out. Connie came flying out of the trailer, just as I emerged from the cabin with Jacobi. Her hair was dripping wet, her face contorted in rage. Schweitzer, who had become bored with walking in the woods, had taken a few shots at some milk jugs with his .357. These milk jugs were left hanging in trees behind the cabin for target practice. The Freemen boasted they would approximate the size and shape of a federal agent's head.

Later Connie told me she thought I had tried to make an arrest and been gunned down by the Freemen.

Little incidents like that kept occurring as the dog days of summer dragged slowly along. Our nerves were fried, and yet we could get no sympathy from the feds in Billings. They had us swinging out there, never telling us the truth. All these years I thought the FBI was the cleanest agency to work for, but I was learning a bitter lesson now. I didn't know what the hell we were in there for—they wouldn't arrest the Freemen leaders, they wouldn't let me arrest them, and they wouldn't let us leave.

We were gathering information, giving the Bureau scenarios, explaining how they could make arrests. The feds wouldn't move on anything. We were told that every proposal went up the chain of command, or we were told they were going up the chain; and one by one all our recommendations came back down the chain—rejected.

I had to get Connie some breathing room. We had lived practically day and night in the very heart of the Freemen empire and we were running out of excuses to be there. I had taken the required course of study a dozen times. A couple of the Freemen leaders began hinting around with questions that if I couldn't bring in the promised mercenaries, why were Connie and I hanging around?

More importantly, we had to pick up our children. They had already been with friends in western Montana longer than the agreed-upon time.

We finally demanded a showdown with our controller in Billings. A tense meeting with Canady at the Artspace coffee shop forced the question: "What the hell is the FBI doing?"

Canady lamely said that, while the FBI still planned to arrest the Freemen at some unspecified time in the future, the delays were caused by other eventualities outside the control of the Billings office. He hinted that the Bureau was placing other assets (undercover agents) in sensitive situations across the country, and that our information might be useful for that purpose.

Connie and I knew the feds had long been tapping the Freemen telephone lines, and along with the reams of hands-on intelligence on visiting militias and white-supremacist leaders, the Bureau was bound to be amassing a substantial dossier on hate groups nationwide. However, Canady still acted as if he were only casually interested in the tertiary information about other groups that we were feeding him on each of our debriefing trips to Billings.

Connie finally exploded in Canady's face. Never one to mince words, she flatly accused the Bureau of toying with us, and reminded the agent that they had us living at risk of death.

After Connie's outburst, Agent Canady was only too happy to give us a few days off to go over the Divide and get our children. I told him we could not return with the family to Winnett. All the good people who had earlier helped us were now highly suspicious of our hanging around with Freemen. We couldn't bring the children back into that environment, so we broached the problem with Canady.

He conferred with Jim Cleaver, the agent-in-charge of the FBI office in Billings, and they decided the Bureau would put us up in a safe house. Again we asked why this was necessary: "Why not just send in the HRT now?"

"We're all getting our orders from the top," he said.

"You mean Louis Freeh?" I asked.

"No! The top!" the agent snapped.

"You mean the White House?" I drilled him for an answer.

The veteran agent just stared at Connie and me, with a small grin on his face.

I think the apartment the Bureau agreed to rent for my family was just an attempt to appease us, a distraction from the real issue. We were now being used to generate much wider intelligence on the militia movement, but the Bureau did not want us to know of the expanded assignment.

Canady finally conceded that the FBI wanted us to remain on the job for a while longer, and that the Bureau would cover the expense of a safe house in Billings for several months. But he wanted the motor home left at the cabin in Roundup and for us to make frequent visits. He suggested I might stay overnight in the motor home at the cabin on a regular basis, while Connie settled our children into the safe house in Billings.

We asked again about settling up our payment, and Canady said the agreement would just be extended on a month-to-month basis. To Connie and me that meant the agreed-upon $25,000 each for sixty days would be prorated for however long we stayed under cover.

Meanwhile, Canady gave us our monthly expense money and a little extra to go over to pick up our children. We checked into the HoJo Motel in Billings, called the Freemen cabin to report that we had to go out of town on personal business, and began looking for an apartment in Billings. The Bureau located a place, paid a $300 deposit, and advanced the rent for July, August, September, and October.

We moved the children to Billings when we returned from western Montana. The Freemen leaders had been told the truth about our picking up the kids, and also that Connie and the children would be living near relatives in the city.

This was the first time Connie and I had lived in anything that resembled a city since fleeing the drug bust gone awry in California eight years earlier. It was the first experience our children ever had living in a big town. And we all hated it. Our love of the woods and wide-open spaces, and the years we had lived in tiny towns or in the wilderness of Montana had not prepared us for city life, especially not for apartment living.

At the same time that we were resettling our family in Billings, I was driving hundreds of miles a week, dropping in on the Freemen at Roundup almost daily. Sometimes I stayed overnight in the motor home. I began to see members of the Clark family at the cabin on more and more occasions. I heard talk that the operational headquarters might shortly be relocated to their sprawling ranch near Brusett to the north.

I also picked up conversations indicating that the Freemen leaders were shifting their focus from a takeover of Winnett to a takeover of the equally tiny hamlet and county seat town of Jordan. The Clark ranch was closer to Jordan, and there had already been one thwarted attempt more than a year earlier to set up an ad hoc Freemen government there.

Based on these reports I took several trips up to Brusett to reconnoiter the Clark ranch. It was located at what felt like the very end of the world on a 960-acre farm. There were an unusual number of buildings on the property, including nine houses in various conditions of habitability, along with a handful of outbuildings. While this was a family farm, the cluster of buildings gave it the appearance of a village.

The one geographical feature about the place that bothered me most was the bleak, open terrain surrounding the buildings. The structures were highly defensible, with clear fields of fire in all directions. There was not a tree on the property large enough for a man to hide behind. If the Freemen ever holed up at this complex there would be no way, short of calling in the Army's combat tanks, to dislodge them.

Schweitzer had a sizable following of Freemen and sympathizers in Garfield County and nearby Petroleum County, and was anxious to move from Skurdal's cabin at Roundup to a location more central to his manpower base.

I relayed this information to the FBI, but got little interest from the busy agents in Billings. I warned of the impending move from Roundup and the much more impregnable features of the Clark ranch.

Tension was also mounting in Roundup, the closest town to the cabin where the Freemen leaders maintained their routine during July and early August 1995. Townspeople were getting pretty fed up with the continuing threats and delays in arresting the Freemen.

The Freemen expanded their harassment of locals, and in one outrageous incident filed a lien against a local Lutheran minister who dared tell his congregation that the hate messages issued in the name of God were nonsense. Even with the regular income from gasoline, cafe meals, and motel rentals generated by a steady stream of visiting militias, the patience of the citizens and local authorities of Roundup was at an end. They were tired of seeing their sleepy, once-peaceful streets invaded by heavily armed strangers. On any given day a gang of bullies with rifles slung over their shoulders or sticking out of car windows would disrupt the normal activities of the community.

The groups attending the seminars were now mostly small delegations, primarily leaders of state militias. Even though they were from many different states, there were usually a dozen or more people scheduled for each of the three-day sessions.

When classes were over they would pour into town in groups, and they were as rowdy as cowboys coming off a trail drive from the Wild West days of an earlier era.

Several different delegations from Texas came up during late July and early August, and they were especially boisterous and obnoxious. In the past I had known many Texans, and counted some top Western musicians from that state among my friends. I had always found their bragging to be tongue-in-cheek. But these Texans from right-wing organizations claimed immunity from all laws except those of the former Republic of Texas. They claimed they had proof that Texas had not been legally annexed by the United States in 1845; therefore, they were already a sovereign nation under occupation by foreign troops and agents of the United States.

I could hardly sit and listen to such malarkey being spouted by grown men in serious conversation. It was all I could do to keep from screaming, "Just listen to yourselves talking such nonsense!"

So I can imagine the bewilderment at the local pubs in Roundup when these armed Texans came into town.

Local officials of Musselshell and Garfield Counties appealed to the U.S. Justice Department in Billings, but nothing happened. The lives of everyone—citizens of Roundup, lawmen, and city-county officials—seemed to be suspended in some lawless limbo.

On my trips into town I drew suspicious stares, and people who had been friendly before made every effort to avoid me. Word had spread that I was *one of them* now and, of course, I was certainly in no position to tell them otherwise. I was tempted to just corner some old friend and explain that Connie and I were in the same limbo as the citizens of the towns of Roundup, Winnett, and Jordan. The truth is, our situation was considerably worse, because we were now suspended between the deadly forces at the cabin and an FBI bureaucracy that was secretive, at best. People who had once been our friends now shunned us.

Meanwhile, at the cabin the seminars were being conducted on an almost round-the-calendar basis. No sooner would one group complete the program than the next group would arrive. The course of study had changed, too, as the type of attendees changed. The Freemen had added emphasis to the part of the program that dealt with taking over local communities. Visitors were urged to develop smaller cells of warriors, the "tempered spearheads" of any assault on community law enforcement and federal facilities.

Schweitzer had picked up guerrilla-training manuals that suggested these small strike units should be autonomous and number only four or so members. Only the leader of each squad should know the names of those in other squads. He preached that this was the structure of the Irish Republican Army and noted that the IRA's secret cells had thwarted the best British antiterrorist experts for years. He suggested the larger, more public militias were the equivalent of the Irish rebellion's political arm, the Sinn Fein, while the terrorist cells of the militia would be the counterparts of the IRA death squads. Such a structure would work just as well in Kansas or New York City, the Freemen leaders told the visitors.

Of course, the Freemen continued teaching financial-terrorism techniques, using fraudulent liens on property and bogus checks and money orders. And everything was served up with generous dollops of the hateful Christian Identity religious teaching.

During early August alone, in her less frequent visits to the cabin with me, Connie took the license numbers and partial names of visitors from Washington state, California, Idaho, Wyoming, Colorado, Arizona, Louisiana, Georgia, Kentucky, West Virginia, North and South Carolina, Ohio, Michigan, and Oklahoma. Some states were represented at different times by units with more precise geographical locations in their names, such as the Militia of Northern Michigan, or by identifying numbers, such as the 100th Militia of Georgia. There seemed to be different groups from Texas at the cabin all the time, but they did not have the word *militia* in their unit names.

Before we left the cabin and the operation, we had encountered units with every sort of name affixed to their state of origin. There were groups that called themselves armies, clans, teams, volunteers, cells, republics, rangers, networks, brotherhoods, priesthoods—but most identified their units as militias.

The main thing these units had in common was the linkage they were establishing right here in an isolated cabin in the Bull Mountains of Montana. A powerful nationwide network was growing rapidly from one nexus—the Freemen of Montana.

The leaders I spent time with at the cabin boasted that they represented organizations back home consisting of as many as three hundred to six hundred men.

And still the Freemen providing this linkage were unable to assemble their own little army of two hundred.

During early August, when I stayed at the motor home without Connie, I used the evenings to get closer to Jacobi, who was still somewhat of an enigma. We spent many hours together, mostly in discussions about the biblical roots of the various movements.

It was in one of these late evening sessions that I discovered the truth about what had been going on back in March when Buzz Jones made the arrests on the streets of Roundup.

CHAPTER 21

All the fraudulent activity the Freemen and their cohorts around the country were involved in was only a sideshow for the real conspiracy. Back in February 1995, Garfield County Attorney Nick Murnion had been closer to identifying the true purpose of the illegal activities than even he or the feds imagined.

When the local prosecutor managed to get a conviction of Freemen member William Stanton under an antiquated state law called criminal syndicalism, he hit the bull's-eye of the plot. Criminal syndicalism was a Montana law that had been enacted back in the 1800s. The law was used against vigilantism. It was imposed against miners' unions by large Eastern landlords, or against sheepmen by cattle barons fighting over territory during the grazing land wars.

Like the renegades of the Old West, the Freemen had technically declared their own territorial government, and any land they could hold was no longer considered by them to be a part of the United States.

Shortly before the day Deputy Jones arrested the Freemen in Roundup, a judge had sentenced Stanton to ten years in prison on the syndicalism conviction. Now I learned why this was such a big deal to the Freemen.

One evening Jacobi and I were sitting at the dining table discussing theology and common law. We had been talking about judges. The look on his face began to change. He dropped his head and stared at the table; I could tell he was gritting his teeth, his jaw was working, and he began to mutter.

I said, "What?"

He said, "We missed that goddamn judge, the judge at Roundup. The son of a bitch had put an edict on us, banning our filing any more of the liens and any other paperwork with the county clerk."

Hearing Jacobi curse was a signal that he was seriously enraged, because as the biblical leader of the Freemen, he seldom used anything except the mildest expletives and never took the Lord's name in vain.

"The sheriff also stole our weapons and ammunition," Jacobi continued, and again began cursing under his breath, so angry he could hardly talk.

Over and over he said, "We missed that goddamn judge!"

"What do you mean, you missed him?" I said.

In recounting the story to me, Jacobi became more and more agitated. He became so angry in the retelling that spittle was flying from his lips and dripping off his chin. He banged the conference table and my arm with his fists.

"That goddamn deputy, Buzz Jones, it's all his fault, and we are going to kill him for it," Jacobi said. "That deputy is going to be gunned down whenever we find him alone. He doesn't even deserve a trial, and besides he will mostly likely resist arrest, anyway."

Jacobi finally calmed down enough to tell me the whole story.

The two deputies in Roundup had actually thwarted a much more deadly plan. Without knowing it, the local lawmen had not only saved at least one judge's life, they had also prevented a general uprising by the Freemen and their supporters. True, the Freemen had planned to kidnap, try, and hang the district judge. But that was only the beginning of the plot.

"It would all be over by now," Jacobi choked. "We would be living in our own free land, right here and now."

The Freemen who had been arrested, along with others waiting in cars outside Roundup, were on their way to bring the judge out to the cabin. They planned to incarcerate him in a dungeon under the cabin until his trial and hanging. The incident, which would be videotaped, was to be the signal event for the takeover of Winnett, the seizure of all public lands and buildings in northeastern Montana, and the establishment of the new Freemen Justus Township domain.

Several times during his recital, I tried to get Jacobi to tell me how many others were involved than those arrested, and who they were. He ignored my questions.

I found the story so incredible that I could only nod as I heard it unfold. When Jacobi looked to me for approval, I finally mumbled, "What dungeon under the house? Where were you going to keep the judge?"

"Not just the judge, but the county attorney and anyone else we could get our hands on." Jacobi scowled.

He took me by the shoulder into the storage room, which adjoined the computer room on the first level of the cabin.

Jacobi raised a hidden trap door in the floor that opened onto a dank crawl space under the cabin. I stuck my head into the musty space while Jacobi shined a flashlight. To my surprise I was staring into a ragged pit, twelve feet deep. It was just a big hole in the ground. The mouth of the dungeon was covered with spider webs.

"We were going to let him think things over for a while in the hole, then we had twelve tried and true men ready to give him the requisite two-hour trial," Jacobi said. "By our law, white males have a right to a two-hour trial. You know that!"

He blurted out the rest of the plan. Simultaneous to the hanging, the Freemen and their allies—whom I now had to assume were members of various militias in the Montana and Washington area— would move to occupy the town of Winnett.

He closed the trap door and we went back to the conference table.

"We were going to videotape the trial and the hanging with that very rope over there." Jacobi pointed at the noose hung on the wall behind the lectern. "The tape was going to be distributed all over the country to let these bastards know we are serious."

Jacobi went on to describe what the justice system would be like for the innocent citizens in the region they intended to take over. He reiterated the plan that I had frequently heard to starve out the old people, force them to leave their homes and ranches because all food and supplies coming in would be assigned to the loyal Freemen and their militia foot soldiers.

But public officials captured in the new Freemen territory would not be given the option of leaving. They had already committed treason. These officials were to be given the mandatory two-hour trial and hanged for their past treasonous conduct. Anyone else who resisted would be shot on the spot or, if they were white men or women, instantly tried for any infraction and likewise hanged.

Having just looked into the dark hole of hell under the floor of the cabin, the tone of this tale was eerily like some surreal horror movie.

Jacobi's sobering confession convinced me that Connie and I were in more danger than we had believed. From that moment I knew we had to get out. I had always worried about the possibility of a sudden mistake that could lead to a knee-jerk reaction and a shootout. Now I knew that retribution would be meted out by the Freemen in a premeditated and deliberate manner. These people, demented by their hate for the government, were capable of anything. If they even suspected we were spies, we would be murdered, and I was sure there were plenty of other dark holes like the one I had just seen in which our bodies could easily disappear.

Schweitzer, Petersen, and Skurdal drifted in to sit at the table. Having heard the name Deputy Jones, they all joined in the macabre discussion.

Skurdal said, "Everyone hates Buzz Jones so much it would be a shame to just gun him down. He should be brought out here and have his skin cut in strips. I would personally pull his skin off with pliers before we hang him."

"Yeah, he's not bonded, so he's in a constant state of treason," Petersen added. It seems that many of the complaints the Freemen had filed against sheriffs and deputies involved some obscure Montana law that said all the constabulary had to post bonds with the county. Apparently no one did this anymore, but it was all the proof the Freemen needed that no local lawman had any authority.

The Freemen's plan to take over territory was alive and well. Only the location of the town for the takeover had changed. The Freemen were definitely planning to move against some small community, and in the very near future.

On my next debriefing I revealed the whole plot to Agent Canady, and his canned answer was that the FBI already had enough on the Freemen to put them away for thirty years. The blueprint of an insurrection and the possibility of a major armed confrontation with the United States government seemed to be of little interest to the Bureau. Canady did not want to complicate anything. (Later, however, after a score of Freemen and their supporters barricaded themselves inside the Clark ranch and the standoff at Brusett began, the topic would come up again. At that time the FBI would be interested.)

During my conversation with Jacobi, I was especially interested in who had provided the unseen manpower back in March 1995. I asked about the role of the Montana militia in the conspiracy to grab the judge.

"Was John Trochmann with you on this kidnapping?" I asked, as casually as possible. The Montana militia leader had been arrested with Jacobi and other Freemen at the time. This produced a flurry of cursing against the militia commander, and epithets of "traitor" and "FBI snitch."

I never did get a satisfactory answer to my question about why Trochmann was with the Freemen that day, or confirmation that the powerful Militia of Montana had any role in the planned insurrection.

I was sorry that I mentioned Trochmann because his name reminded the Freemen sitting at the table that I, too, had not produced the manpower I had bragged I could supply.

My failed promise to deliver mercenaries produced one of the oddest events of our whole undercover operation. I had been telling the Freemen I was having trouble getting the ex-combat men to come to Montana because they weren't interested in the promised twenty-acre homestead sites. They wanted payment in gold, I said, since these men of war no longer trusted the federal monetary system. I felt sure this would hold the Freemen at bay for a little while, since pulling together enough gold bullion to pay off a small mercenary army was an impossible demand.

The new requirement for large amounts of cash to purchase gold to pay for my imaginary mercenaries became a sore spot for the Freemen leaders. The Freemen put out word on their grapevine that a large war chest of gold bullion was urgently needed.

Two days later, what I can only describe as the Odd Couple drove up to the cabin in brand-new vehicles. The man—I'll call him Charlie—was driving a new Ford crew-cab pickup with a dealer plate from the Seattle area. His girlfriend followed minutes later in a new Ford Explorer utility vehicle. I was introduced to the young couple, who told me they were from a town near Seattle, Washington.

They were there to show off their purchases, and bragged to Schweitzer that his bogus money orders had worked perfectly. They had used the fraudulent checks to purchase the vehicles.

I could tell Schweitzer was more irritated than pleased that the young couple had used his fake paper to buy the cars, when the Freemen themselves were isolated in Roundup and having a more difficult time getting anyone to take the phony financial documents.

Schweitzer was openly offended that the hard currency of his illicit labors was going for such frivolous things when he needed the cash for the cause.

The Seattle visitor's girlfriend quickly became as much an object of loathing for Jacobi as her extravagant boyfriend was for Schweitzer. Jacobi's ire was raised when the young woman announced that she was a professional clairvoyant. She went about the cabin in a feigned trance reading the Freemen leaders' auras. This clearly upset them. The Freemen could not abide pushy women and barely tolerated women under any circumstances. Now a brazen young woman who went around touching the armed and dangerous leaders was daring to read their destinies through some invisible auras. It was just too much for men who had been practically monastic in their self-imposed solitary confinement for more than two years.

Jacobi complained that such a dubious gift as clairvoyance could have connotations of witchcraft. He kept his distance from her, just in case she might really be a witch.

The ditzy young woman made several attempts to approach the brooding ex-cop, and for a while I worried that he might just pull his revolver and dispatch her to Valhalla or wherever young witches go after being shot.

Leaving this far-right, far-out Samantha to torment the leaders,

I worked on Charlie to see what his connection was to the Freemen and how he had acquired enough of the fake checks to buy what looked like about $60,000 worth of new vehicles. Jacobi fled the cabin and the haunting Samantha and joined us outside.

He mentioned that Schweitzer was upset by the young man spending all his money on cars when the Freemen needed to raise a large amount of gold in order to hire my mercenaries.

Charlie beamed and said, "*No problemo*, Chief. I know where you can get all the gold you could ever want."

This really got Jacobi's attention. He was so thrilled with the prospect that it would not have taken Samantha's special gifts to read his mind.

"There's millions in gold bullion stashed over at Butte in one of the old sealed Anaconda copper mines," Charlie assured us. "It was hidden there by the Jew Rockefellers."

Charlie told a story that one of his great uncles had worked in the copper mine back in the 1920s, and that the copper ore had also yielded tons of gold. The gold had, according to his family legend, been separated and poured into giant ingots. It was just sitting there waiting in a sealed mine shaft. He claimed his family had tunnel maps of the exact location of the mountain of gold bullion.

"The only hitch is the Jews—you know how tight-fisted they are," Charlie said. "They keep a heavy guard detachment posted just out of sight inside the mine." It would take a small army to shoot through the guards and get the gold.

I was greatly relieved to hear that, although I seriously doubted there was any such trove in the first place. In the first place, I had been to Butte on several occasions and seen the poverty of ruined landscape shrouding the town. If there had been a mountain of gold stashed anywhere near there, no detachment of guards could keep it secret.

In the second place, the Freemen didn't have the small army Charlie said it would require to get the gold. And without the gold there couldn't be any way to get the small army. There you have it.

Déjà vu, Catch-22 all over again.

★ CHAPTER 22 ★

By August, the Freemen of Montana, much to the delight of the four leaders in the Roundup fortress, had become a national resource center for the burgeoning American militia movement. They found themselves besieged by so-called patriot groups and individuals who wanted instruction, training, refuge, funding, or all of the above. These petitioners offered nothing in return, except possible ego gratification for Schweitzer, who fancied himself the patriarch of a vast antigovernment movement.

Instead of sending soldiers for the small private army the Freemen coveted, militia commanders who attended the seminars offered only promises. Scores came for training in the fraudulent money schemes, but instead of enriching the Freemen cause, they carried away bales of bogus checks and counterfeit money orders. Hundreds of millions of dollars in worthless paper, signed by Schweitzer and Skurdal, was issued from the rustic cabin in Montana, to be passed in major operations in California, the Carolinas, Missouri, Minnesota, Texas, Washington, and Oregon. Authorities would spend years trying to trace all the bogus paper and cash the schemes generated.

But very little cash actually came back to the Freemen coffers, and the leaders frequently fought over what to do about this reversal of fortune. Schweitzer, as chief justice, always prevailed by telling the others it was their God-given duty to help train and fund the nation's militants. His rhetoric sounded noble, but the fact remained that the Freemen needed large sums of money to carry out their ultimate goal of carving out an independent republic in Montana.

So, when a flashy con man came into the picture with a scheme to internationalize the Freemen fraud, the leaders fell for it hook, line, and kitchen sink. Their greed would ultimately be their undoing, but at the time they welcomed this most unlikely scam artist to the bosom of their brotherhood.

Connie and I arrived back at the cabin after a day of shopping in Billings for office supplies needed in the Freemen communications center. Of course, we had also stopped by the Artspace coffee shop for a debriefing with Agent Canady.

While we were unloading the supplies, Petersen asked Connie to stay over rather than drive back to Billings. Skurdal even chimed in that if we stayed over we could use the spare bedroom so Connie would be more comfortable. Of course, that was out of the question because of my sleep talking. My nocturnal rantings had grown so bad that even when we were sleeping in the trailer, Connie would often stay awake half the night to make sure no one eavesdropped on my dreams.

But Connie came up with a ready excuse to get us away from the cabin. She said she needed to relieve a baby sitter, so I would have to drive her back to the city. Just about the time we were to leave, a most strange entourage arrived at the cabin.

Two of the seediest-looking men I ever saw drove up in a battered old truck. The men were from Lewiston, Montana, the county seat of Fergus County and another stronghold of Freemen. They looked like something from the Dust Bowl era, in patched bib overalls, ragged shirts, battered hats, and cracked high-top work shoes.

In contrast to their appearance, the most bizarre person I'd ever seen at the cabin jumped out of the pickup behind the two hobo look-alikes. This man, in his late thirties, needed only a couple of cameras hanging around his neck and a funny straw hat to fit perfectly on a cruise ship vacation. He was dressed in a short-sleeved rayon shirt emblazoned with huge, garish tropical flowers. He wore white knee-length shorts and sneakers without socks.

His name was Derrick States. He claimed he was from Honolulu, but not a native islander. He quickly informed us, however, that Hawaiian natives considered him to be the great savior from a legend that predicted a white man would rise up to free the original South Seas islanders from Yankee domination. Within a short time of his arrival he had already arranged permission to stay at the cabin in the spare room. With his smooth line he had convinced Schweitzer that he was not only the savior of the native Hawaiians, but also someone who could deliver the Freemen from their financial dilemma.

Derrick States convinced Schweitzer that he had international connections and could move millions and millions of dollars in bogus checks overseas into the Far East. He said the greed of the yellow races knew no bounds; therefore, they would soak up all the fraudulent money orders the Freemen could produce on their laser printers.

It's a common myth in the underworld that you can't con a con man, but I was amazed at how glibly this obvious con man conned the con men inside the cabin. I had long since learned that criminal minds absolutely thrive on even the most preposterous schemes, and will believe anything if it is aberrant enough.

Derrick took an instant dislike to me because I questioned his basic premise that a white guy could lead a small army of rebellious Hawaiian natives. The man's arrogance was so complete that he just brushed aside my skepticism and had Schweitzer, Skurdal, and Petersen eating out of his hand. Jacobi stood back and observed the unfolding scam with his usual dubious calm, while the others fantasized about the great cash potential promised by this character.

States soon had Schweitzer's approval of a plan to take a suitcase full of the bogus Freemen checks and money orders. He promised the Freemen the lion's share of the cash he would raise, stressing that he was an honest guy who could be trusted to keep only a small percentage of the take. He assured the Freemen that even his small percentage would be used only to arm the Hawaiian rebels of his waiting island army.

I saw Connie, ignored as usual, sitting off in the corner taking notes.

When we left the cabin that evening, the four leaders were busily printing out reams of money orders amounting to millions of dollars. We had heard States tell the Freemen of his plan to catch a flight out of Billings the following day. Connie wrote the flight number and all the details in her notebook.

When we arrived back in Billings late that night, we were so excited we had the FBI office roust Canady from his home for a late-night debriefing at the Artspace coffee shop. Our new information was of such interest to the feds that a rare meeting was set for us to meet with other agents at the Bureau offices the next day.

To Connie and me, Derrick States seemed like just another oddball character in the Freemen setting, but the FBI obviously knew a lot about more about him. The men who gathered for our morning session at the Billings headquarters included field supervisor Jim Cleaver and a handful of other stern-faced agents. They were excited, and Canady told us that the Bureau already had quite a dossier on Mr. States. It seems he was known to the Bureau as a con man specializing in secessionist schemes for his own illicit financial gain.

At the meeting, field supervisor Cleaver took the opportunity to publicly praise—as public as the Bureau would ever be with undercover operatives—our performance on the Freemen case to the other agents in the room. As hard as we had worked, and as voluminous as the intelligence was that we had been bringing out over the past four or five months, this latest bit of information seemed the least important to Connie and me. But it generated the greatest excitement to date from the assembled federal agents. As the meeting broke up, Canady commented that he was going to have to pay Mr. States a visit.

A week later Tommie Canady dropped a hint that he had been to Hawaii since our last debriefing. I asked him what happened with our mutual friend Derrick States.

The agent just grinned and said, "Derrick loves me!"

Months later we would learn that the Bureau had caught up with the colorful con man after he had crossed many state lines and half the Pacific Ocean with his suitcase full of fraudulent paper. Faced with spending much of the rest of his life in a federal prison, Derrick States was easily rolled over by the Bureau. He would later play a key role in bringing the Freemen operation to an end and the Freemen leaders to arrest. Greed is often its own reward.

★ CHAPTER 23 ★

Close on the heels of the encounter with the man from Hawaii, Connie and I were faced with an encounter of a far different, and perhaps more significant, sort.

This next contact would prove to be as potentially deadly as the Derrick States contact had been sleazy. Geographically, this new intelligence was coming from the opposite end of America—our intelligence-gathering would now span half an ocean and the entire North American continent, from Hawaii to West Virginia. This was no longer a simple assignment to arrest a bunch of local criminals.

The brazen, nationwide fraud scheme centered at the Freemen cabin was overshadowed, in our minds, by a plot of insurrection, and the next visitor to arrive at the cabin was to provide the proof.

Floyd Raymond Looker, self-described commander of the six-hundred-member West Virginia Mountaineer Militia—with followers in West Virginia, Ohio, and Pennsylvania—was prepared to make a deal with the devil in an unholy quest to bring down the government of the United States.

The day he and a henchman drove up to the cabin in Roundup, Commander Looker did not seem like a commanding general. He had a military bearing, but he came to the cabin broke. The stoutly built Looker, who sported a large, trim moustache, closely cropped military-style haircut, and aviator-frame spectacles, had all his worldly possessions loaded into his car.

At first, as far as I was concerned, he was just another of the supplicant leaders coming to the Freemen in hopes that their illicit financial scheme could be used to raise the huge amounts of money they needed to sustain some shadowy militia units back home. I soon learned otherwise.

Because he came with hat in hand begging for money, Schweitzer did not immediately take to the tough-talking general of the Eastern army. Commander Looker boasted of his manpower and a three-hundred-acre training facility near the Pennsylvania–West Virginia border, but he confided that he was temporarily strapped for funds and couldn't even pay his mortgage or utility bills.

He bragged of a well-armed seasoned army of more than three hundred, with an equal number of recruits in training. In addition, Looker said he provided training facilities for as many as fifteen hundred more from Ohio and Pennsylvania militia groups. The cost of providing combat training to militiamen from throughout the Appalachian Mountain area had almost financially ruined his own Mountaineer unit.

Schweitzer tolerated the swaggering Looker, just in the event that he might be able to deliver the two hundred men the Freemen needed for the takeover of Winnett or the new target, Jordan. But it was clear there was a strong personality clash between the two supreme leaders.

Looker told us he had almost been elected to various public offices on several occasions as both a Democratic and Republican candidate. The fact that he was down on his luck did not keep him from playing the role of the general, and he moved right into the cabin as if he owned it.

Connie and I saw the personality clash developing and we worked to feed the friction. Just in case Looker was real and actually had a small army to contribute toward the Freemen cause, I wanted to be close to this man. Looker was asking for a few million in Schweitzer's bogus money orders and, in return, promised to deliver some men when the time was right.

Connie and I were still hoping our plan to bring in the FBI's own HRT under the guise of visiting militiamen would be accepted by the Bureau, so I wanted to make sure that no substitute manpower would be provided to the Freemen.

We got to know Looker very well—perhaps too well.

When Looker learned that I was an experienced explosives man he took an intense interest in me. He said the West Virginia Mountaineer Militia was sitting on several hot federal targets, including buildings and office complexes in Washington, D.C., and nearby locations in the suburbs.

At one point he elaborated on a chillingly plausible scheme that could cripple the nation's law enforcement establishment.

"Every fingerprint in the country is maintained by the Federal Bureau of Investigation," Looker pointed out. "If we brought down that building, the entire FBI would be out of business."

I put on my best subservient act, fawning on my leader Schweitzer and proving to Looker that I was the type of dedicated fanatic that could be counted on to do anything my leader ordered me to do. My act, repugnant as it was to me, paid off time and again, because it led these egotistical radicals to spill their guts to me or Connie.

Looker confided that he was in command of the finest, strongest, and most deadly militia in America, and he wanted me to join them.

But the Looker-Schweitzer relationship continued to sour. The second afternoon of the West Virginian's visit erupted in a confrontation during a break in one of the training sessions. With everyone outside the cabin for a smoke, we heard Schweitzer and Looker yelling at each other at the top of their lungs.

Schweitzer absolutely refused to give Looker any of the bogus money orders, even though the West Virginian said he had an arms pipeline to Argentina and could easily move huge amounts of the phony paper into South America.

Even at the risk of offending Schweitzer, I stayed close to Looker and his aide-de-camp over the three days they were at the cabin. Before they finally left—empty-handed I might add—I had a firm invitation to move to West Virginia and join the Mountaineers as a paid member of the command staff. I never asked what I would be paid with, since I knew the braggart was out of money and could hardly pay his own upkeep.

When Looker determined he was not going to get any financial assistance from the Freemen, he headed west toward Hayden Lake, Idaho, to put the arm on the leaders of the Aryan Nations. I took down all the information necessary to contact him later when he returned home, and told him I was definitely interested in moving to West Virginia to accept his offer to become the chief demolitions man and a command officer on his staff.

As soon as Looker left Roundup, Connie and I rushed to Billings to report this new intelligence to Canady. One mention that the FBI's own facilities were being discussed as a potential target sent the Bureau people in Billings into communications orbit with head-quarters in Washington.

In our debriefing, Canady said the Bureau knew nothing about the tristate group, and would almost certainly want me to go to West Virginia and join the Mountaineers as soon as we finished up here in Montana.

I looked at Connie and said, "Well, I guess I'd better dig out my camie BDUs [battle dress uniforms]."

Canady said, "That's not exactly the capacity we want to send you in."

"I'm versatile," I said.

Canady sent the word up the line, and I waited to hear the results. I am not sure, even today, if I would have gone into the West Virginia operation—certainly not for the paltry bucks that I was expecting to get for the Freemen job. Going into unfamiliar terri-tory in a situation where I would be without any backup could mean certain death at the slightest misstep.

We waited to hear from Washington about whether they wanted me to go inside the West Virginia group. Coincidentally, another vis-itor to the cabin may have played a role in the ultimate decision.

About the time Looker left, one of the Ohio militiamen from the larger, earlier delegation was spirited out of Ohio by two of his hench-men. The Ohio militiaman, whose first name was Joe, was a federal corrections officer. He had been caught helping several white supremacists gain their release from the prison where he worked, and was being investigated for that offense. Now he had compounded his misdeeds with another—felony theft of government property.

On his way out of the prison he had filched a footlocker full of antique common-law books from the prison library. Schweitzer, who had studied every scrap of old common-law information he could get his hands on, fairly salivated when he saw this cache of material.

The fugitive's plight was all but forgotten in the excitement over the new information contained in the old law books. The Freemen wanted these books, which they believed would hold the legal key to the future of the movement and prove to everyone that their cause was not only legal, but Constitutionally correct.

Joe's wife called while he was at the Freemen cabin and warned him that federal agents were looking for him and the books.

Schweitzer said the books absolutely could not be returned before they were copied. The Freemen leaders sat around and tried to calculate how big a job it would be to photocopy the tomes. There were tens of thousands of pages. They decided such a task was impossible.

I volunteered to take the rap and claim responsibility for stealing the books from Joe, so he could return home and face the lesser charges of aiding in the illegal release of the felonious supremacists.

"Absolutely not!" Schweitzer said. "We will not allow one of our own to be implicated. Joe will just have to go home and face the music like a man. It's a small sacrifice for the cause."

Poor Joe was, therefore, sent packing to his fate with the feds. The volumes of old common-law statutes remained the proudest addition to the Freemen library.

The Freemen leaders' avid pursuit of legal justification for their criminal endeavors, albeit from any oddball documents, has always puzzled me. They seemed perfectly willing to snatch judges and hang them, skin deputies alive, shoot blacks on the street, and yet they—particularly Schweitzer—fervently cloaked these outrageous misdeeds in some nutty interpretation of a Bible verse or a twisted reading of the law. This same zeal for justification seemed to permeate the ideology of most of the visiting militia fanatics.

No criminals I had dealt with in the past had ever evidenced such concern. Those common criminals and their defense lawyers would take any opportunity to beat a rap on a legal technicality, but they never believed their own justifications, as did the Freemen and their followers.

Despite bringing this new treasure of legal documents to the Freemen, poor Joe was disposable.

Before Joe left he acknowledged to me that he had trained with an Ohio militia unit at Looker's base in West Virginia, and that he knew Commander Looker personally. With petty crimes pending against him, I believe Joe set himself up as the perfect candidate to become a rollover for the FBI.

Connie and I passed all this information along to the Bureau in Billings. A short time later, Agent Canady informed me that Washington was not interested in my going under cover inside the West Virginia Mountaineer Militia.

The episode with the West Virginians did not end with our contact at Roundup. In October 1996, a few months after the Freemen of Montana leaders were arrested, more than a hundred federal and state lawmen raided the headquarters of the West Virginia Mountaineers. Looker and six of his top officers were arrested.

This full-fledged domestic terrorist organization had sold blueprints of the FBI's Criminal Justice Information Services Division at Clarksburg, West Virginia, to an undercover FBI agent. The agent was posing as a buyer for a Mideastern terrorist organization that planned to blow down the huge complex. Every fingerprint and major case file on America's criminals is housed in that gleaming new facility. A successful bombing of the complex would virtually bring law enforcement in the United States to a halt, and create untold havoc throughout the justice system.

The arrest of this group in West Virginia provided the first proof that elements of the American militias harbor such a depth of hatred against the U.S. government that they will use any means to overthrow it, even sell out to foreign terrorists intent on attacking Americans on our own soil.

In conversations I overheard and participated in with the leaders passing through the cabin at Roundup, a disturbing pattern of international linkage with terrorists of all types began taking shape.

As horrible as this reality may be, more astounding to me is the the fact that powers in Washington either refuse to acknowledge the truth or are deliberately withholding the information from the American people. The pattern of disinformation by denial from the FBI and its parent, the Department of Justice, on the subject of domestic terrorism was gradually revealed to me.

Newspaper accounts related that an FBI agent had been introduced to Looker by an Ohio militiaman whom the FBI had turned, and who went under cover about August 1995. I've often wondered what kind of deal poor old Joe, the corrections officer from Ohio, was able to make. I never heard anything about him after he left the Freemen cabin.

I found one particular newswire story about the capture of the Mountaineer leaders to be most revealing and typical of the denial that a national conspiracy of domestic terrorism exists. To me, the following account is absolutely chilling:

WEST VIRGINIA MILITIA
SUSPECTED INFORMANT

CLARKSBURG, W. Va. (AP)—Leaders of the West Virginia Mountaineer Militia were suspicious that federal authorities knew of their plans to blow up three federal buildings.

They even ordered one member to remove his shirt one day to prove he wasn't wearing a wire.

They asked on the wrong day, according to court documents.

The member was an informant who had been secretly recording members conspiring to destroy the FBI's Criminal Justice Information Services Division complex in Clarksburg, about 80 miles south of Pittsburgh, and two other government buildings in West Virginia, the documents say.

The information he provided led to the arrest Friday of seven men linked to the militia on conspiracy charges. They were being held Saturday pending detention hearings this week.

The informant had gone to the FBI 16 months ago after becoming disenchanted with the group's activities, which included making and testing homemade explosives, U.S. Attorney William Wilmoth said Saturday.

At least one militia member, according to the informant, believed the FBI complex contained a clandestine operation that might be a command center when the government turned against the people under the "new world order," the documents said.

Prosecutors do not believe the alleged conspiracy was linked to antigovernment groups in other states.

"I do not want it to appear to be some nationwide conspiracy or anything more grave than the charging documents show. As far as we could tell, it was localized," Wilmoth said.

In reading the article so many months later, I had two thoughts. First, the Justice Department spokesman was spouting the official "big lie" about the operation being an isolated incident.

Second, had I gone under cover with the Mountaineers, that insider could have been me. I wondered if I would have been so lucky. Chances are I would have been wearing a wire the day the Mountaineers forced the guy to take off his shirt.

On such a razor-thin game of chance is the life of an undercover operative sliced.

CHAPTER 24

The situation with the Freemen was tense enough without our worrying about taking on another assignment. As each day in August ground along at a snail's pace, the Bureau—much to our dismay—dropped even the pretense that it was interested in arresting the Freemen leaders. Every debriefing ended in instructions to get more information about the militia members and individuals from other groups who were now flowing in a steady stream through the Roundup cabin.

Connie and I suspected the diverse information we were bringing in was of such interest that the Bureau might actually be postponing arrests just to keep open their newfound pipeline into the nation's militias. Repeatedly, we were told by our happy handler at Billings that the stuff we brought the Bureau was checking out.

The wiretaps were apparently sizzling hot, too.

For what amounted to a minimal investment, the FBI now had the resources to build a national file on potential terrorists they had previously known little or nothing about. While the larger, better known, and supposedly more dangerous organizations like the Aryan Nations and the Aryan Republican Army continued to foment revolution and made attempts to network with the sprouting state militias, I had good reason to believe the feds were unable to establish any reliable pipeline into their headquarters at Hayden Lake.

Our source in the Bull Mountains was therefore one of the best—if not the only—intelligence operations the Bureau had going on a national level. We had, quite honestly, stumbled into this cauldron of hate. Even Connie and I were amazed at the depth and breadth of information we were able to obtain.

The Bureau, while denying it to us, obviously liked this information more than they wanted to arrest the Freemen. We could have had their Hostage Rescue Team inside the cabin for a bloodless arrest at any time. One team member checking by telephone on some detail of such an arrest told me they had built a mockup of the cabin back at Quantico, rehearsed for weeks, and were ready to roll.

So someone in the Bureau was not even leveling with its own tactical people, who also thought the arrest was imminent. The HRT asked me to get an estimate on the exact time it would take a team to storm from my motor home onto the porch and through the front door into the cabin. They thought about staging a backup team in the motor home to rush the front door at the time the tactical unit made the arrest inside. As we had recommended, the actual arrest would be made by agents, inserted as visiting militiamen dining with the Freemen.

I estimated the time by rehearsing a dash from the trailer to the front door and reported it. Even with my bum leg I could make the sprint in three seconds flat.

But still the Bureau would not give the go-ahead for the arrests, and our personal situation at the cabin was rapidly deteriorating. Upon later reflection, I believe the problem lay more with the growing tension among the Freemen than any suspicion of why Connie and I were still hanging around.

Even though she usually did not stay at the motor home more than one or two days a week, and I made more and more prolonged trips to Billings, our frequent visits were becoming a little awkward to explain. Jacobi began watching me like a hawk.

And there was an unfortunate incident involving Petersen. One evening he and I were discussing a Bible quotation that the Freemen had discovered to prove some new nonsensical point. Petersen was taking notes when his ballpoint pen ran dry.

I took a cigarette lighter and heated the tip. In the process, some of the plastic melted. So I pulled out the cold-steel pocketknife I carry, opened the razor-sharp four-inch blade, and began to shave the melted plastic from the pen point. Petersen leaned his face close to observe the big blade and I jokingly said, "If I had one of my seizures now, this knife would slit your throat."

I regretted the joke immediately.

Petersen jerked back, his face ashen. Like the other Freemen leaders he was so paranoid that someone was coming to kill him that he rarely got near me after that. In fact, he joined Jacobi in silently watching my every move around the cabin.

Skurdal had taken an uncomfortable interest in Connie's activities, to the point that she became wary of taking notes. She would try to memorize names and license plate numbers and not write them down until we had left the cabin.

Schweitzer and Skurdal were also openly arguing. Skurdal would carp at Jacobi or Petersen about some real or imagined lapse of cabin protocol, and Schweitzer would jump him. Finally, Schweitzer told Skurdal that if he didn't shape up and stop being so grumpy all the time, they would all move out and leave him alone at the cabin.

This threat quieted things down for a few days, because Skurdal's greatest fear was to be left in the mountains alone. He knew he would be arrested the minute his guardian buddies left the premises.

The three other Freemen were hardly speaking to Skurdal, so he turned his full attention to Connie whenever she was there.

She drove up to the cabin one afternoon after having lunch with Cherlyn Petersen, Daniel Petersen's wife. They had been to Roundup to pick up groceries for the cabin. Cherlyn left and Connie hung around for a while to see if I wanted to ride with her back to Billings or stay over at the motor home.

The water tank on the motor home had sprung a leak, with a little help from me, and I had been talking about driving it off the property to have it repaired. I planned on using that excuse to get the thing away from the scene, in the event the operation was either shut down or the FBI's Hostage Rescue Team wanted to load up its backup assault unit to carry out the operation we had discussed.

Skurdal complained about the mud puddles the leaking tank was causing on the adjoining driveway, so I knew I would have no problem explaining why I suddenly wanted to drive off in the big thing.

Anyway, Connie was loitering around the cabin. I had lured

Petersen into a discussion of the Freemen's warped religious theories, in hopes of making up for the recent unpleasantness over the incident with the knife.

We had been in deep discussion for about thirty minutes when Petersen commented that Connie had been gone from the big room for quite some time. I knew she had not left the property without checking on my plans, so I searched the places in the cabin where she should be. I looked in the kitchen and across to the computer center. Connie was nowhere on the main level.

Jacobi was cleaning his police revolver at the big table when I asked, "Where's Connie?"

He didn't respond at first, but he stopped polishing his pistol. Finally, he told me he thought he had seen Skurdal escort Connie up the stairs.

A pang of terror tore through my chest. Connie had complained only the day before that she was beginning to feel nervous around Skurdal. She said during the last three or four visits he had been telling her progressively more off-color jokes and trying to get her to take walks with him around the property.

Now all I knew was that Connie was absent and Skurdal was nowhere to be seen.

I remembered spying on the barrel-chested, ex–oilfield roughneck watching porno movies via satellite TV late at night.

I remembered him tossing railroad ties several feet from a pickup truck with no apparent effort at all.

I remembered that these guys had been without women for almost two years.

I saw red.

When I jumped toward the stairs leading to the second floor of the cabin, Jacobi snapped closed the cylinder of his reloaded pistol and raised the weapon. I thought it was aimed at me, but I had already decided it would take more than a .357 Magnum slug to keep me from taking those steps three at a time.

Jacobi saw the glare of determination on my face, and he shouted "Go!" pointing the muzzle of his revolver toward the stairwell. He bounded behind me up the stairs.

I was thinking as we reached the second floor that if anyone was going to get shot today, it would be Skurdal, and either Jacobi or Petersen would pull the trigger. They were both fed up with the cabin's proprietor, and neither Jacobi nor Petersen would have stood by for a minute if Skurdal or any other visitor to the cabin tried to harm Connie.

We found Skurdal towering over Connie in a corner of one of the upstairs bedrooms. He had just cracked a joke about hanging a basket from the rafter over his bed.

I had heard the smutty story before, used to described a sex toy in Hong Kong whorehouses frequented by U.S. sailors on shore leave, so I snarled, "And why would you need such a big basket for the puny flowers around this place?"

Skurdal wheeled around. His complexion turned bright red when he was confronted by me, Jacobi, and Petersen standing in the doorway.

Connie came across the room to me with a relieved look on her face and said, "Let's see the rest of the upstairs, and then Dale and I have to go."

She was cool as a cucumber. I later asked her what she was going to do if Skurdal had further pressed an attack on her.

"I would have disabled him for life," she said coolly. And I believe she would have. I know she could have.

On the way out of the cabin Petersen mumbled something about "goddamn women always being trouble."

Connie got into the pickup and I slid into the driver's seat of the motor home. We drove to Billings.

I placed a cell phone call to the Bureau and asked for Tommie Canady. Instead, I got Jim Cleaver, the Billings field supervisor, and told him we were pulling the motor home out.

He asked why, clearly concerned.

"It's getting a little crazy," I said. "I'll explain tomorrow."

I hung up, hoping the bastards would also worry a little about their precious operation. But I didn't count on it.

CHAPTER 25

Connie's unpleasant and potentially dangerous brush with Skurdal caused us to take serious stock of the operation and our own safety. We felt as if we were spinning our wheels anyway, and each incident, no matter how significant or unimportant, was like straining at gnats.

Our commitment to the Bureau for sixty days of undercover work had long since been fulfilled. There had been no attempt at an arrest of the Freemen leaders. Our experience warned us that when a deep-cover operation goes off track, someone is likely to get hurt in the wreck. This one was off track big time. We now had no idea what the FBI's true agenda might be.

A gut feeling—call it instinct or chalk it up to experience—told me the thing was getting too dangerous for me to continue taking my wife inside the Freemen stronghold.

The next morning I called Canady and said, "We have to talk."

"Can't it wait?" he asked irritably.

"No, let's meet," I insisted, and we set a time.

Connie and I waited at the Artspace coffee shop for an hour past the appointed time. Agent Canady finally arrived in a huff, and before we could say anything he began grilling us on what I had told Cleaver in my brief cell phone call.

I told Canady "Nothing," because that is exactly what I had told the station boss.

He asked where the motor home was, and I said, "It's back of the Shopko parking lot," out in the Homestead Industrial Park.

"I'll have it picked up," the agent said. "Give me the keys."

"Look, Tommie, we need to know what's going on here," I began.

"What happened at the cabin?" he asked

I quickly recounted the incident with Skurdal. Connie broke in to explain that she thought it was just a minor event.

"The bigger picture is more important," Connie said. "What's this operation all about?"

The agent ignored her.

"Dale, do you think it's too risky for Connie to go back up there?" he asked, as if she wasn't at the table.

"Could be," I answered. "Now that the RV is out, there's no way she'll be staying over again, anyway."

I did express a concern that the Freemen had been talking about my participation in some clandestine operation. On several occasions one or another of the leaders had said it was a pity to waste my demolition talents.

"The main problem I see with Connie going up there now would be if they sent me out on a job," I said. "She'd have to stay back at the cabin. If the job involved something heavy, like blowing something up, I couldn't do it. They'd figure out I wasn't for real, and Connie would be a virtual hostage."

Canady became highly agitated at the thought of such a hypothetical scenario. "Let's go back to the office," he snapped.

Once we were settled in his office, Canady immediately resumed the discussion about Connie being left at the cabin with one or more Freemen while I was sent on an illegal operation with some of the others.

"We already know they tried to grab the judge at Roundup," I pointed out. "They have been talking about gunning down Deputy Buzz Jones the next time they can get him out of Roundup. There's also been a lot of talk about grabbing County Attorney Nick Murnion up at Jordan."

The agent was clearly uncomfortable with this line of conversation. His simple little intelligence-gathering operation was being overcome by the reality that he was dealing with something far more sinister and dangerous than a bunch of check-forgers.

"When push comes to shove I'll have to make a quick decision," I said, enjoying the agent's discomfort. "I'll either have to go along with a felony or neutralize the Freemen I'm with. That's the only way I could get back to the cabin in time to get Connie out. Probably have to take out whatever Freemen were still at the cabin, too."

I also related another incident with a Freemen member, which I believed proved the gang of radicals had decided it was time to commit open mayhem, or even murder.

During my last visit to the cabin Richard Clark had shown up in a state of high dudgeon. He paced about in his clean-pressed Levi's and shined cowboy boots, ranting against a local highway patrolman.

It seems Clark had been pulled over by the patrolman for a minor traffic infraction, and instead of taking a ticket, had pulled a gun on the officer. I told Agent Canady the only thing that had prevented a shootout with the authorities was the fact the officer had backed down, got back into his patrol car, and driven away.

"We know about that already," Canady said. "The cops up there have been ordered not to act against individual Freemen."

"So the bastards have carte blanche to do anything they want!" I responded incredulously.

Canady paced his office, obviously upset with the talk about bloodshed.

I was tempted to tell him that if there was any shooting it would be because of the Bureau's procrastination in making the arrests when they were practically handed over on a silver platter.

"Okay, we'll lower her profile at the cabin," Canady said, "and ease Connie out of the routine. Start winding her part down. Say she can't get away from the children."

"We've already decided that," I said, trying to cover the mounting sarcasm in my voice.

I waited for the right opportunity to inform the agent of another decision I had already made. I was not going back in the cabin without a weapon. Agent Canady had refused several times to let me carry a pistol, concealed or otherwise. I was not going to show up suddenly with my 10/22 carbine hanging around my neck.

"It's beyond time for me to pack an equalizer," I said, as casually as possible.

"Out of the question," he snapped.

"I'm not going back in without a gun," I said finally and stared the agent down.

He stewed about it for a minute or two, then realized the argument was over.

"I don't want you out here carrying it on the street." His argument was waning. "Maybe just when you're actually at the cabin."

"I'm plain and simply not going in there without a gun," I said finally.

He exploded, "Okay, okay, but if you shoot one of my Freemen, I'll make you drag him out to the woods and bury him yourself."

Connie and I talked about that comment throughout the night. It haunted the rest of our operation. It had become clear to us that Tommie's whole concern—probably the only concern of the Bureau at that time—was for the FBI's public relations image. We were right back to the same old paranoia that had prevented a clean arrest early in the operation. No matter what else happened, the only thing that mattered was preventing a repeat of the incidents that had so tarnished the Bureau's image at Ruby Ridge and Waco.

These Freemen leaders had clearly gone well over the line of normal criminals, and yet they were being treated with kid gloves. They were terrorizing communities in half the small towns of eastern Montana, not to mention teaching Terrorism 101 to half the militias in the country. All the Bureau could think about was making sure its hands didn't get dirty.

I told Connie, "As much as I feel I owe my country, I'm not going to get my ass shot off doing PR for the FBI." I immediately went to a Billings gun dealer I had known for a long time and purchased a second Glock .45. Now we had one for me and one for Connie.

"And something else, Hon," I told my fellow agent and trusting wife. "We're going to wind this puppy down ASAP." She nodded in agreement and gave me one of the famous smiles I had not seen on her face for several months.

★ CHAPTER 26 ★

Two days later we went back to the Bull Mountains fortress.

The mood was noticeably different. When we drove up, Schweitzer met us outside the cabin and solemnly asked me to come inside. He ordered Connie to stay in the pickup.

The tension in the air was so thick I could have cut it with my cold-steel folding knife. I glanced at Connie as she got back into the pickup. We had any number of prearranged hand signals that had served us well in life-threatening situations in our years of battling druggies.

Connie scratched the tip of her nose and brushed her blond hair off her left ear. That meant she would be waiting with the motor running in the pickup. I rubbed the back of my neck in acknowledgment and patted my right side at belt level. She knew I had received her message, and that my Glock was under my denim jacket on my right hip. Since I depended on my left arm, I holstered a weapon butt forward on my right side or at the small of my back.

I entered the cabin escorted by Schweitzer. Skurdal was sitting on the couch and did not greet me. He looked down at the floor and didn't even raise his head to acknowledge my arrival in the room.

Jacobi and Petersen were seated at the big conference table, each with a soft drink at hand.

I noticed they were armed, as usual, but no one had a gun laid out on the table or otherwise at the ready. That was a good sign they were not prepared for a shootout—at least not at the moment.

But I calculated how I could draw my Glock and move around the room taking one shot each to immobilize the four men before they could shoot me.

"Dream on," I told myself. There was no way I could drop all four of these guys before at least one of them drilled me. These were no pushovers; I had seen each one perform some degree of marksmanship, practicing with their various side arms behind the cabin. I'd be lucky to get two of them.

But that would be okay—Connie would at least hear the gunfire and have time to get out of the area. As sad as it was for either of us to think about losing the other, we had long ago agreed, for the sake of the children, that at least one of us had to survive whatever situation we were in. We had no relative we wanted to raise them. Our own childhoods had been too traumatized by our kinfolk, no matter how good their intentions.

Connie knew that if she heard gunfire she could wait no more than thirty seconds. If I had not come out of the cabin door, or whatever place I might be when shots were fired, she was to haul off down the road. If I survived, she'd see me later. If not, we kept an emergency road kit in the closet of our home and she was to grab the kids and keep running as far and as fast as our little cash reserve would take her.

We had used the escape plan on two occasions when previous jobs went wrong, except on those cases we had managed to get out together. This time it didn't look certain.

So I took a seat at the table and chatted about some minor current event I had heard on the news driving up. Schweitzer, almost casually, cut me off with an announcement.

"By the way, Dale, you've been elected a justice. A full justice of the court."

He could not have stunned me more had he hit me in the face with a dipper of ice water on a hot day.

"Wow!" I was genuinely pleased, but not at the appointment to the inner court. My exclamation came from my great relief at not having to fight a bloody battle to save my life.

But the three Freemen at the table took it for real enthusiasm at their announcement and offered hearty congratulations.

"We have to swear you in, and the ceremony is going to take a while," Petersen announced solemnly.

I thought of Connie sitting out in the pickup waiting to hear the doomsday gunshots.

"Can I just go out and tell my helpmate this wonderful news?" I asked humbly. "And could I take her one of those Pepsis? She's probably dying of thirst."

I knew my wife was dying, but it wasn't from thirst.

The Freemen leaders just beamed and said sure.

I went out and told Connie that I had just been made a full-fledged justice. "That's what all the secrecy is about!" I almost shouted.

The relief on her face brought tears to my eyes. What was I doing putting her through this agony again? All my wife really wanted was a normal life, raising kids, going to church, running our own little business. At that moment I was angry—at myself, at the Freemen, at all the hate groups in the country—but most of all at the self-serving Federal Bureau of Investigation.

"Go back inside and get it over with," she said in a soft voice, choking with relief. "Too bad you're getting such a fine promotion just when you're quitting your job." I saw her trying to force a smile.

"You know me—it's not the prize, it's the fun of the chase," I said, also forcing a smile.

I went back into the cabin and noticed that Skurdal had joined the others at the table for the swearing-in ceremonies.

A Bible was produced and I was ordered to put my hand on the holy book to swear an allegiance.

It was a little awkward for a few seconds when they asked me to raise my other hand for the ceremony. Since I obviously couldn't do both, Schweitzer settled on my raising my hand in a solemn salute to him.

"Do you pledge allegiance and loyalty to the supreme court of Musselshell County and to the republic under its jurisdiction under common law?"

"I do," I responded as seriously as circumstances would allow.

"The supreme court of Musselshell County now officially appoints you a full justice under the jurisprudence with full responsibilities and privileges. May Yahweh be with you! Amen!"

After the official session of the justice court was concluded, I received pats on the back all around. Even Skurdal came out of his shell for a moment to welcome me into the brotherhood of Freemen of character.

I started for the door on somewhat wobbly legs. My bunged-up right knee was shaking, and I was afraid it might collapse under me.

Schweitzer stopped me before I reached the door.

"There's just one thing, Dale. Your first order is to go over to western Montana and take out this black federal official that's been giving our people trouble. Will you handle that for us?"

Jacobi stared at me from across the room, a malevolent grin on his usually featureless face.

I nodded and responded, "It's a great honor to be made a justice, and I accept the responsibility humbly. But what if I had declined the honor, or decline now?"

Jacobi spoke up. "You'd be placed in the hole for a few days before we hanged you."

"Well, we wouldn't hang you immediately," Petersen chimed in. "You'd be left in the hole for thirty days of discipline and then we'd ask you one more time."

The conversation lightened just a bit, but the Freemen leaders said I knew full well what my duties were because I had diligently gone through so much instruction.

They told me more about my first assignment. In a day or so I was supposed to go to Great Falls with some other Freemen and help grab a black federal officer. I asked his name, and Schweitzer said my escort would have all the details.

The reason for the delay of a day or two was that the Freemen had ordered new badges for justices and constables, and we would need the badges to make the arrest of the government man.

After we dispatched the black man, my next assignment would be to go with the same team up to Jordan and bring in County Attorney Murnion. He was to be brought back to the cabin for trial. After all, he was a white man and entitled to his two hours before the bar of Freemen justice.

The black official was to be shot and his body hidden in the mountains so it would never be found. Murnion would be hanged right there at the cabin.

They escorted me to the storage area adjoining the computer room, and through a small window I was shown an old wooden scaffold that had once served as a swing for children. It was just outside the cabin. They planned to raise and shore up the frame to withstand the weight of a body struggling with a noose around its neck.

The makeshift gallows and the noose now hanging on the cabin's main room wall were to get quite a workout in the coming days.

The Freemen leaders began talking over each other rapidly and wildly about others they would try and hang.

Jacobi wanted Deputy Buzz Jones. Petersen was excited about hanging Sheriff Busenbark of Petroleum County.

"I'd like to pull the rope on him slowly," the grandfatherly Petersen said. "Let it go and do it again and again until he dies."

"That deputy [Buzz Jones] should be hanged up there naked," Jacobi said. "Peeling his skin off in strips."

The Freemen leaders stood around fantasizing aloud about a variety of tortures they would administer on the law officers and prosecutors. I knew they had been drinking colas and not liquor, and was astounded by grown men who seemingly reveled in describing such gruesome punishment for their enemies.

They didn't mention how they planned to dispose of all the bodies, but some key victims would be used as examples and their bodies left hanging from lampposts.

Before I left the cabin, almost in a daze, I was given one additional instruction.

"It's open season on that son of a bitch Buzz Jones," Jacobi said. "If you see him on the road on your way home to Billings, you have authority to kill him. As much as we'd like to spend time on him, he needs to die now."

Connie and I wasted no time in driving back to Billings.

At the earliest opportunity, we briefed Canady on the whole affair. He just asked to see my badge and I told him it was on order to be presented to me later. The agent showed very little interest in the bizarre events of the day. After all, the Bureau already had its fraud cases made.

The next day I called the cabin and told Petersen, who answered the phone, that Connie and I had some business in Billings and would not be up that day.

Petersen said that was fine because they had some errands for us in town, too. He said his wife, Cherlyn, was driving down to look at a new copying machine and desktop publishing program. She wanted to come by our house and pick us up to accompany her on the shopping trip.

"We don't even know where you live," Petersen said, being a little too obvious in the innocence of his question. Since Connie and I had moved into the apartment the FBI had provided us, we had made sure that no one knew its location. I had to think fast.

"Just a second, let me check with Connie about our schedule," I lied.

I took Connie by the arm and with finger to lips, shushing her, I led her to the kids' bedroom and closed the door.

"It's Petersen," I whispered. "He wants to send Cherlyn over to pick us up for a trip to the computer store." I saw the flash of alarm on Connie's face. This was a threat to her most avidly protected secret, the safe haven of her children.

"No possible way, never," she hissed.

"Okay, what do I tell him?" I asked.

"Tell him we're staying with my grandmother, and since we'll be out shopping anyway we'll just meet Cherlyn at the computer store." I patted her cheek in appreciation. My wife could always come up with a plausible solution on an instant's notice.

Back on the phone I told Petersen the arrangement.

He was not altogether pleased, but in no position to argue.

"Okay, what's your home phone number?" he asked. "So Cherlyn can call and set a time."

I was ready for that one.

"Just call us on our cell number," I said. We conducted all our communications by an untraceable cell phone that was several layers removed from us. "Connie's grandma is somewhat of a crank about anyone using her phone. She won't let us touch it."

Petersen grumbled, but we made an appointment and met Cherlyn at the computer store. We carefully took down all the serial numbers, make and model of the new copier, and name of the desktop publishing program to turn over to the FBI. After the purchase we bid Cherlyn a cheery good-bye, separated at the door, got into our pickup, and drove away. When we left the parking lot, Connie turned in a direction away from our true destination.

I looked through the rearview mirror and, as suspected, saw Cherlyn's car following us about a block behind. I told Connie. "I know," she replied.

She made two quick right turns and drove through an alley. A block away she fell in behind Cherlyn's car at a safe distance, out of sight. We followed the Freeman's wife as she zigged and zagged looking for us, until she finally gave up and headed her car back toward Roundup.

⋆ ⋆ ⋆

Connie and I were alarmed by the Freemen's clumsy effort to send Cherlyn to find our house in Billings. This following close on the heels of my being named a justice of the court just didn't ring true. The four leaders had obviously set some murderous chores for me as a test. Did they want me to commit a crime, a very major crime, so they could be assured of my loyalty? Or were they probing to see if I really was who I claimed, a loyal Freeman who would kidnap and murder for the cause?

We did not have to wait long for an answer. The following day Canady called and told us not to leave the apartment.

I told him I was just about to drive to Roundup and the Freemen cabin.

"Don't leave the fucking house," he barked into the phone. I knew something was up, and from the staid agent's expletive, it was not good.

Within a matter of only a few minutes, Canady and two other

agents were banging on the apartment door. We let the three breathless agents in, and they went over to close the blinds in the living room.

Canady took out a pocket tape recorder and reeled it back to start. They began playing a fairly high-quality audiotape.

It was Petersen's voice talking to Lyle Chamberlain, probably at his ranch up at Cat Creek near Winnett. Petersen was saying that there's something wrong with "that pair"—clearly meaning me and Connie. Petersen asked Chamberlain questions about how he first met "the Jakeses," discussed our children, and ended by instructing Chamberlain to do some further checking out in western Montana, where we had lived prior to moving to Winnett. He also told Chamberlain to check a little deeper around Winnett.

From the conversation on the tape, the Freemen wanted to know more about my previous job as a logger. Chamberlain was asked if he personally knew one of the Clark family grandchildren who worked on a tree skidder for the logging company.

The big question the Freemen discussed was, "How do the Jakeses live, where do they get their income?"

It was now almost four months since we had left our part-time jobs at the Kozy Korner Bar and Cafe to move onto the Freemen property.

When the taped conversation was concluded, Canady instructed me to go outside with him and look around. We left the apartment. There were a half-dozen people on the streets in front of and beside the apartment complex. Normally the street would be empty at this time of day. Two men sat talking in an unmarked car across the street. I recognized them as Jim Cassaria, the young agent the FBI had attempted to insert into the cabin two months earlier, and an agent named Tim Healy, an undercover man we had briefed on several occasions. Healy would soon play a key role in the Freemen case.

Up and down the street I observed an unusual number of yardmen puttering around the apartment lawns, and it seemed every utility company in town was reading meters at the same time.

"How odd," I commented to Canady.

"What's odd?" he asked.

"We're finally getting some maintenance done on these ratty apartments you assigned us to," I said.

"Screw you, Jakes," he retorted.

I laughed as Canady and I walked back into the apartment.

"Hey, they don't know where we live," I said. And I related the story of evading and then following Cherlyn, the Freemen's snoop, until she left Billings.

Back in the apartment, Connie and I assured the FBI agents that if all the Freemen were curious about was our income, we already had made up a good cover story.

"When they check the timber company they'll find I suffered a serious injury," I told the agents.

"We can say we're on welfare waiting for disability insurance," Connie said. "The Freemen already know all about Dale's previous head injury. He uses that all the time. And they know he's got a really bad leg that needs surgery in the worst way."

Both of these stories were absolutely true.

"All I would have to do is rip off my shirt," I added. "I've got scars from my neck to my waist, and lower down, too, if they asked me to drop my pants."

But Canady was adamant. "You're out—you're not going back, even for one minute."

The more I argued that I should continue the operation, the more angry Canady became.

Finally, we left the apartment with the agents and went to the FBI office in downtown Billings. Jim Cleaver joined us in a conference room.

I argued my case for keeping the operation open. As much as I wanted it over, I wanted it concluded with the arrest of the Freemen leaders.

Canady would not budge on the issue. Twice his boss and other agents at the meeting agreed with Connie or me that we could still maintain some part of the operation, albeit slightly altered for security purposes.

I said, "Tom, I really think we can go back in and calm the fears of the Freemen."

The agent glared at me. "No!"

Connie piped up, almost cheerfully, "Okay, then, so when do we get paid? The last thing we want to do is stick around here."

The other agents in the room grumbled about ending the operation so suddenly and discussed possible alternative scenarios to put another undercover agent inside the Freemen cabin. It was generally agreed that no good alternative presented itself. Then the other agents began to argue that Connie and I were probably not burned anyway.

Field Supervisor Cleaver suggested we go over to Noxon to look in on the Militia of Montana while things cooled off at the Freemen cabin.

Canady adamantly refused to hear of our getting involved with the Montana militiamen and Trochmann's bunch. That suggestion was dropped.

I wondered why Canady had such a powerful position that he could seemingly overrule the head of the Billings office with impunity.

Finally, with most of the agents in the room on our side, including the special agent-in-charge, Connie and I prevailed on Canady not to abruptly pull us out, thus burning the Freemen operation.

I argued successfully that if we just suddenly disappeared without any explanation, the Freemen leaders would know for certain that moles had been at work inside their operation. There is no telling what they would have done, but going deeper underground was most likely. The FBI had already blown every opportunity to make an easy, bloodless capture.

If their undercover operatives were now revealed, all the wiretaps and a lot of the months' worth of intelligence would have gone down the drain.

There was only the slightest risk that the Freemen were really suspicious of us, and even if they were, the only way they could prove it would be with Canady's assistance through our sudden, unexplained removal.

So a compromise was reached, which took us physically off the Freemen property but maintained our contact and cover.

With the agents' general consensus, I called the Freemen cabin on my cell phone, right from the FBI conference room to the cabin. It was kind of eerie sitting across the table from a half-dozen FBI agents talking to Freemen chief justice LeRoy M. Schweitzer.

I told Schweitzer that the family business I had mentioned a few days earlier had turned serious. My father in Phoenix was on his deathbed, I said. The family needed me to come down right away to take care of some estate business.

If Schweitzer loved anything it was complicated legal matters. He offered me any assistance he could if I got into problems with those "damn shyster lawyers" in Arizona.

Schweitzer said he had to run and that he would put Petersen on the phone to get all the information about where I could be reached in an emergency.

I repeated my story about the deathbed to Petersen and said, "My family needs me immediately."

"Your family must come first—by all means, go for as long as need be." It was the only hint of compassion Connie or I ever heard uttered by a Freemen leader.

I thanked him and hung up before he had time to get the information Schweitzer had wanted on how to reach us. Poor Petersen, he was constantly failing in his assignments to get an idea of where Connie and I could be found. I knew he would catch hell from the chief justice for his dereliction of duty.

Connie commented as we left the FBI building that I was probably putting Petersen in a bad spot with the other Freemen. She liked that, since to reveal even a hint of our location would risk her little chicks' safety.

"Frankly, my dear, I don't give a damn," I said to my wife, doing my best Gable impersonation.

★ CHAPTER 27 ★

In the freelance undercover trade, a job well done can be measured by three benchmarks. First, of course: Did the operative come out alive and undetected? Second: Was the intelligence gathered of high value to the contracting law enforcement agency? And, finally: Were the bad guys put out of business?

In late August 1995, Connie and I believed the Freemen operation was completed and at least our part of the mission highly successful.

We had gone in, worked diligently for four months—twice as long as our original commitment—and fulfilled the first benchmark of success. We came out alive and undetected.

We provided information that the Freemen had hosted or were scheduling seminars for militia units and other far-right groups from at least forty-six of the fifty states. The evidence was becoming clear to me. The conspiracy was national in scope, deadly and dangerous. Contrary to every previously published report, at least some elements of the American militia movement were organized and linked. There might not yet be a national leader directing the phantom cells, but their common ideology of hate and their antigovernment agenda were turning these clandestine organizations into a cohesive force for terrorism and insurrection.

Assuming the job with the Bureau was over, Connie and I began packing our belongings at the apartment and called to see when we would get our money. I had been under cover almost five months, and Connie four, so we reckoned the Bureau owed us around $75,000.

When we called Canady about settling up our account, the agent mumbled something about the operation not being over until the Freemen were actually incarcerated, and said he was now putting us on consultant status. Meanwhile, we would continue to receive a $2,000 stipend or advance—and the FBI would pay for the safe-house apartment in Billings.

During this hiatus I kept contact with the Freemen leaders by telephone, reporting the imaginary ups and downs of a dying father in an imaginary nursing home in Arizona. My fictional family business was a tangled mess, and I would not be returning to Montana for quite some time.

The Freemen taking my calls at the cabin told me they were extremely busy, and did not seem too concerned that their new "justice" was taking a long sabbatical.

Throughout the operation we were referred to by the Bureau as "golden." This is trade jargon for deep-cover human assets of great value to the contracting agency. The Bureau debriefers, including the tactical-assault unit and the behavioral analysts, used this term countless times during the summer of 1995.

Tommie Canady frequently stopped taking notes during one of our sessions to tell me or Connie, "This is incredible . . . priceless." He would come back a week or two later to tell us that the Bureau had confirmed our intelligence on militia personalities or operations. Intelligence gained at the Freemen cabin was confirmed by agents back at the locations where the militia units originated.

At one point I half-jokingly asked, "Does that mean we'll be getting more money?"

Canady put down his pen and somberly replied, "No, it means you're doing your job."

So, having been ordered out of deep cover by the FBI—alive and undetected—we were satisfied that we had accomplished the second benchmark of our mission: Intelligence gathered was of high value to the contracting law enforcement agency.

All that remained for this operation to achieve a perfect score was to put the bad guys out of business. And that certainly was not, by any stretch of the imagination, within the scope of our assignment. We had created a half-dozen completely doable scenarios for taking down the Freemen leaders. At every operational level of the Bureau our recommendations had been accepted and praised, and gears had been set in motion for implementation. The plans were nixed at "the top" for political reasons, not because they were faulty.

Why didn't the arrests happen? We never got an explanation from anyone at the Bureau, only the repeated statement, "We are getting our orders from the top." This lame excuse became and remained a sore spot between Connie and me and our handler, Agent Canady. We wanted this band of criminal malcontents arrested so the people of Winnett, who had been so kind to us, could have their lives back.

Thus, from our standpoint, an important part of our business with the Freemen was still unfinished. We were bitterly disappointed.

Agent Canady, for some reason that remains unknown to us to this day, played on our dissatisfaction about the arrest, too. On the one hand, he wanted us out, and on the other hand, he obviously wanted the additional information we were bringing.

Connie and I used the last few days of August 1995 for R and R, but we also stayed in touch with both the Bureau and the Freemen.

One day Canady dropped by our apartment, ostensibly to check up on our well-being. We chatted about our plans to pull out of Montana very shortly and relocate near some small town in Alaska. Canady talked again about his impending retirement, and once more reminisced about his own dreams of Alaska as a great place to live out his days.

He talked to our children about how great the FBI was as a career and showed them his identification card and badge. He even took our son to his car and showed off the communications equipment, and then he took the kids to McDonald's for lunch.

All in all, Connie and I were pretty satisfied that at least our contribution had been a successful, final operation. Even though it was certainly not a walk in the park—being an undercover informant on the very best day is rotten, dirty work—our faith in the system was restored. After all, at the end of our last operation eight years earlier—the one that finally drove us out of the business—we had been exposed and almost killed, then double-crossed on our payday. But that fiasco had been sponsored by a local-state task force, not the Federal Bureau of Investigation.

Dealing with the FBI is different, I reminded Connie. I recounted our conversation, when we were being recruited for the job, recalling Canady's indignation when I questioned whether the Bureau would hassle us over the final payday.

"The FBI pays its bills," I crowed to Connie, aping the agent. "That's what Canady said, and that's what the Bureau stands for."

I am an eternal optimist. Thank heavens my lovely wife is an eternal pragmatist. The harsh reality was about to drop rudely onto our heads.

On our next encounter with Canady his disposition was markedly changed. No more warm and fuzzy Agent Friendly—he was now Mr. All Business, if seeming somewhat embarrassed. From that point on, Canady was never to get on a personal level with me or my family again.

Suddenly, the spokesman for the Bureau was nitpicking the operation. He was evasive about what we were supposed to be doing. He hemmed and hawed every time I brought up money, often snapping that our rent was paid through October and "things" take time.

I protested that we had done everything we were instructed to do, plus a helluva lot more.

"I asked you to find a place in the cabin to put in some ears," he groused. "You never did."

I reminded him that he had yanked us out prematurely, and that we had found a dozen places in the computer room and other parts of the cabin to place electronic listening devices. No bugs had ever been provided for me to plant.

"What was I supposed to do, buy bugs on the open market?" I responded to the ridiculous nagging. It was true that Canady had told us to look for places to plant the listening devices. I reminded him that he had said the Bureau's tech man was coming out to talk to us—that the bugs could be made to look like anything we wanted them to, that they could be as tiny as need be. But this had never happened, and then we had been ordered out.

The gripe about the bugs was typical of the inane criticism of what had earlier been deemed a seamless operation. I knew the Bureau knew that the big snafu had been the failure to close the case, and the FBI wouldn't dare try to blame us for its own failure to make the final arrests.

But to my amazement Canady even tried that. As September began, I told our handler that we really wanted to get on with our lives, that we needed the payday. I pointed out that we could not get jobs around Billings because the town was well populated by Freemen. In fact, we were already slipping around trying to stay out of sight, making hurried trips to out-of-the-way stores for our necessities.

"Well, I can't get your settlement until the arrests are made." Canady floated that latest canard. It went over like a turd in a punch bowl.

"What do you mean, until the arrests are made?" I asked incredulously. "When we signed up you said our payday was not contingent on the actual arrest."

Canady nodded and mumbled that it was usually a policy that an operation was not considered concluded until the final arrest. He said in some cases it was not considered complete until after the undercover informants had actually testified.

I became pretty angry at the direction the conversation was taking. Canady told me to calm down.

"You're in shock," he suggested.

"I'm not in shock, I'm pissed! We gave you every kind of opportunity to arrest them," I said. "But now we've missed them . . . and I've never missed before."

He grinned and said, "But you've never been involved in anything this politically sensitive before. Everybody in Washington is involved in this case."

Connie and I had already come to the conclusion that the Bureau's real agenda went far beyond merely making an arrest of the Freemen leaders. Once the feds found out what a wealth of new intelligence on the radical elements of the militias was in the Freemen's pipeline at the cabin, our assignment had been drastically changed. The only problem was that no one had bothered to tell us.

In the aftermath of Waco and Ruby Ridge, we were just tools in a political and public image face-lift. Granted, the FBI and Department of Justice and the ATF and Treasury Department were severely hamstrung by numerous congressional hearings. The law enforcement agencies' ability to gather information on citizen hate groups, even if they could physically penetrate these phantom cells, was greatly hampered by ultraconservative congressmen parroting the National Rifle Association theme about "jackbooted thugs" in the federal law enforcement branches.

The pendulum had swung far to the other side. Federal law enforcement efforts abruptly went from aggressive enforcement against these hate groups and individuals all the way over to hands-off anything and anyone, no matter how criminal.

In their G-men's eyes, everybody from congressmen to the man on the street hated them because of Waco and Ruby Ridge. They were forced to close ranks in a sense, and take a defensive posture. And this paranoia was partly justified. The Bureau was in a lot of trouble with many congressmen and senators. Attorney General Janet Reno had even offered to resign, and many critics, including myself, thought President Clinton should accept her resignation.

The FBI badly wanted to show its critics that it was really the world's most professional law enforcement agency, but the brass didn't seem to know how to prove that the Bureau was chastened and changed.

Tommie Canady often told us there was a "new FBI" operating under new rules. Under the new rules an agent couldn't even shoot an escaping felon. Under the new rules of engagement the agent had to run the bad guy down and tackle him or let him go. Unless the bad guy shot first, the agent couldn't even pull his gun to make an arrest.

The more we heard agents talking about these new rules of engagement, the more Connie and I wanted to get out and get gone.

"My God, law enforcement won't be able to function," I told Connie after one lecture from Canady. "There's just going to be chaos. What are they supposed to do, walk up to a bank robber and ask, 'Please come with us'?"

A few days after the disturbing meeting over our pay, Canady called to tell us that field supervisor Jim Cleaver wanted us to stay on the payroll. We weren't going to be terminated with the conclusion of this operation.

But we still expected to get paid for the assignment before we started under some new arrangement. The Bureau was again talking about our returning to western Montana and getting inside Trochmann's Militia of Montana, or even some of the more firebrand groups in Idaho or eastern Washington.

Connie was adamantly opposed to continuing. I was ambivalent about the new proposition.

So I told Canady, "We'll consider something else, but let's get this settled first." I mentioned some numbers, and Tommie said he would have to prorate the final figure to cover the time we were actually on the job.

He was playing one-eyed jacks are wild, no-peeky, aces-out-of-the-deck poker with the numbers, and I got angry again.

"Just keep the apartment, and we'll keep giving you your $2,000 a month until we sort this out," the agent told me.

I turned to Connie after that unpleasant exchange and mentioned that I was beginning to have an uneasy feeling about our pay. Connie just stared at me, but I could see behind her big blue eyes that she was saying a loud and clear I told you so.

Despite my wife's mounting doubts, I still chalked up the delay to bureaucracy. So I returned to my routine of calling the Freemen, ostensibly long distance from Arizona.

On one such call toward mid-September, I was chatting with Petersen about being further delayed in our plans to return to Montana. Toward the end of the conversation he said, "Well, you had better hurry back. We won't be at this phone number much longer."

I tried to be casual about the explosive statement.

"Oh, you're changing the phones," I said. "Good idea. Why not give me your new numbers now?"

"No, we're leaving Roundup," he replied. "We're moving headquarters up to the Clark place."

"When?" I asked.

"Soon," he replied. "Soon. I've gotta go now." He hung up.

★ ★ ★

The long-simmering feud between Skurdal and the other Freemen leaders holed up in the cabin at Roundup for two years came to a boil in September. Schweitzer, Jacobi, and Petersen had finally had it with Skurdal's tantrums. The leaders just wanted to go to another place and the Clark family had long wanted the Freemen operation moved to its sprawling ranch 120 miles north in Garfield County. I picked up information that the other leaders were even considering leaving Skurdal behind in his cabin in the Bull Mountains. Alone, his certain fate would have been immediate arrest.

Connie and I contacted the Bureau after each of our telephone conversations with the Freemen. Of course, with their wiretaps they, too, were aware that the move was about to occur, but by this time there did not seem to be any interest on the part of the FBI in initiating an arrest. I had warned them weeks before that such a move was possible, and had also given the Bureau my assessment of the tactical problems the Clark ranch would pose.

Two days before the exodus, the Bureau did alert Musselshell County Sheriff Paul Smith that the Freemen were about to leave the Bull Mountains, but I imagine the sheriff, like any reasonable person, could only rejoice in the news. I assumed the Bureau had done the decent thing and warned the local authorities up at Jordan that the thugs were headed their way.

Acting on information provided by the Bureau, the local sheriffs and county attorneys, without any help from the federal agencies, assembled two SWAT teams consisting of local deputies from surrounding counties and a trained tactical unit from the Yellowstone County sheriff's department at Billings. The locals wanted to intercept the Freemen when they left the cabin and arrest them on the open roads.

With information pinpointing the exact time of the move, the two teams were assembled in Roundup the evening of September 28, 1995. At the last minute, orders came from "a high authority" in the Department of Justice that the SWAT teams of local lawmen were to stand down.

The SWAT teams were waiting inside the Musselshell County Courthouse. But Sheriff Smith, on orders from the FBI in Billings, told the unit commanders to take their squads into the basement and remain out of sight.

Around midnight a heavily armed convoy of six utility vehicles, pickups, and sedans pulled out of the log cabin fortress onto Johnny's Coal Road. The caravan turned north onto the two-lane Highway 87 and drove defiantly onto the main street running through Roundup.

It passed directly in front of the courthouse, within thirty yards of the two local law enforcement teams. Schweitzer, Petersen, Jacobi, and a chastened Skurdal were accompanied by a dozen of their most ardent followers—all armed with their heaviest weapons. Though it was the middle of the night, the move was brazen, even for the Freemen.

At that time, local authorities who had been besieged by Freemen fanatics for more than two years finally had enough manpower and firepower to equal the bullying outlaws. Could the locals have stopped the convoy and taken the Freemen out on the open highway? There certainly would have been some resistance—possibly, even probably, some bloodshed. But it would have ended then and there.

Later I spoke with one of the key officers who had been involved that night. From him I learned that local officers considered the FBI's interference to be an outrageous dereliction of duty. The idea that these criminals could just roam at will on the streets and roads, penetrating the hearts of the towns unchallenged, was too much for the lawmen to stomach.

While one county, Musselshell, was temporarily relieved of the Freemen problem, it was dumped on nearby Garfield County. Montanans pride themselves on taking care of their problems, not shoving them off on their neighbors. And local authorities and the citizens they were sworn to protect were enraged by these buck-passing orders from the FBI.

At daylight on September 29, Sheriff Smith and remnants of the SWAT team went to the abandoned Freemen fortress. They were accompanied by agents from the FBI.

I had warned the Bureau that Skurdal had repeatedly threatened to burn down the cabin before he would let anyone take it from him. The place might be booby-trapped, but I doubted it.

The Freemen's explosives expert, me, was away on a mythical sabbatical, and I knew that any device the others were capable of making would be very crude. However, since I was not on site, I cautioned that some visiting militiaman could have rigged some very unpleasant surprises for the feds moving in on the abandoned cabin.

But what the local authorities and the FBI found was a completely empty cabin. Even the carpets in the living room area had been ripped up from the hardwood floors. Furniture, a huge stock of weapons and ammunition, computer and telecommunications equipment, printing and reproduction machines, files and cabinets, books and cases, and a massive quantity of printing paper and other supplies had been loaded on numerous vehicles and moved out, right under the noses of the authorities.

The convoy of Freemen drove unchallenged through the towns and hamlets of Roundup, Flatwillow, Winnett, Mosby, Sand Springs, and Jordan.

County Attorney John Bohlman, who had himself been a target of one of the Freemen's hanging warrants, expressed the relief the community felt now that the Freemen were gone. Bohlman told the local media the following day: "I am sure the IRS will take over the property and will make sure they [the Freemen] don't come back."

The IRS did move immediately to take possession of the cabin. But the Freemen problem was not solved. The trouble had just moved a few miles to a more secure fortress where their operation could be expanded.

Despite all the information Connie and I had given the Bureau concerning the Freemen's plans to set up an armed republic—waiting only for the extra manpower they needed—they were allowed to establish their township near Brusett on the sprawling Clark ranch. It wasn't exactly what the Freemen leaders had wanted, but with its nine buildings, roadway control, and isolation, Justus Township, the capital of the Freemen Republic of Montana, was created without any resistance.

Local citizens had been assured by the Justice Department in

Billings and the FBI that they intended to solve the Freemen problem. The locals felt the federal government had simply fed them and their communities to these armed and dangerous terrorists.

The day after the Freemen move I asked Canady why it had been allowed.

"We didn't have time," the agent muttered.

I reminded him that I had informed the Bureau days earlier that the move was imminent, and that I knew they had wiretap confirmation even before that.

"Well, I mean we couldn't get permission in time," he responded.

The Bureau remained paralyzed and the citizens were paying the price.

With the move to Brusett, the center of attention for the Freemen problem was relocated from Roundup to Jordan. Jordan is the county seat of Garfield County. But local officials there were certainly no strangers to the Freemen problem. If anything, the Freemen had more supporters in that area than at its previous stronghold in Musselshell County.

As far as the Freemen leaders were concerned, the first step in their insurrection was a complete success. There is no wonder that they were emboldened by the weakness of their sworn enemies.

A long, cold winter's reign of terror was about to begin in eastern Montana. It was to be a bitter winter for my family, too.

CHAPTER 28

Safely ensconced in their new headquarters of Justus Township, the ranks of Freemen quickly swelled from the handful of leaders to dozens.

The Freemen leadership cadre was also immediately expanded to include several members of the Clark family. The patriarch, Ralph Clark, his brother, Emmett B. Clark, and Emmett's son, Richard E. Clark, all strengthened the justice court.

There were other members of the Clark family in the community, but many relatives would have no truck with the radical Freemen movement, and preferred to go on with the family business of running their farms.

John P. McGuire, wanted on a felony charge from California, joined the group. William L. Stanton's son, Ebert W. Stanton, moved his family onto the property. The elder Stanton was the Freeman convicted of criminal syndicalism the previous spring. That action had set off the face-to-face confrontation in Roundup that brought Connie and me into the Freemen operation in the first place.

Wives and children of some of the Freemen also moved into the compound. Local authorities received reports that other fugitives from as far away as North Carolina were holed up at Justus Township.

I received word shortly after the move that Skurdal was being kept under house arrest and on short rations in a log cottage on the property, but I guess he preferred the rough shed to a jail cell.

Ralph Clark was made the marshal or constable of Justus Township, with orders to arrest anyone who trespassed.

It was not long before he had the opportunity to enforce the borders of the new republic. In November 1995, a news crew from

ABC television defied the No Trespassing signs. The crew was first run off the property, but when they moved to a new location to film the buildings in the township, several pickup trucks with armed men surrounded them. The men flashed badges and confiscated more than $60,000 in camera equipment. This time they drove the media people off the property for good. Pleas for the return of the expensive equipment were ignored, but the incident created a national press furor.

Newspeople from around the country began to drop in to the rural community of Jordan, an area of Montana never before in local memory visited by the national media. The media news noses were sniffing out another potential disaster like Waco.

During the autumn and until the cold Montana winter set in, more militia types visited the Clark compound with impunity. The Freemen began pushing hard on local officials and neighboring ranchers. Throughout the winter, local citizens became increasingly angry that their government would do nothing. The number of death threats, liens, and armed confrontations in nearby towns continued to grow.

Garfield County Sheriff Charles Phipps and County Attorney Nick Murnion were once again in the thick of Freemen occupation of their county. Both Phipps and Murnion had million-dollar bounties on their heads, issued by the Freemen leaders.

Sheriff Phipps asked a Freeman who was visiting Jordan to pick up groceries if he could collect the million-dollar bounty himself by going out to the Justus Township. The surly outlaw replied, "Sure, you can collect, but you won't live to spend it. We're going to hang you."

Local authorities—humiliated by their inability to do anything about the lawless bunch of thugs from all parts of the country roving around their community—put on a false face of calm to the public. Sheriff Phipps still had no deputies and only the tiny, two-cell jail. He told visiting reporters, "As long as they [the Freemen] are not a threat to the public, there's no urgency."

This was not the real situation, and County Attorney Murnion, frustrated by the federal government's inaction, had petitioned President Clinton directly for assistance.

Montana officials were also slow to aid the beleaguered county authorities. State Attorney General Joseph P. Mazurek told the press in September, "We'll do everything we can not to put officers or others in harm's way."

U.S. Attorney Sherry Matteucci, obviously getting her orders directly from Attorney General Janet Reno, issued a press statement about the Freemen. "I think federal law enforcement has always been very reluctant to go knocking down doors. Law enforcement by its nature requires considered, planned, cautious action that is based on probable cause of evidence. It takes time to do it right and that's what we want to do."

The federal prosecutor's pacifist comment was certainly an understatement; by that time the Freemen leaders had been rampaging over Montana and their criminal cohorts had been committing felony fraud across the nation for well over two years. There had been little or no interference from the federal government.

In November, the frustrated Murnion—joined by his protégé, Musselshell County Attorney John Bohlman—traveled to Washington to testify before a congressional committee.

"I believe this group has declared war on our form of government," Murnion testified. "They are in open insurrection."

The locals' pleas for help were answered the way government usually answers a citizen request it does not plan to fulfill. The government participated in a feel-good public hearing.

The U.S. attorney and the Montana attorney general appeared on the front page of the Billings paper flanking John Trochmann, commander of the Militia of Montana, at a conference called "The Enemy Within: Civil Disorders in American Politics." It was the local version of what amounted to a blue-ribbon commission.

When I heard that Trochmann was a featured speaker at the conference, I called Canady and suggested I attend.

"It would be a good chance for me to get closer to the Militia of Montana," I said. "We've been thinking about moving back over to western Montana, anyway."

"Don't even think about it," Canady said. His voice was suddenly highly agitated. "I don't want you anywhere near the Montana militia."

While federal and state authorities were schmoozing with Trochmann at the Billings conference—which was sponsored by Rocky Mountain College and the Institute for Peace Studies—the Freemen's seminars were going full blast. Back-to-back sessions were being conducted by Schweitzer at Justus Township. The Freemen were oblivious to what was going on in the world outside.

At the Billings conference, Trochmann, who had been arrested with the Freemen in Roundup in early March, denied the Montana militia was involved in what was going on up in Brusett.

The Billings conference was clearly a public relations dog-and-pony show for all three of the organizations: the federal government, the state government, and the Militia of Montana.

At one point the Montana state attorney even bristled at a question that Montana had become a haven for radicals.

"I don't think we are a bastion of extremism," Mazurek said. "Let's not let ourselves become one." He said it was the citizens' duty to learn all they could about the ideas of the Freemen, whom he described as "racist, sexist, and, oftentimes, just plain goofy."

Tell it to the hard-pressed citizens of Jordan, Winnett, and Roundup, who had endured open and unchallenged physical and financial terrorism for more than two years. The local citizens I talked to did not characterize the Freemen's operations as "just plain goofy." After years of unrelieved terrorism, they had good reason not to be amused.

Every time I talked to my contacts who were going in and out of Justus Township, or talked directly by phone with a Freeman inside, I was told of the amazing success of the expanded illicit operation. It was estimated that more than fifteen hundred trainees passed through the seminar during the last months of autumn and the early days of winter 1995.

One Freeman boasted that Schweitzer had announced he now had disciples in forty-six states. As it turned out, the fake checks were indeed spread all over the nation and began showing up in banks from coast to coast. Estimates have been published that the Freemen created and distributed more than $150 million in bogus checks and money orders. One man was arrested after successfully passing $500,000 in bogus checks to buy a half-dozen cars and a condominium in Hawaii.

The federal government's key law enforcement agency was not only turning a deaf ear on the pleas of the citizens from a few rural communities in Montana, it was also turning a blind eye on one of the most far-reaching criminal conspiracies against the nation's banking institutions in history.

The Bureau had exacerbated its own problem. As Connie's and my intelligence had accurately shown, the Clark ranch—now called Justus Township—was a formidable fortification to assault, and the Freemen's forces had grown at least fivefold.

★ ★ ★

Considering the trauma faced every day during the winter of 1995 by so many people Connie and I had known, I am reluctant to describe the travail forced on my own family by the federal government.

But almost parallel to the inaction by the FBI in the Freemen case, Connie and I were left in operational limbo during that cold Montana winter. We maintained telephone contacts with the Freemen and militia leaders from other states, and passed information on to the Bureau.

Despite all assurances to the contrary, our monthly advance, expense reimbursement, and safe-house rent were suddenly curtailed by Canady at the end of October. In fact, we did not even receive our back expenses or the $2,000 monthly advance for that month.

We found ourselves cut off from any source of income. But I was still confident we had a substantial payday due us from the FBI. It was probably just a paperwork glitch.

When I went calling for the cash that was due us under our agreement, Canady informed me that he could possibly get a little cash in the interim since our previous information had been so good. He was not interested at all in the bits and pieces I was able to pick up by phone at the time. That is, until the day I heard that a phantom militia cell was planning an assault of some type on the dignitaries attending the upcoming spring conference of governors to be held in Cleveland. The President of the United States would be the keynote speaker.

I had heard through the grapevine, and through contacts I maintained with an Ohio militia leader, that some group planned to target several governors of both political parties.

Ohio militiaman Joel Steelwill, who videotaped one of the Freemen seminars in Roundup, had assumed a ranking position with that powerful militia group after the death of Mike Hill. Steelwill confirmed that some activity was planned around the governors' conference and invited me to bring over a delegation from Montana to join in "making our presence felt" at the conference.

I met Canady at the Artspace to give him my report. When he heard about this veiled threat to the conference attendees, he leaped up, knocking over his chair, and rushed from the coffee shop. On the way out he shouted to us, "Stand by!"

A short time later, he returned to tell us the situation was covered and that the Bureau, the ATF, and the Secret Service were on top of the rumored threat.

But despite his pleasure at the new information, it did not break loose any more money.

The next time I called Canady about our pay situation, he suggested Connie and I come in to the FBI office and talk. Canady said the Bureau was interested in our attending a Freemen-type seminar, billed as a four-day common-law school, and scheduled at a lodge on Lake Eufaula near Checotah, Oklahoma. It had been advertised nationwide and was likely to draw a large crowd of militia members.

I had informed the Bureau about the meeting. One of the Freemen had sent an advertising circular about the seminar to my mailbox. For security reasons, we always kept at least one rented mail drop.

Even though the seminar sponsors included two of Schweitzer's rivals (Dennis Smith and Gerald J. Henson from Oklahoma), the Montana Freemen leader, along with Dale Jacobi, was to be on the program via telephone hookup. Schweitzer was to teach a course called "Uniform Commercial Codes. Step-by-step." Jacobi's course was listed as "Bible History, Common Law as it relates to you and your heritage." Other topics, as described in the brochure, included:

- ★ Becoming a Sovereign
- ★ Common Law Court Set-up
- ★ Exposing Emergency War Power Acts
- ★ History of Common Law Trusts
- ★ Our Future in Common Law
- ★ America Past and Present (Early History, Constitution, 13th Amendment, United States of America vs. United States)

The program was to be a well-organized blueprint on how to plan and execute a successful secession.

Speakers were coming from all over the country. Connie and I had met a number of them, and felt that we could easily get into the big conference without jeopardizing our cover story. We could have driven up to Oklahoma from our pretended sojourn at my supposed family home in Arizona.

We agreed to cover the seminar for the Bureau, but made a point to note that it was an extra job for extra pay, and not covered by the Freemen job agreement. We reasoned that we needed this interim money while our paycheck ground through the bureaucratic mill somewhere between Billings and Washington, D.C.

Several days went by and the registration deadline passed. I called Canady to remind him that I had to make the reservations, and he casually informed me that the Bureau was no longer interested in the meeting.

I told him again that we really needed our payoff so we could get out of the apartment in Billings.

We heard nothing more for several days and received no pay. So I called again. By now we were confronting a really tight financial problem. While we watched our savings dwindle, neither of us could take a regular job in Billings for fear of exposure.

This time Canady said there was a short job for a couple like me and Connie down in Utah. Another group, similar to the Freemen or perhaps even associated with the Montana operation, had opened shop outside Salt Lake City. We almost certainly knew some of the people involved. There had been a number of seminar participants from Utah over the months we had been inside. No names were mentioned, but Canady said he had talked to the agents in Salt Lake and they were interested in our coming down for a new undercover operation.

Canady had described our success in Roundup to the special agent-in-charge in Salt Lake City.

"Salt Lake thinks you would be perfect for the job," Canady assured us. "You could just move right in down there. These subjects are expanding the operation really fast. It's just like the Freemen deal. In fact, they were trained at Roundup."

We waited to hear on that assignment, which we had been assured would be of short duration, but nothing happened. I finally asked about it and Canady said the Bureau had made other arrangements.

Connie told me she thought Canady had his own agenda. She had me believing our controller was running some sort of rogue operation.

"It could be that Tommie never mentioned our agreement to the Bureau," she said. "Maybe he just personally used us without getting authorization for anything except the $1,000 apiece we've been receiving."

I told her not to worry, the FBI didn't operate that way. We—the Bureau and me—had a handshake for $25,000 each for sixty days of work, and by now we had been under cover for seven months. Even if they quibbled about the exact date the operation had terminated, the payday had to be substantial. However, I must admit, Tommie Canady's evasiveness every time I brought up our pay was beginning to concern me, too.

And I had another bigger concern at the moment. By early November my bum knee was stiffening to the point that I could barely hobble.

My injured knee blew out on December 8. I was walking across a room and my leg folded sideways under my weight. I had to have emergency surgery immediately. I had put off a far less serious operation since injuring the leg in the logging accident a year before. Now there was no more postponing it.

The surgery on the leg was massive, involving bone work as well as muscle and tendon repair. When they finished, my leg was reattached with seven large screws.

During the period of convalescence at the hospital and therapy afterward, we got further and further behind, finally borrowing from friends.

I was in a wheelchair through January 1996, but as soon as I got out of the hospital I resumed my telephone contacts with the Freemen and various militia leaders I had met at the Roundup cabin.

By the time I was walking again in February, the blast from the Arctic had pretty much put an ice cap on Freemen activities at what everyone was now calling Justus Township. It was as if everyone had gone away to escape the bitter Montana winter.

I read an article in an Eastern newspaper that made fun of the Freemen for misspelling *justice* in the name of their township. I commented to Connie about how little the media, at least the mainstream national media, knew about what was happening in the militia movement.

Absolutely no one had got it right about the Freemen and what they were really up to.

The Freemen knew perfectly well how to spell *justice*, and, in fact, had it engraved on their new badges.

Apartment-bound during my continued convalescence from surgery, I was tempted to write a letter to the editor about the meaning of Justus Township, but Connie suggested we really didn't need exposure in the newspapers.

About the same time I recovered my mobility, the Freemen began to stir from their relatively long hibernation inside Justus Township. With winter thaw not far away, the agriculture-based life cycle of Garfield County began. It was approaching plowing and wheat-planting time on the Great Plains.

The only problem was that in taking over a large chunk of northwestern Garfield County, the Freemen had not just laid claim to adjacent federal lands. They had also warned local farmers whose property adjoined Justus Township that they would be trespassing if they tried to plow their own property.

This was the proverbial straw that broke the camel's back for the farmers and ranchers in the Jordan-Brusett area. They had suffered threats of death by shooting and hanging and other types of physical harm, false liens filed on their homes and property, rowdy visitors waving guns on their streets, and all other sorts of insult and affront.

An attempt to stop or in any way interfere with the very life cycle of the farming community would not be tolerated.

It is true that most of the men and women of Jordan and the surrounding communities were terrorized by the Freemen, by their sheer force of numbers. And the citizens have a strong mind-your-own-business tradition. And it's true that folks of the eastern Montana ranch and farm country are a peaceful people. But it is also true that the hardy people of this farm and ranch country can be pushed only so far.

Their elected officials had tried every legal means, every kind of cooperation with federal and state authorities. Every logical remedy to deal with the Freemen and their growing band of followers had failed. So, like the practical folks they are, the Montanans decided they would deal with the problem so they could get on with spring planting.

Sheriff Phipps agreed to meet with a delegation of farmers and ranchers in early March 1996.

There had been no vigilante committees formed in this part of Montana since around the turn of the century. But every man, boy, woman, and girl in this neck of the woods learns to handle a gun before they learn to drive a car.

The assembled ranchers, farmers, and townspeople told Sheriff Phipps it was past time for words and promises. It was now time to act. Since the feds and the state would not help, they would oust the Freemen themselves.

Sheriff Phipps listened to his constituents' well-grounded complaints, conferred with County Attorney Murnion, and said he would not allow them to go outside the law as vigilantes. Instead, he would deputize them all.

Two large posses, deputized by the legal sheriffs of Garfield and Petroleum Counties, were created. The Freemen inside Justus Township might have semiautomatic assault weapons, but the new posse members had a fairly good arsenal of personal hunting rifles and shotguns. One rancher even went to an army surplus store in Billings and purchased several .30 caliber World War II–vintage M1 Garands.

They were going out to the Clark ranch to clean out the Freemen. If there was bloodshed, too bad. This was their homeland to defend.

Local authorities did, however, contact the FBI, the U.S. Justice Department, and Montana public safety officials to advise them that they were taking the last legal remedy available to them.

When I heard that posses were going after the Freemen, my first reaction was horror at the prospect of so many good people risking their lives because of the government's bureaucratic inertia. My second thought was overwhelming admiration for the sorely tested citizens of these communities. My third thought was anger that private citizens would have to take the bloody brunt of such an action. Noble as their motives were, these oldsters, teenagers, and untrained middle-aged men would face far superior weaponry when they moved over the wide-open terrain surrounding Justus Township.

My final thought was how stunned the Bureau would be when they found out the citizens had had enough, and were going in to do the Bureau's job.

"I'd like to be a fly on the wall at the Bureau office in Billings," I told Connie. "I'll bet the phone lines are sizzling."

"I'd like to be a fly on the wall at the White House," Connie replied. "It will be the phone lines to Washington burning today."

CHAPTER 29

On the morning of March 26, 1996, I went outside our apartment to pick up the *Billings Gazette*. When I opened the paper I was stunned by a big black headline: FBI Moves on Freemen. The entire front page was covered with the story of the FBI's arrest of LeRoy Schweitzer and Daniel Petersen—identified as Freemen leaders—and a man named Lavon Hanson.

Connie and I watched local television news reports and talked about the arrest over breakfast.

Schweitzer and Petersen, along with the third man arrested, were whisked to the Yellowstone County jail in Billings, where they were held without bail. The *Gazette* said that Schweitzer and Petersen were not cooperating with their jailers, refusing to be fingerprinted or photographed. I thought at the time this would be only the beginning of the Freemen's disruptive behavior. They recognized no court—federal or state—as having any authority over them. In fact, for them to cooperate with authorities would be an act of treason.

Schweitzer and Petersen were in the hands of Satan, as far as they were concerned.

I clearly remembered Schweitzer at the blackboard instructing his disciples about the current government.

He would scrawl "DEMOCRACY" on the board in large letters, the chalk screeching on the slate from the force of his anger. Then he would chop up the word to "DEMO," then add an "N" to make "DEMON."

"See, this country is built on evil!" Schweitzer would scream. "It's really a DEMON-OCRACY!"

Schweitzer and the other leaders preached that judges at all levels were especially traitorous, and must be the first persons to be purged when the militias took over their communities and set up the new townships and republics.

Every Freemen leader, and almost every Freemen follower and sympathizer, had had some bad experience with either a federal, state, or local judge.

Now Schweitzer and Petersen were in the hands of the greatest demon of them all—a federal judge.

Connie and I believed it was finally over. I did not call the Billings FBI office to offer assistance at the time, because Agent Canady had made it clear he did not want our continued involvement with the Montana Freemen. But we planned to call later in the week to remind him and the Bureau that our payday had come—we were owed and due our settlement. The last excuse, the arrest of the first of the Freemen leaders, had been accomplished.

Skurdal and Jacobi, along with a couple of dozen Freemen, family members, and visiting militia types, were still holed up inside Justus Township. But with their supreme leader Schweitzer in custody, it was surely over now.

Connie and I were wrong on every assumption.

First, we were not going to get our pay as a result of the arrest. Second, the Freemen operation was far from over. In fact, a wild new phase of the undercover operation had only begun.

A couple of days later, when it became clear that the Freemen inside the Clark compound were not coming out, I called Canady's office. All I had on my mind was getting at least a partial payment so I could get my family out of eastern Montana. We were prepared to have to wait for the full balance of what the FBI owed us.

In calling around to my Freemen contacts in the Roundup and Winnett area, I heard troubling stories that the scores of Freemen and more radical militiamen were planning murderous revenge for the arrests.

Threats of murder were pouring into the switchboards at the sheriffs' offices in Musselshell and Garfield Counties. CB radio operators monitored broadcasts from ham operators identifying themselves as Freemen supporters and stating that assassination squads were headed for Roundup to begin killing people until the Freemen leaders were released.

I learned that County Attorney John Bohlman, who had been one of the first to move against the Freemen while they were still at the Bull Mountains cabin, immediately moved his family out of Roundup to a safer location.

Connie and I decided it was a good time for us to move ours for the same reason. All we needed was the money we were owed.

But Canady did not return our calls.

In the meantime, I learned the details of the arrest of Schweitzer and Petersen. Indirectly, the bloodless arrest had been a result of Connie's and my intelligence operation.

The Hawaii con man Derrick States, captured months before on information provided by us to Canady, had indeed been turned by the Bureau. Shortly before the arrest of Schweitzer and Petersen, States had introduced Agent Tim Healy to the Freemen leaders as a communications expert named Mike Mason.

Schweitzer wanted a shortwave radio tower set up in Justus Township so the Freemen could maintain radio communications with the outside world, independent of telephone and electrical lines. The Freemen already had plenty of electrical capacity from gasoline-powered generators hauled onto the property.

A construction crew composed of undercover FBI agents led by Healy moved in the supplies for the antenna. On the morning of March 25, the agents lured Schweitzer, Petersen, and Freeman Lavon Hanson out to the proposed radio-tower site.

Months before, we had proposed a similar scenario to isolate the leaders outside the cabin for just such an arrest. The agents had rehearsed the plan until they were grabbing the Freemen in their sleep.

The agents posing as the work crew had split into groups, so several agents covered each one of the three men. On a given signal, they simply surrounded the unwary Freemen and slapped on the cuffs. They were practically being hauled off to appear before

U.S. Magistrate Richard Anderson in Billings before any of the other Freemen in the compound were the wiser.

One of the participating agents told me they had overtrained for the arrest, and by the time it actually happened, it seemed like just another exercise.

"It was like watching one of the training sessions," the agent told me. "I almost forgot my part."

The arrested Freemen were ordered held without bond.

But that left more than two dozen others inside the compound. Shortly after, the handful of FBI agents and Montana state troopers at Brusett were joined by nearly a hundred federal agents and an assortment of other law enforcement officers.

The longest and most costly standoff in American history had begun. From the first day of this standoff the FBI, through U.S. Attorney Sherry Matteucci's office, announced there would not be another Ruby Ridge or Waco. This was to be a peaceful standoff, if the definition of *peace* can be twisted to describe hundreds of heavily armed men staring at each other down gun barrels.

The FBI's Behavioral Science Unit, including the shrinks who had interviewed Connie and me in Billings in June 1995, was to be in charge. The FBI's Hostage Rescue Team was relegated to something amounting to sentry duty.

FBI Director Louis Freeh announced later in a Washington press interview that the FBI used a new tactic in the Freemen standoff. "In Montana, for the first time, we were all on the same sheet of music," Freeh said, a bizarre quote for the macho leader of the world's preeminent law enforcement agency. "In fact, the negotiators [behaviorists and profilers] were calling the shots and the tactical teams were in the background."

That approach was fine with me. Of course, I did not want to see unnecessary bloodshed. But I also knew from experience that the Freemen leaders and their followers inside and outside Justus Township weren't necessarily going to waltz to Freeh's kinder, gentler song.

It soon became clear, even to the Bureau, that the militants inside were not coming out just because some of their leaders were in jail. News media representatives swarmed into the area, renting every available car, truck, and utility vehicle for miles around.

FBI and ATF agents quickly took every motel room in the area. One local resident commented, "There haven't been this many feds in this part of the country since General Armstrong Custer and his 7th Cavalry."

And in this case the modern-day cavalry was also on unfamiliar turf, just as the pathetic Custer had been at nearby Little Big Horn in 1876, 120 years earlier.

The Bureau took over the fairgrounds at Jordan for a command center, but generally the small community was not set up for an international news event.

A number of ranches in the area equipped bunkhouses or cleaned up cabins that were usually rented only during hunting season. When the hordes of newspeople converged on the scene, they were left with nothing to rent but rooms in private homes. Unfamiliar with the Freemen's reputation for hating the media, many newspeople blundered into the roadblocks set up by the FBI surrounding Justus Township. Another TV crew venturing onto the ranch had its camera equipment confiscated by gun-toting Freemen. After that, the FBI's perimeter was strengthened, as much to keep the media from wandering into rifle range of the holed-up Freemen as to contain the fugitives inside.

The news media quizzed every citizen of the community, and ABC's *PrimeTime Live* somehow secured a videotape of the Freemen leaders, which had been made a day before the arrest of Schweitzer. On the video a plan to kidnap local officials was discussed.

"We'll travel in units of about ten outfits, four men to an outfit, most of them with automatic weapons, whatever else we got—shotguns, you name it," Schweitzer preached to the other men. "We're going to have a standing order. Anyone obstructing justice, the order is shoot to kill." The tape was aired nationally, and suddenly hate groups began coming out of the woodwork.

Most ominously, the national media began to air reports from all over the United States that armed militia groups were headed for Montana to reinforce their beleaguered compatriots inside the compound. The Bureau's only source of information about what the militia movement intended to do about the Freemen standoff came from the newspapers and television reporters. The Bureau was aware that there were buildups of militias in the area. They knew that there was increased activity over on Duck Creek at Rudy Stanko's feedlot, which was called the Freedom Center. The main house on the feedlot property served as the Freemen headquarters in Billings. But the Bureau had no idea what any of these groups were planning to do. In fact, the Bureau didn't seem to know what it was going to do, either.

When it became clear that these Freemen and their supporters were not only declining the invitation to dance but wouldn't even come to the ball, Connie and I got a call from Canady. Our agent-handler did not admit it, but I knew the Bureau didn't have the slightest clue what was going on, either inside or outside Justus Township.

Canady's call to our apartment came on April 15, a Saturday, as we watched the unfolding drama at Jordan. Ironically, the call came a few minutes after Connie and I had been joking that it was time to pay our taxes and the paperboy.

Canady said the Bureau was having to use all its manpower to concentrate on what the Freemen were doing inside Justus Township. He wanted us to infiltrate Freemen headquarters in Billings; the Bureau also had a report that the Freemen outside the compound were establishing a second front on a nearby ranch.

I was sorely tempted to say I told you so, but politely listened to the agent's request.

Canady acted on the phone as if it was old home week, with a lot of "how you doing, buddy" camaraderie. He did not mention our hassle over back pay. He asked only if we were willing to go back in. This call came almost exactly on the one-year anniversary of our first going under cover for the Bureau against the Freemen.

The agent wanted us to go to Winnett and check out the rumors about the sudden influx of militias in the area.

"There's a report of a large group of people we don't know assembling at Chamberlain's for a big meeting," Canady said.

Agent Canady sounded almost paranoid about the gathering militias.

He said repeatedly the Bureau had to know "immediately" if the outside groups were planning to "hit" the Bureau.

Suddenly, we had new stature in the eyes of the Bureau. During the first weeks after we went back under cover, everyone was calling me sir and taking my calls—whether to the Billings office or to the FBI command center at Jordan—on a priority basis.

Despite our smoldering anger over nonpayment of fees from the previous operation, we agreed to go back under cover for the Federal Bureau of Investigation.

We were assured that all the financial problems would definitely be worked out as soon as this crisis passed. Agent Canady said the Bureau would even overnight us a couple of grand to get us back to work immediately.

"I'm going to get you back on a regular pay schedule, too," Canady assured us.

I did tell Canady that I felt like a sucker for agreeing to work with him on this new assignment, but that the bite of my old patriotism bug was stronger than my skepticism.

Connie and I talked it over and decided we really had no choice but to do this job, whatever our personal feelings about the Bureau's lapse in business ethics. There was every possibility that we were the only people anywhere who could prevent this standoff from turning into a bloodbath. At least we knew we could get inside the Freemen and militia groups converging on Garfield County, and hopefully douse the sparks before they became flames.

I had carefully maintained my contacts with the Freemen and militias, despite the Bureau's ham-handed attempt to yank us out without a cover story. The last thing that had happened, before our phony sabbatical to Arizona, was my inauguration as a "justice" of the Freemen's supreme court. So, as far as any Freemen or sympathizers knew, I was one of the highest-ranking Freemen outside the compound, and not under arrest. This dubious distinction would come in very handy in the days ahead.

★ CHAPTER 30 ★

On April 16, 1996, Connie and I suddenly reappeared on the scene, as far as the Freemen were concerned, after a long sabbatical in Arizona. At least our months of having to slink around Billings were over and we could move about the neighborhood more freely.

Our cover story served us especially well, for now I could say I had rushed back to be of service to the cause after hearing that my fellow Freemen were under siege by the hated feds at the Justus Township compound. I told them my father had died and the family business affairs were concluded.

We reported for service as dutiful Freemen. Other Freemen knew I had been made a full justice and Freeman of character, so I was readily accepted as a ranking authority.

I first called on the Freedom Center in Billings to present my credentials and test the waters. I was not sure just how safe we would be, but I was welcomed by the Freemen at the center with open arms. Connie and I then made a number of calls to Winnett, where it had all begun a year earlier.

During the hiatus since the Bureau had cut off our pay, our insurance and license tags had lapsed on my pickup, so I made the Bureau rent us a car for the operation.

FBI agent Robinson was Canady's assistant during the operation, and he delivered the rental car. We headed north to Winnett.

Suddenly Agent Canady took a paternalistic interest in our safety. In our next meeting with him he was extremely nervous about the potential for a confrontation, and reminded us of the threats that were flying around the countryside.

When we arrived at the Kozy Korner in Winnett, we saw three

new Ford Explorers parked at the curb across the street in front of the post office. Connie and I went into the bar and were greeted as if it were homecoming week.

We regaled those in the bar, not knowing if they were friend or foe, with stories of having been in Arizona on family business for the past several months. At about four o'clock, two clean-shaven young men in khaki pants and blue windbreakers stuck their heads into the bar, looked around, and left.

They had FBI written all over them, so Connie and I were glad they didn't come right up to us to ask if we were okay. We knew they were checking on us for Canady. But we didn't know if they were checking on our safety or had come to make sure we were on the job.

We hung around the Kozy Korner, hoping Lyle Chamberlain would make an appearance. We wanted our reintroduction to the Freemen to be seamless, and knew that if there was any hint that we had been "made" we would find out from Lyle.

Lyle Chamberlain was one of the rare adherents to the Freemen movement who had an unblemished reputation for minding his own business. He had once told me the Freemen did not want him involved in any of their illicit activities so that he could qualify for election as a county commissioner at some time in the future.

While Chamberlain talked the talk, he never, as far as I knew, participated in any of the illegal activities. He personally did not need to engage in any of the fraudulent schemes because his sprawling ranch at Cat Creek was not under foreclosure. I had often heard him say it was better to sell off small parcels than pay taxes, so he had managed to stay above the tax liens or heavy mortgages that had forced many of the Freemen followers and sympathizers into confrontations with the government.

A true frontier type, Chamberlain was a man of few words, but when he spoke he did not hesitate to say exactly what was on his mind. If he smelled anything rotten, he would say it.

When Lyle didn't show up at the bar, I went to a pay phone and called. I reached the lanky, bushy-bearded Freeman at his home, and he welcomed us back to Montana. Chamberlain said all the counteraction was taking shape on his ranch at Cat Creek, just west of the standoff site.

We made arrangements to meet him and several other Freemen at the ranch the following day.

That evening I talked to Canady by phone. He was in the FBI tactical center on the Jordan fairgrounds.

The agent sounded exhausted, and he also expressed genuine and deep concern for our safety.

"You are going into the tiger's lair," he cautioned. "If you take your wife in, I don't want you to let her out of your sight."

We got up early the next morning and drove a circuitous route toward our destination. I did not want anyone following us, including the FBI agents we had spotted the day before. We went through Winnett at about daybreak, and took back roads—almost trails—toward Cat Creek. We stopped occasionally in blind spots and waited to make sure no one was behind us.

I had been to Cat Creek many times on logging jobs and had even hunted on Lyle's property. I knew the land, the low foothills of the mountains, the creek beds. Lyle's family ranch had once been a sprawling spread of several thousand acres. Over the years he had sold off parcels of twenty or thirty acres at a time. The ranch headquarters is in a beautiful place, right on Musselshell River in a small mountain valley.

But Lyle's ranch complex is an eyesore in the otherwise bucolic valley. It consists of a main house and several outbuildings and barns, along with rusting storage tanks, broken farm equipment, and general debris left over from a more active era when it was a working ranch.

I saw the vent pipe of an underground bunker I knew to be buried near the main house. The bunker, which was stocked with arms and ammunition, water, food, and survival equipment, had been dug by Lyle and his brother. I was at the ranch when they were digging the hole. They planned to drop a rusty old water tank in the hole and fill over it.

I had built a number of survivalists' shelters when I had my landscape-logging company on the western slope of Montana, and warned them the tank would collapse. They asked my advice on shoring it up, and I told them how to do it.

Down the road from the ranch is the ghost town of Cat Creek. It was an old oil-field town during a boom in the 1930s. What's left of the oil field makes a good living for one family; the whole field is owned by Lloyd Carroll, who minds his own business, raises his family, and tends his depleting oil patch.

I am sure Carroll was amazed when convoys of 4x4s, filled with armed men dressed in camouflage uniforms with full field gear, began to descend on his little ghost town.

Connie and I were not prepared for what we saw when we entered the Cat Creek ranch.

Militia leaders from several heavily armed groups and a half-dozen states were already assembled at the ranch. We soon learned that word had gone out over the Internet to militias everywhere to come to Montana, "but stay clear of the standoff."

The main militia units were given careful instructions on how to drive to the ranch without passing FBI surveillance or news media located at Jordan.

A sophisticated communications center had been set up at the Cat Creek ranch, headed by the self-described American patriot freelance writer Dan Wooten from Rathdrum, Idaho.

Connie and I were greeted at the main house by Lyle Chamberlain and Wooten. Wooten handed me a business card that identified him as a constitutional tax consultant. There is no question that Wooten has excellent connections—from top news-media personalities to government officials. A native of Tennessee, he had been a key campaign leader in one of Al Gore's bids for the Democratic nomination for president.

Moreover, Wooten is an expert communications man with extensive knowledge in computer technology. Shortly after we arrived, a UPS truck hauled up and unloaded additional computer and modem equipment. I thought at the time that UPS really could deliver anywhere in the world, and that the company should have had an advertising crew shooting a commercial here.

Wooten also claimed he had a CNN reporter standing by on

media hill at Jordan. The reporter, according to Wooten, would alert the militia headquarters at Cat Creek the minute the feds moved against the Clark ranch. Later we were able to get the name of this reporter, but never ascertained if she was a willing conduit to the militia or just an unwitting dupe.

As a justice of the Montana Freemen, I was given immediate access to everything going on at the Cat Creek headquarters. Connie followed me around like a dutiful, subservient hausfrau. Her temporarily retired notebook was once again in full service as she recorded names, license plates, telephone numbers, Internet passwords, and conversations.

As the day wore on, more and more militia leaders arrived at the Chamberlain ranch house. Everyone was abuzz over the report that Norm Olson, commander of the Northern Michigan Militia, was on his way with a large contingent. The rumors were fueled by a television broadcast aired on the Sunday-morning talk show *Face the Nation*.

Olson, who wore combat fatigues with the stars of a major general on the lapels, had angrily denounced the FBI's action, even though it was peaceful. He charged that militia leaders who were urging other groups to stay away from the confrontation, such as the Montana militia, were "moderates who believed the treachery" the FBI was putting out at its press conferences.

Connie and I quickly ascertained that a major ideological split within the ranks of the militias was playing out across the country, and the first signs were showing up here at the Cat Creek ranch.

Everyone arriving on that day, and in the days to follow, either was totally against the criminal activities of the Freemen or came to join a shootout with the federal government, no matter the justification.

Most of the militia leaders said they were coming to put themselves and their units between the Freemen and the feds to avoid a repeat of the Davidian standoff that had resulted in so many deaths at Waco. But others were trying to figure out ways to get through the FBI roadblocks with their arms and supplies, to prepare for a final day of reckoning.

Commander Olson's inflammatory comments on *Face the Nation* raised the tension level considerably.

"When the first shot is fired," he almost shouted over the nation-wide show, "we have the possibility for an armed revolution. We have inaugurated Operation Certain Venture . . . we are gathering material . . ."

He said a relief column of militias was assembling to begin a drive to Montana.

The Michigan militia officer was the first to publicly call for April 19 to be the new D-day. It would be the second anniversary of the end of the siege at Waco and the first anniversary of the bombing of the federal building in Oklahoma City. He likened the militias' drive to Jordan to "a Normandy invasion, a landing on the beach."

He said on the CBS network: "If this is going to be the place where the second American revolution finally culminates in war, then it's good for a battlefield commander to be there to look at the logistics, to look at the needs, and to find out exactly what the situation is on the ground."

Talk at the ranch was much the same, with one group arguing for intervention by the assembling militias, and others recommending a wait-and-see approach. As sunset neared, word was received at the ranch that Commander Olson's party had become lost somewhere in the vast high plains and would not make it to Cat Creek that day.

What's a general to do?

The conversation turned to John Trochmann, commander of the Militia of Montana. Trochmann had issued an appeal for all out-of-state militiamen to return to their homes and let local authorities take care of the situation.

Several militiamen called him a traitor and an FBI stooge. A discussion among the leaders about sending a squad to arrest Trochmann ensued.

I saw this as my first chance to spread a little oil on troubled waters. I announced I had information that Trochmann's own men were rebelling and would take care of him themselves. Of course I had no such information, but I figured I could do as much good putting out disinformation as I could gathering real information for the Bureau.

Shortly after sundown, a tall military figure in a starched combat uniform with a pistol on his hip came striding into the house, followed by his adjutant. It was "Major General" Norm Olson. He had finally found his way.

He let it be known to everyone who would listen that if it came to battle, he was here to take over the field command. He kept talking about the "dogs of war" being loosed.

None of the other militia leaders at the Chamberlain farmhouse rushed to relinquish their commands to this self-appointed general.

Meanwhile, sixty miles away near Jordan, other militia members were stumbling into FBI roadblocks as they headed for Cat Creek, lost on back roads. Two heavily armed Oregon militiamen were stopped and turned away.

Not all those approaching the roadblocks were lost. Two militiamen, one a fugitive from Oklahoma, eventually did elude the roadblocks and slip into the compound. Two armed local Freemen members tried repeatedly to join their leaders inside, but were stopped at checkpoints. They argued with the agents, but were sent away.

These militiamen eventually drifted into the Cat Creek ranch with tales of their confrontations. They complained that the agents were not dressed in their distinctive black assault uniforms, but wore hunting togs and colorful baseball caps. Polite but firm Montana highway patrolmen also manned some of the checkpoints.

And to the chagrin of some of the visiting militiamen, local ranchers pitched in to assist the lawmen. About thirty men from the Jordan area, who had earlier planned to join the vigilantes to oust the Freemen, volunteered to drive in their own vehicles to stop cars with out-of-state license plates. They explained to the unwelcome visitors that this was their home country and they did not appreciate the intrusion by outside troublemakers.

Many militia members were actually surprised by the grassroots support of the locals for the federal officials who had finally come to do their jobs. A Jordan bank hung a sign in its front window reading, "Good-bye, LeRoy. Hello, FBI."

The low profile kept by the agents was clearly disappointing to the militiamen. The ones coming for a fight wanted to face off with the "jackbooted" feds in Darth Vader–looking armored suits and helmets.

An Ohio militia leader, Don Vos, arrived with a small unit of heavily armed men. This group was itching for a fight. Shortly after arriving they asked where they could dig in. These hardened combat-trained militia members went out to literally dig foxholes near a barn to sleep in, despite the below-freezing temperatures each night.

Earlier in the day, another group of militiamen had used a front-end loader to scrape a ditch in the barnyard. They shoved an old school bus body into the ditch to serve as sleeping quarters and filled dirt around it for insulation from the cold Montana winds.

There were others arguing with a voice of reason—most notably Scott Bowman, an attorney from Ohio. Bowman said he had come out only to assure himself that there was nothing going on but negotiations. He would have a major role in keeping the lid on things in the days ahead.

I spent several hours talking to Bowman. He said he was going into Jordan to meet with the FBI and volunteer to help work out a peaceful settlement.

Bowman repeatedly expressed fear that the Bureau was intending to storm the Clark ranch. I tried to calm his fears without revealing that I knew the Bureau had no intention of such a rash act, at least not in the foreseeable future.

Wooten said he might accompany Bowman because he wanted a way into the compound to get an interview with the Freemen still holed up there for airing on the patriot radio stations.

As each of the state units dropped in on what had now become the Freemen standoff's counterforce command center, they left word where their units would be billeted. Connie tried to get a copy of this roster, but was unable to do so on this first day back under cover. We did hear a dozen towns around eastern Montana mentioned in various conversations, and were led to believe that for each delegate at the Cat Creek ranch, there were a dozen or more militiamen either on the way or already resting at another location.

It was getting late, and Connie and I had already decided we were not going to stay overnight. We had not come prepared, and we badly needed to get away from the Cat Creek ranch to file a verbal report with the Bureau.

We knew by now the FBI was getting pretty nervous about all these groups converging, and we did not want any preemptive action. We also knew that no immediate action was being contemplated by the militias, either.

The intelligence-gathering game had begun in earnest, and this time its main value would be preventive. At the new headquarters, I overheard militia leaders numbering about twenty discussing their on-the-ground strength. Their battle plans were chillingly efficient. The FBI did not know it, but while they were surrounding the Freemen at Clark ranch, dozens of heavily armed militia units from several states were surrounding the FBI.

These militia units were stationed in camps hastily thrown up—from the North and South Dakota border to such places in Montana as Circle, Miles City, and Billings to the south, Lewistown to the west, and the Fort Peck Lakes to the north.

The first three weeks of the standoff between the Freemen and the Federal Bureau of Investigation were by far the most dangerous, because heavily armed men on both sides were gripped by paranoid distrust.

The Justice Department's plan to simply wait out the Freemen proved correct in the end. The standoff was costing an enormous amount of money—estimates of $300,000 per day were often mentioned in the media. Costly as it was, this huge government expenditure was not shocking in a jaded society accustomed to seeing its tax money spent on $600 toilet seats. The real tragedy was that the government had once again created the potential for another bloody mistake like Ruby Ridge or Waco.

The media never dug deep enough into the situation to discover that the standoff was entirely unnecessary in the first place.

And the hundred-plus newsmen and newswomen converging on the scene at the Clark ranch never had a clue that a threat of far greater disaster was building. A short drive away they could have filmed the massing of scores of armed militiamen. Instead, the newspeople huddled in their warm vans, sipping hot coffee and lapping up Bureau and Justice Department press releases. They had come in hopes of an entertainment event that would provide great ratings.

The newspeople busily tried to get to high ground to poke their long lenses at the farm buildings and the children playing in the yard. They interviewed every willing citizen of Jordan and the surrounding farms, and attended news conferences held by the U.S. attorney in Billings. Every so-called hate group expert and politician and nationally recognized hatemonger they could find became an instant expert.

Fortunately for everyone, they were missing the bigger story playing out beyond the defined boundary of the standoff. I say "fortunately" because, had the media broadcast that an army was building for a showdown in Montana—which it was—such press reports would undoubtedly have only escalated the arrival of groups from around the country.

But the media was already becoming bored, and decided this was a nonstory about a handful of nuts out in the boondocks of Montana. Thus, the news types practically missed the opening page in a new chapter in America's history, the dawn of a new American phenomenon: homegrown terrorism.

A single incident, one thoughtless act, one provocation by an overzealous law enforcement officer, or a deliberate assault by a radical superpatriot or even a lone lunatic, could light the match that would consume the whole place.

All the elements were there: the angry lawmen, the fanatical militiamen, the lone lunatic—the fuel for a major conflagration.

Connie and I were the unwitting keepers of the box of matches. We had unintentionally been thrust into the middle. We were the only eyes and ears in both camps; and we saw and heard a bigger confrontation in the making.

The ominous black date of April 19 loomed—the anniversary of both the fire that destroyed the Branch Davidians at Waco in 1993 and the bombing of the federal building in Oklahoma in 1995. Connie and I also faced an anniversary: one year inside the hate congregation of the Freemen of Montana.

Connie made herself useful in the center, typing, running

errands, and filching copies of as many lists as she could. The foot traffic through the center had become so heavy that she stopped trying to take down the license plates of the visitors' vehicles and concentrated on conversations, E-mail, and telephone calls that came through the converted ranch house.

I spent most of my time at Cat Creek meeting with the arriving and departing militia leaders, trying to find out where their groups were billeted or bivouacked.

Well before April 19, the various militias had men in place surrounding the FBI and ATF at Jordan. These units were tightly linked by radio, and a code was established to notify the units in the outlying countryside the minute the feds moved in force against the Freemen compound.

We learned that the Cat Creek command and communication center also had eyes on the FBI at Jordan and received regular reports on every move the government made. It took a little time to figure out where this information was coming from.

Based on bits of conversations I overheard, I suspected that certain elected officials with strong sympathies for the militia movement in other parts of the state were learning everything about FBI plans in their visits to the government command center at the Jordan fairgrounds, and were passing the information on to the militia leaders. Try as I might, I was unable to learn who was reporting inside information to some of the militiamen.

We did finally learn how information about the FBI and ATF operation was getting inside the siege lines to the Freemen still holed up in Justus Township.

At various times family members of some of those inside the Clark farm would drop by the Cat Creek ranch, chat with Freemen briefly, and then leave. On one occasion I saw a militia leader give a document to one of these family members.

The FBI, early in the standoff, had cut all telephone lines between the Clark ranch and the outside world, keeping only one line intact between the Bureau negotiators and the Freemen. The Freemen were not answering this phone, primarily because they refused to recognize the authority of the government even to negotiate with them.

The Bureau was smug in its belief that the Freemen were sealed off tightly and unaware of anything except what they were able to get on television reports. And the media was being kept totally in the dark by the FBI. Nut cases from all over the Northwest and surrounding Plains states drove to the standoff site—most with no affiliation to any organized militia group. They were stopped at what the Bureau called its IACs—Identification Access Checkpoints.

There was a lot of railing and ranting at the checkpoints, but these very vocal agitators were easily repelled. This led the Bureau to believe its containment plan was working just fine.

After several days of relative calm on the siege line, the Bureau was apparently convinced that early reports about a potential threat from outside militias were false.

But the real menace, the organized militia units, were out of sight and thus out of mind. This made Connie's and my job doubly difficult, because the Bureau simply did not want to believe the reports we began delivering.

Over the next tense days we regularly turned this information over to an increasingly agitated FBI. Agent Canady had changed his tune from fear of an outside attack to absolute denial. With each new bit of information he became more cool—even angry—toward his moles, clearly not wanting to hear the information we were bringing him. He would often break out into a tirade of skepticism that the militias had come to Montana because of the standoff.

Meanwhile, the Freemen inside the Clark ranch had also put up their own barbed wire barricades to keep others out. Several media members tried to talk with them, but after another TV crew had its camera seized, these efforts stopped.

After this incident the FBI made everyone else approaching the Clark ranch sign a form acknowledging that they were traveling at their own risk. The form stated that the signee knew he or she was in an area "which is extremely dangerous due to the presence of persons charged with federal and state crimes." Others were warned that if they attempted to take certain items such as food, arms, or ammunition into Justus Township, they could be charged with aiding and abetting felons.

Under the guise of my cover as a Freemen justice, I began asking around about getting messages to Skurdal, who was now believed to be back in his former leadership role in the compound. I was told that would be no problem, that several of the family members visiting those inside were regularly carrying coded messages from the militia leaders to the Freemen leaders. The drop point was a residence in Winnett.

"We want them to know there's an army outside supporting them," the militiaman told me.

Of course, Connie and I immediately informed the Bureau that their information blackout was being penetrated by a few of the family members they were allowing to travel into and out of the compound, ostensibly to visit the children inside.

Suddenly, this leak was plugged when family members were denied access to the buildings inside the ranch.

The FBI was not entirely remiss in taking this hard line, because I knew a number of Freemen and sympathizers were using children as a ploy to gain access to communicate with Skurdal, Jacobi, and other hard-liners inside the Clark ranch. One Freeman even took his own daughter to the FBI barricade with a teddy bear for a little friend on the inside. I knew the real purpose of that visit was to deliver a message concealed in the bear from Cat Creek to the Freemen leaders.

But the ploys did not work, and cutting off family visits did disrupt the vital links between Freemen and militias on the outside and the Freemen holdouts on the inside.

However, to counteract the loss of this channel of information, militiamen worked on plans to use especially skilled individuals from within the militia organizations to slip into the compound under cover of darkness.

I had reason to believe one enterprising freelance writer, who published regularly in *Soldier of Fortune* magazine, made such trips, undetected, on more than one occasion. However, this ex-Army Green Beret was going in to get a story, not to serve as a messenger boy for the militias.

CHAPTER 31

An ideological dispute arose at Cat Creek between what Michigan Commander Olson scornfully referred to as the "moderates," and the representatives of the more zealous groups—such as his fragmented Michigan militia and the Ohio cell headed by Don Vos.

The radical elements argued that a stand had to be made in Montana to prevent the federal government from using the Freemen standoff for an excuse to begin dismantling the patriot movement nationwide. Others argued that the militias could exercise good sense on this occasion and prove to the rest of the country that the movement was not fanatical and not a danger to the public.

One of those arguing most effectively for constraint was Scott Bowman, who identified himself as a spokesman for another Ohio group.

Bowman's argument was to present the Freemen with an alternative to a shootout. He wanted to advise those inside of their rights, and assure them that the militias would demand they get full and fair hearings through the court system.

The Ohio lawyer and three or four militiamen from his unit, made it clear to others at Cat Creek that they were not white supremacists, nor had they come to Montana to participate in an armed confrontation with the government. While this group was armed with the best equipment of any of the militias at Chamberlain's ranch, it also was the most vocal in its commitment to prevent another Waco.

John Trochmann also sent representatives to the area to monitor activities at Jordan, but at the same time he issued a press announcement urging out-of-state militias to stay home. He even praised the FBI, much to the chagrin of most of the assembled militiamen, issuing a statement that read: "I think the FBI has been handling it very patiently. I admire them for their patience. And they've had a tremendous amount of pressure from the public, from the local law enforcement, and from their superiors in the FBI and Justice Department. I think they're caught between a rock and a hard place, and they're doing the only thing they can do."

This statement created a further split within the ranks of the Militia of Montana, and several of these disgruntled members appeared at the Cat Creek ranch, ready to join whatever group intended more direct confrontation with the feds.

Not only had I been introduced to the militiamen as a Freemen justice, but Chamberlain had also told some of the leaders that I was a top-notch demolitions man. At one point I was approached for consultation on part of a plan to "neutralize" the FBI's siege operation.

Since the perimeter of the standoff was scattered over a considerable territory—covering several thousand acres of the ranch and a half-dozen country roads—the FBI's communications links were vital. The Bureau had set up a tactical center with a small cellular phone tower on the Claude Saylor ranch. Saylor, who during the season was an outfitter for hunting parties, had opened several cabins to house the FBI tactical-assault teams. The cellular phone tower on Saylor's ranch was one of the prime targets of the radical militia.

I was asked what it would take to bring down the tower and ruin the equipment so it could not be reinstalled quickly. A team was assigned to carry out an attack on the tower before the militias moved over the several roads onto the Clark ranch to take up positions between the FBI and ATF and those inside the ranch.

I told the militia leaders it would not be necessary to send in a squad for this assignment, that I could handle the job alone. I knew, by volunteering to do this job, that if it came to a shootout, at least the Bureau's cellular link would not be cut.

The mission to bring down the tower was not an isolated event, but part of a much larger and more dangerous plan. After several days at the patriot command center at Cat Creek, Connie and I noticed a number of Freemen and visiting militiamen undertake an odd activity.

We had been observing, listening, and duly reporting that a good number of the arriving militia units were fully intent on starting a small war. Then we learned that there was a radical plan unfolding to reinforce the compound at Justus Township with an armed invasion.

A bus, tractors, and trucks arrived in the muddy barnyard at Chamberlain's ranch.

Welders began fixing rusty steel sheets from stock tanks or scrapped equipment to the sides of tractors. Even though the last snows had fallen and the spring thaws set in, snowplow blades were reattached to heavy trucks to be used as battering rams. The Freemen and the radical militia units were building crude armored vehicles—makeshift tanks. The vehicles were to be loaded with food and ammunition. These ragtag armaments with additional soldiers riding atop them would crash through the FBI and ATF perimeter in a relief column for the holed-up Freemen.

These fanatics were prepared to shoot their way into Justus Township, if need be. The leaders were pretty sure they could just drive in, but the steel plates were welded onto the vehicles just in case.

The plan to rush reinforcements into the compound also required that the attacking force be able to communicate their plan to the Freemen holed up inside. Otherwise, the defenders could mistake the relief convoys for an FBI-ATF attack and fire on their own rescuers.

Someone had to get word inside that the armored convoys were coming, and an exact date and time needed to be set. The target date was April 19.

While militiamen with welding skills continued to mount steel plates on the farm vehicles, plans for a swift run into the Justus Township were being completed. The idea was to crash through the roadblocks, which in most cases consisted of only a couple of vehicles and two or three agents or state law enforcement officers. The lead vehicles to be used by the militias were the large snow-removal trucks. The snowplow blades would clear the cars blocking the roads.

An old bus, armored with the sheet-metal welds, would be loaded with armed militiamen. Following the militiamen would come trucks loaded with supplies, including food, water, blankets, and other necessities to extend the time those inside could hold out.

Once again, the main problem was manpower. Only a small cadre of the hard-core militiamen was actually willing to smash into the compound unless the surrounding FBI agents did something provocative.

Again, I volunteered to bring in several score of mercenaries—those same mythical men I had promised the Freemen leaders for several months before their flight from the cabin at Roundup. Again, I saw the opportunity to bring in the FBI's tactical-assault teams, the HRT. If the militia supporters of the Freemen were actually going to try to break through the perimeter in armor-sided farm vehicles, it would certainly be preferable to have these vehicles well staffed by planted FBI agents.

The problem now was the number of militiamen on hand to do the work themselves. It was only a matter of sorting out which of the militias were here to fight and which were here to assure a peaceful conclusion.

In the early weeks of the standoff, the number of militia members scattered around Cat Creek—and reportedly on surrounding farms and ranches of Freemen or Freemen sympathizers—ranged widely from two hundred to more than a thousand. At any given point it was also impossible to tell what percentage of these were moderates and what part answered to one or more of the fanatical leaders present at the headquarters.

Supreme leader Schweitzer finally had the militia manpower he had coveted to establish his long-sought Freemen republic, but the little army did him no good. He was locked away in a jail cell in Billings with Freemen leader Petersen. The other primary leaders, Skurdal and Jacobi, were sealed up and incommunicado inside Justus Township. And on the outside, the militia leaders with armed troops on the ground were widely split on what to do. It is doubtful from the disdain these militiamen had for the Freemen that they would have obeyed orders from Schweitzer anyway.

Many of the militiamen at Cat Creek were vocal in their opposition to the Freemen ideology and considered the four leaders little better than common criminals.

To further confuse the issue, strong voices of reason were now being funneled into the Cat Creek command post, and generally over the news media. The well-known "patriot" spokesman, Bo Gritz, who had helped end the Randy Weaver standoff at Ruby Ridge, and Weaver's lawyer, Gerry Spence, issued statements complimenting the FBI's handling of the Freemen standoff.

The Tri-States Militia, an umbrella organization claiming to speak for a number of militias in Midwestern states, charged that the Freemen were misusing the patriot movement to conduct their own criminal activities. Tri-States' spokesmen urged "constitutional militias" to go home. Trochmann's Montana militia had earlier issued its warnings to these visitors to let Montana handle its own problems.

The United States Militia Association, headquartered in Idaho, issued a press statement disavowing the Freemen as common criminals and urging all militias to stand down. Another Idaho group, calling itself the Freemen Patriots, issued a counterstatement, warning that the standoff at Jordan was a trap and that regular Army Special Forces Units were deployed to wipe out those militia members assembled around the area.

The militias on the ground, whose leaders were reporting regularly at the Chamberlain ranch, were in a high state of nervous anxiety. Everyone watched the skies for the long-expected black helicopters. Rumors of an impending attack on the militias by either the FBI and ATF or worse—regular U.S. Army troops—were rampant.

So, on April 17 and 18, leading up to the doomsday of April 19, confusion reigned supreme at Cat Creek. The problem with confusion, when it rules among scores of heavily armed men, is that very serious consequences may occur.

As Connie and I left after dark on April 18, we were also in a state of dread. The most likely scenario would be that, because of the panic, someone would just start shooting. But we had done all we knew how to prevent the potential conflagration.

The last thing I saw in my rearview mirror as I drove out of the Cat Creek ranch was the sparks of arc welders affixing armor plating on a commandeered road grader and a big grain truck.

We stopped at Winnett and called Tommie Canady, finally getting through to him at the FBI command center at the Garfield County Fairgrounds at Jordan. I told him about the arming of the vehicles and the plan to bust into Justus Township.

I also told him I could probably get several dozen FBI HRT men inside Cat Creek, and suggested that these government men could then easily arrest the holed-up Freemen. Once inside, the HRT men could follow pretty much the routine rehearsed for the planned arrest at the cabin. I suggested that three or four agents could position themselves with each of the few armed men inside the Clark ranch and just cuff them on a given signal.

Even though there were a couple of dozen people still inside, I doubted that more than a handful were actually armed and willing to fight. The rest were women, children, and seminar trainees trapped inside when Schweitzer and Petersen had been arrested. Several of these noncombatants had already voluntarily walked out of the compound.

"What! What have you done now?" Canady fairly shouted the question into the phone.

I repeated the information and my suggestion. The agent became enraged.

"We don't have any warrants to arrest anyone at Cat Creek!" The agent continued to fume. "I want you to leave them alone."

I was incredulous. Here we had been days inside the militias' operations center and brought out solid eyewitness information that large numbers of armed men were building what amounted to tanks to attack the FBI and the ATF. I repeated that armed convoys of trucks, road graders, tractors, snowplows, and an armored bus were preparing to come blazing down on them.

"And, by the way, Tommie, I'm not going to harm any of the militiamen at Cat Creek." I had to put that little dig in to assuage my own frustration at his reaction.

Canady just cursed me.

If ever I saw the messenger beheaded for his message this was the most outrageous case. I was very tired at the time and sorely tempted to tell Canady that I hoped the first busload would drive up his backside.

But instead, Connie and I drove back to our apartment in Billings and called Cat Creek to tell the militiamen and Freemen gathered there that I could not raise the volunteer mercenary army I had promised. At the moment I didn't care what they thought about my reneging on the offer.

Several hours later Canady called me at the apartment in Billings. He at least recognized that a violent confrontation, not against the Freemen trapped north of Brusett but against the lawmen outside, might be possible.

Agent Canady finally ordered Connie not to go back to Cat Creek because of the mounting possibility that a big gun battle might occur. He asked me if I was armed, and I said, "Lightly."

The truth was, Connie and I were both armed to the teeth from the first day we went back under cover at the ranch.

I told Connie that Canady had suggested she not go back.

"I'm glad to be ordered to stay at home with the kids," she admitted. "This whole thing is getting too outrageous."

Then, to my surprise, she broke into open laughter. I could not help joining in. We both laughed until tears were rolling down our faces. Whether it was a release of tension or the ludicrousness of the situation, I do not know. We never stopped to ask each other, "What are you laughing at?"

But the next two days were to be anything but a comic opera. The isolated Freemen standoff in faraway Montana was about to take an uglier turn of significant danger to a larger number of citizens of the United States.

CHAPTER 32

On April 18, the eve of the dreaded anniversary date of the disasters at Oklahoma City and Waco, I donned my camouflage fatigues and loaded up on Meals Ready to Eat and field equipment, in preparation for whatever might happen in Garfield County. Since Connie had been ordered by the Bureau not to return to the militias' command center at Cat Creek, I felt I had lost half my team.

There was little additional information to be gained at Cat Creek, and the Bureau did not seem to be that interested in what the militias were doing, anyway. But I hoped I could lower the level of tension and help avoid any misstep that might lead to a shooting incident.

When I arrived at the Cat Creek ranch I was confronted by a bedraggled army. Damp and cold warriors had stopped work on their makeshift tanks. I believe the miserable Montana winter thaw had as much to do with taking the fight out of the gathered militias as anything the Bureau was doing.

The one hundred–strong FBI and ATF team and scores of local and state lawmen surrounding Justus Township were just as cold and wet as the militiamen.

The dozens of newspeople had already interviewed every living soul in the region except, of course, those snuggled warm inside the farmhouses of Justus Township. The media had taken to cannibalizing itself for new story material.

The Bureau's standoff team, headed by Deputy Director Robert "Bear" Bryant of Washington, was gaining the edge. Bryant was no stranger to long, cold sieges, having led one against a polygamous Mormon cult in Utah some years earlier. Waco had also taught the lesson of rotating the line troops, and agents were put out on the muddy checkpoints for no more than two weeks at a stretch. Thus, the government agents on their stations were relatively fresh at any given time, compared with the die-hard militiamen.

The militia units had come in with little backup. Only one group from Ohio had arranged for rotation, with replacements scheduled to arrive on a regular basis during the early weeks of the standoff.

A rumor flew through the ranks of the militias that April 19 was to be the day the "jackbooted thugs" of the FBI and ATF would attack them. In response to the rumor, a defensive mood had replaced the bravado for smashing through to the compound with a relief column. When I arrived on April 18, the leaders at the Chamberlain ranch house were planning tactics for defending themselves and their positions, not breaking into Justus Township threescore miles away.

I strolled into the midst of the militiamen gathered in the yard of the ranch house, listened for a few minutes, and then realized I had a golden opportunity to defuse the situation for the expected April 19 D-day. My credentials as a Freemen justice served me well in this case. The militiamen listened eagerly to my suggestions as they gathered in clusters around the farmyard, stomping their feet and swilling coffee to take the edge off the wet cold.

Satisfied that the rank and file bought the plan, I took it to the leaders inside.

If the feds were actually going to attack them it would be under cover of darkness, I told the little knot of leaders standing around a kitchen table in the ranch house. Therefore, the units should be deployed as soon as possible in small groups around the perimeter of the Cat Creek ranch. Those units deployed in outlying areas should be called to the ranch so that all the manpower could be focused where needed on short notice. I learned that another group of Freemen at Lewiston had been joined by a few militiamen from Idaho and Washington, and had reportedly amassed a small armory of heavy weapons in that close-by Montana city.

I hoped that consolidating the various militia formations scattered around eastern Montana would prevent some small band from taking action on its own or stumbling into a fed roadblock, thus creating a confrontation.

"But with all these units in the hills around the ranch," I cautioned the leaders, "we have to be careful they do not mistakenly shoot each other. I strongly recommend they build sizable camp-fires so our other militia units will see their positions."

I knew most of the militia units had at least one set of night-vision goggles or binoculars, and that the bonfires would render these optical enhancers useless. There was always a possibility that some overly ambitious SWAT team of local lawmen might come over to the Cat Creek ranch for a look-see at the militias. And I knew that local farmers and ranchers were still pretty anxious to get the standoff resolved. Planting time had been indefinitely post-poned in the vicinity, and the Bureau would not let farmers in the area begin working their property. There were roving vigilante bands of idled farmers antsy to get on with their lives.

I also knew the Bureau was not telling Connie or me every-thing on its agenda. I doubted it, but there might be some FBI or ATF tactical-assault team roving around the hills. I did not want the militias spotting such teams, if they did exist.

Of course, the militia leaders at Cat Creek had no reason to suspect my motives. They thought my plan was good, and by mid-afternoon units began arriving at the ranch. They were in every sort of utility vehicle, four-wheel-drive pickup, and van. Several of the militia units even had horses, pulled behind their vehicles in trailers.

My ploy was certainly going to keep them busy relocating their troops, digging foxholes, and preparing to spend this worrisome night out of harm's way. By harm's way, I wanted to be sure the mili-tias stayed as far away from Jordan, Brusett, and the Clark ranch as possible, until the April 19 anniversary had passed.

By my calculation the closest FBI checkpoint at Jordan was about fifty miles from the Chamberlain ranch, a comfortable buffer between the armed camps.

My little plan was enhanced, by accident, I'm sure, when a flight of three military helicopters passed swiftly over the ranch at mid-afternoon. These were not the mythical black helicopters that haunt the imaginations of right-wing fanatical leaders. They were National Guard copters, one with a red cross painted on the side. But the militiamen were certain they were spying for an impending attack during the coming night. The FBI had a small airstrip and several helicopters were located at their command center.

Some of the militiamen in the barnyard raised their automatic weapons in the direction of the copters, and I held my breath. Nothing happened. But when the Guard helicopters cleared the area, their presence put new vigor in the digging of defensive foxholes around the Cat Creek ranch.

Late in the afternoon, with the redeployment well under way, I needed to call in my report to the Bureau. I had done everything possible at the time so I bid farewell and drove away from the ranch. I covered my retreat by telling the leaders I was going out on extended recon and would call in if I spotted anything unusual.

I had no idea if my plan would work or not, and half expected to get up the next morning to hear on the news that a conflagration had started.

I called Canady from Winnett as I drove south toward Billings, but could not locate him. Whoever answered the phone at the FBI command center at the Garfield County Fairgrounds said that Canady was at home. Since this date was critical, I assumed that meant Canady was back at FBI headquarters in Billings. So I left word that to the best of my knowledge the militiamen at the Cat Creek ranch were bedding down, if nervously, in defensive positions to watch the anniversary pass peacefully.

During the height of tension, fate took an unfortunate twist. Halfway between Billings and Winnett en route to Cat Creek, the transmission in my pickup locked up. Ironically, or I should say ludicrously, I had to use my own vehicle after Connie left the operation because the FBI, knowing I did not have a valid driver's license, would not let me drive a car they rented. The Bureau's Mickey Mouse nitpicking over such niceties in the midst of a potential life-and-death catastrophe drove me bonkers.

The red tape had its costs that day when solid intelligence was the most critically needed. All hell could be breaking loose at any minute and I had to have my vehicle towed back to Billings. By mid-day I had returned to the apartment in a state of near panic. The day would be over before I could rent another vehicle in my wife's name and make the long drive north to Cat Creek. There was no choice but to use Ma Bell to "reach out and touch" the situation over the wires.

So, on April 19, I spent the day frantically working the tele-phone. I called Cat Creek and told Dan Wooten, who was still man-ning the computer terminals, that I had established eyes and ears at the FBI command center and would be filing regular reports to him.

He reminded me that he also had eyes and ears among his news media acquaintances on media hill nearby at Brusett. I one-upped Wooten's sources by asking him if his eyes and ears had reported that the FBI was also dug in, not mobilizing, and, in fact, there was practically no movement at Jordan.

On my next call to Cat Creek, Wooten said his source at CNN had confirmed my report. Since I had made up the story and was actually calling from Billings, nearly two hundred miles away, I was surprised but pleased.

The anxiety was still high throughout the day. I called the FBI compound at Jordan again, looking for Canady. Then someone told me he was at home, sick in bed.

I told the agent on the other end of the line, "This is Talon. I have to talk to him."

There was silence on the line for a moment, then extensions were picked up, with several voices chattering questions at once.

I explained again that the militias were hunkered down fifty or sixty miles away and not moving. There was an audible chorus of sighs, which I took to be relief.

"So there's no reason for you guys over at Jordan to get aggres-sive," I said. "If you just cool it, which I know you will, then nothing is going to happen today or tonight. They think you guys are going to hit them. If you don't send anyone driving around over there, it should be quiet."

About an hour after that call my phone rang. It was Canady.

The agent was chuckling between coughs. "I hear you got every-one calmed down over at Cat Creek."

"I hope so," I said. "And at Jordan, too."

"Yeah, at Jordan, too," Canady said. "Thanks a million—a great job."

"It's not over yet," I said, cautioning my handler not to unleash his dogs at Jordan.

He indicated that the FBI was planning nothing out of the ordinary for the day, adding, "I don't think my compadres got much sleep last night."

"Nobody did," I said.

"I'm sick," the agent concluded with another cough. "I'm going back to bed."

April 19 came and went without anything unusual happening.

Nothing unusual, that is, unless several hundred heavily armed, adult white males dressed up in combat regalia and body armor watching for each other through binoculars in a bucolic American farmland can be considered unusual.

CHAPTER 33

On April 20, Connie and I rented another utility vehicle and headed north to Cat Creek. Our own pickup remained locked in the garage without current license plates and in need of transmission work. Connie was planning to stay over at Winnett and visit with friends while I made a brief appearance at the ranch.

En route we encountered Lyle Chamberlain driving his beat-up old pickup on the road just outside Winnett. Connie was driving our rented 4x4. The Bureau's ridiculous ban on my driving a vehicle without a legitimate license continued to stick in my craw. I had several licenses under different cover names, but none was legit.

Connie slammed on the brakes and fishtailed the utility vehicle in a U-turn to come up behind Chamberlain. My intention was to flag down the big cowboy for a chat—actually to find out what errand of mischief he might be on that would take him away from the visiting militiamen he hosted at Cat Creek.

Apparently, Lyle did not recognize the car and kept driving. Suddenly another pickup roared up behind us, passed, and swerved between our car and Chamberlain's. I did not recognize the driver of the vehicle trying to cut us off. There was a near collision.

I pulled my 10/22 from a backpack and laid it on the floorboard at my feet. I also unholstered a Glock .45 and chambered a round, laying the automatic on the seat. I told Connie to use it if she had to.

Then Connie recognized the second car's driver as one of Chamberlain's sons.

We waved and pulled past him, also passing Lyle with our lights flashing.

Chamberlain finally pulled into a ranch house driveway. When I got out and approached him, he was sitting behind the steering wheel of his vehicle. His face was pale beneath a big, flat-brimmed cowboy hat. But his voice was firm. From behind the bushy, red-gray beard, Lyle's eyes blazed. "You shouldn't have done that," he said. I saw his .357 Magnum revolver on the seat beside him. "Gawddamn, Dale," he said. "I thought you was the feds."

After everything Connie and I had done to avoid a shooting, our impulsive action in trying to stop the rough-hewn Freemen rancher for a talk could have ruined it all. Lyle calmed down after a few minutes and told me that things were coming undone up at his ranch.

"A lot of them [the militias] are talking about packing up and going home," he said. "Maybe you should get up there and try to talk them into staying for a while."

"Sure," I said. I was thrilled with the news. "I'll get right on it." But I had other things in mind. I would go up to Cat Creek, all right, but it would be to encourage everyone to leave Montana.

At Winnett, I slid into the driver's seat and left Connie behind.

Sure enough, when I reached the militia command center at the ranch, I was confronted by a cold, soggy soldier posted at the gate. I recognized him as one of the Ohio militiamen, the unit making up the largest militia on the grounds. He informed me his group was packing up to go home.

A scan of the barnyard revealed several others tugging and yanking the steel plates from the road grader and old bus. They were dismantling their tanks, leaving ugly scars on the already banged-up equipment.

I hurried into the ranch house to be met by a knot of camouflage-clad men standing around the computers watching the screens.

Then I came upon a piece of the most horrifying information of all—too incredible to believe even after the incredible events of the past week. If my handler at the Bureau was reluctant to believe the reports delivered thus far, he was going to go ballistic when he heard what I would now have to report.

Having had their fill of camping out in barnyards and ditches in the hills, the militiamen were indeed heading home. But they were not abandoning the Freemen inside the siege lines.

Apparently, during my absence on D-day, April 19, the leaders at Cat Creek had decided on a new strategy for dealing with the government's confrontation with the Freemen at Justus Township. After all, it had become clear to everyone that any effort to break through the blockaded Clark farm would be futile. There never was a consensus among the various militia groups on what tactic to use.

The FBI had also refused to cooperate by giving them any real excuse to make an armed show of force. In fact, the Bureau, through press conferences presided over by U.S. Attorney Sherry Matteucci in Billings, had been more than reasonable in assurances that no assault would be made against the Freemen.

"We absolutely intend no harm to the persons who are on the current property. I assure them that we are doing everything possible to make certain that a dangerous situation does not develop up here," Matteucci said in a television appeal aimed as directly at the militiamen outside the siege lines as to the Freemen on the inside. She paraded out senior FBI spokesmen, local law enforcement officials, and local politicians to confirm her peaceful assurances.

Special attention was directed at the media throng concerning the safety of the women and children inside Justus Township. When a half-dozen women and children did come out, the Bureau made a big show of reporting that they had even intervened to have local charges dropped against the participants in the standoff, who had been caught only accidentally when the Bureau threw up its lines around the Clark farm.

In another unusual step, the Bureau announced that it had actually contacted the leaders of many of the known militia units around the country and signaled its peaceful intentions to wait out the Freemen.

Likewise, militia leaders from the mainstream units all over the country had made a great public effort to let the media know they were not in sympathy with the fraudulent financial schemes and other criminal activities of the Freemen. But they failed to tell the press at their conferences that, regardless of their lack of support for the conduct of the Freemen, the militia movement "would absolutely not stand for any government attack on citizens."

As the militia leaders were gathering up their troops on the ranch in preparation for the long drives back to their states, Wooten revealed the new strategy the militias would use to intimidate the Bureau.

A nationwide network alert was being sent over the Internet, by phone, and by fax to units in every state where militias could be identified.

I was surprised to hear the leaders at the ranch confidently reveal that groundwork had already been laid in practically every part of the country for just such an occasion.

Plans had been drawn over the past year by scores of militia units; targets had been identified in metropolitan areas and small cities in nearly every state. These targets were reconnoitered and catalogued for just such a contingency as the Freemen standoff.

There would be dozens, perhaps scores, of small uprisings throughout America if the FBI fired the first shot at the Montana Freemen compound. Right or wrong, some of the more radical militias—whose members had long been itching for an armed confrontation—were waiting for an excuse, no matter how unjustified, to test their combat skills.

Governors, federal judges, and local officials throughout the United States were on these target lists. Federal buildings in large and small cities housing IRS, FBI, ATF, federal courts, and National Guard or reserve armories had all been scouted and filmed. Assault plans and schemes to either seize or destroy the installations had been rehearsed. (The proof of what I heard at the Cat Creek ranch that day would come three months later, when the Viper Cell in Arizona was busted by federal and local authorities. The exact techniques I revealed to the FBI on April 20 from my Montana intelligence were outlined in documents and videotapes seized in Arizona.)

Wooten said he had received confirming E-mail from scores of militia units. The militias were ready and they acknowledged that their units would participate. They awaited only a confirmation from Cat Creek that the feds had launched an assault against the Freemen at the nearby Clark ranch.

I overheard one especially chilling conversation. If the FBI and ATF moved against the Freemen, public officials—from governors all the way down to local county sheriffs—would be primary targets of attack.

"We are going to take out the government, one location at a time," one of the leaders from a Midwestern militia boasted. "We are good to go in every state. What we are doing is legal, constitutional. We're just foreclosing on liens and taking back the people's property."

Another justified the plan for insurrection by citing previous actions of the FBI.

"There won't be another Ruby Ridge or Waco without an answer from us this time. The beauty is, we'll hit everywhere. There's no way the feds can muster a response if we hit in fifty or sixty places at once. We'll take out our targets and then melt back into the community."

"And strike again if they don't get the message the first time," another militia leader said.

The guys at the computers assured the militiamen that every unit reporting in now had the code word to activate the plan. I was able to learn the code words that would launch the nationwide attacks: Project Worst Nightmare. It was an appropriate name for what the militias had planned.

In the blink of an eye, with the stroke of a few computer keys, the "go" order could be simultaneously sent to dozens, scores, or even hundreds of computers in towns and cities across the land. Then armed and trained men in small groups would simply walk out of their homes, offices, factories, fields, and bars and proceed to create chaos on a scale never seen in this country, or anywhere else in the civilized world.

I was impressed. And I was genuinely frightened. Even if they could pull off half or a tenth of what they were boasting about, there would be general panic and great bloodshed throughout the United States. It would be Oklahoma City all over again, only multiplied dozens of times.

The thing that made me the most upset was the demeanor of these men standing around the kitchen table. They were talking in calm, almost jovial banter about insurrection in their own country and overthrowing their own government. I knew many of them personally, and knew that most had once fought in the country's armed services to preserve the very nation they now so glibly talked about destroying.

Their voices were calm and rational, only their subject was irrational and insane. It was as if they were discussing a Super Bowl game or a deer-hunting trip. They were actually talking about real places in their own hometowns that had been pretargeted, and about people they worked with every day who had been selected to be shot, or at the least put into concentration camps.

I wanted out of that place. I wished I had never heard or seen what happened there. I had rarely been surprised at anything I heard from the Freemen leaders. They were a deranged, hateful clan of fanatical criminals. But these men were from every walk of life in middle America.

I made some excuse like, "Nothing left for me to do here," and began saying my farewells.

While the militias were leaving the battlefield in Montana, they were far from surrendering the war. If the FBI and ATF made a move against the Clark ranch, such an action would have actually triggered a catastrophic event. Such a move by the government was to start what amounted to a general insurrection. When I first found out about the possibility of a nationwide militia uprising, I was so astounded by the news that I toyed with the idea of blowing my cover and going straight to the FBI command center at the fairgrounds compound near Jordan.

But reason prevailed and instead I left Cat Creek. I picked up Connie at Winnett, grabbing her out of a coffee klatch with her old friends at the Kozy Korner. We rushed to Billings.

Once there we went straight to the FBI offices in the Western Federal Savings Building for a face-to-face meeting, and I breathlessly told my story to the first FBI debriefer I could find. The man looked at me as if I had come from Jupiter with a report about an invasion from outer space.

As I feared, the FBI was frozen in a state of complete denial.

The Bureau, after all these months, obviously still believed that the militia movement was some loose-knit organization of kooks. No matter what Connie and I had brought them as proof to the contrary, the bureaucratic party line was to minimize the militias as a serious, potentially dangerous group.

I was again the messenger who would be beheaded for bringing the message—a message that I myself hardly believed. Yet Connie and I had documented it over and over again, in detail. We had seen reams of rosters and organization plans, and dutifully reported everything to the Bureau for almost a year. At the Freemen cabin in Roundup we had seen the men, admired their weapons, talked to their leaders; and at the Cat Creek ranch we had observed their operational readiness and tactical skills with our own eyes.

A short time after we made our report to the Bureau at Billings and returned to our apartment, Canady called. He was again in a high state of agitation, but this time his ire was aimed at me.

"I heard about your report," Canady said curtly. "The militias aren't that well coordinated, period!"

I tried to explain the source of the information, the faxes I had actually seen, the talk on the Internet. Each time a unit from another state announced it was in position and ready, the leaders at the ranch had let out a loud cheer: Texas is in! Georgia is ready! It's go for Missouri! I explained all this to Canady, who kept interrupting me with something like "Bullshit" or "Yeah, yeah, yeah."

The Bureau could not be convinced the militias, while operating in tiny cells with no national head, were and are, nevertheless, well organized.

At the height of the tension, when Connie and I were almost daily bringing out intelligence of a national terrorist network, three Georgia men were arrested for stockpiling pipe bombs to be used at the upcoming Summer Olympics in Atlanta and in terrorist attacks on the federal government.

The men, arrested in mid-April, identified themselves as members of a heretofore unknown Georgia militia unit. The men were identified as militia leader Robert Starr III and members Troy Spain and Jimmy McCranie. Connie and I had not run across them or heard anything about their group, the 112th Georgia Militia, at the Roundup cabin. But their modus operandi fit. The more radical militia leaders assembled at Cat Creek cheered the arrested trio's quoted intentions.

The phantom elements of the militias were no longer a bunch of weekend warriors chasing around in the woods. We brought proof that many have a common mission and the wherewithal to carry it out.

Connie and I had been going back to Billings from Cat Creek for nearly two weeks, and pouring this information into the FBI. When Connie was still up at Cat Creek she would write it all down. Tommie Canady kept telling her he needed the information right away. Someone from the Bureau would pick up our notes and reports and deliver packets to the FBI office. Many of the reports were sent by courier to the FBI command center at the Garfield County Fairgrounds. We were told the Bureau did not want the information on teletype or in faxes. It was too sensitive to risk a leak.

Now we had uncovered what I considered to be the most dangerous information of all—a well-designed plan for nationwide insurrection. This was too much for our employers to comprehend. The FBI held the militias, along with the Freemen of Montana, in such low esteem that they refused to believe they could ever be organized enough to carry out such a grand plan.

"Our government has to know this, has to believe it," I insisted to Canady.

But obviously the Bureau, which is primarily responsible for domestic peace and tranquillity, is not prepared to deal with it. There is certainly not enough money in the shrinking federal budgets, even if adequate laws were on the books, to handle widespread uprisings. So, like the proverbial ostrich, its giant head is buried deeply in the sand—exposed butt flying high in the air, with a thousand guns carefully aimed at its tail feathers.

Canady finally moved to cut off our telephone report. He said he had to go on to some "important" matter around the FBI command center in Jordan. But before he hung up he gave me a firm order.

"You're finished at Cat Creek," he said. "Shut it down, right now."

Only the day before he had been telling me how glad he was that Connie and I were back on the job.

Within a few days of the rude rejection of our latest intelligence about the potential for a national uprising, confirmation of my reports began to trickle in from independent sources—primarily the news media.

National television broadcasters aired stories from various points around the country that local militias were issuing warnings of local attacks to be launched if the FBI moved against the Freemen in Montana.

The radical leader of the West Virginia Mountaineer Militia, Ray Looker—with whom I had spent time at the Freemen cabin in Roundup—issued a press statement from Pennsylvania warning that his units were prepared to move against local targets.

A score of militia leaders from a dozen states issued a press release that called the FBI operation "unlawful" and warned that an injury to any of the Freemen inside Justus Township would be considered an act of war. "[We will] no longer restrain our brethren," the press release said.

Commander Olson from the Northern Michigan Militia stepped up threats and continued to hang around Jordan. The Bureau's curious reaction to this man, who led one of the largest, best organized, and most heavily armed militias in America, was to ridicule him. They called Olson and his aide "Yogi Bear and Boo-Boo."

Stuart Waterhouse, a San Antonio–based spokesman for one of the dozen known militias in Texas, told a CBS-TV reporter in a taped interview that "units can hit the FBI everywhere we find the FBI . . ." He went on to describe the militia nationwide as "an army" waiting in readiness.

Finally, the Bureau did seem to recognize that there was a real and imminent danger. Television stations reported that the FBI had issued an alert to law enforcement agencies across the country. The report said the FBI had revealed a document entitled "Militia War Warning," which "calls for attacks of government facilities to shut government down." The alert listed the following targets of opportunity:

★ Federal satellite uplinks and telecommunications centers
★ Military depots
★ Law enforcement communications centers
★ Senior federal law enforcement officials
★ Federal Reserve Board governors
★ Media installations, television networks, and other select media

Oddly, at about the same time the Bureau was issuing this alert to law enforcement agencies, which leaked it to the news media, the FBI issued another alert. They warned Jewish doctors and business executives that a Middle Eastern terrorist organization was planning to murder twelve hundred physicians and businessmen unless Israel pulled its forces out of southern Lebanon.

The irony of the almost simultaneous warnings hit me hard.

Our own homegrown terrorists were emerging throughout the heartland of America. Advocating the same unholy tactics as the long-recognized enemies of civilization—the Jihad of the Mideast, the Red Brigades and Irish Republican Army of Europe, the Shining Path of South America—a new terrorist organization was being born. This time, it was the All-American terrorist militias.

The United States had finally arrived!

★ CHAPTER 34 ★

Connie and I would never know if the intelligence we had gathered on the militiamen assembled in the hills around the Cat Creek ranch influenced the wait-them-out approach taken by the federal government during the early days of the standoff.

And, thank God, the validity of our intelligence did not have to be tested by a firefight between militiamen and feds in Montana.

April 19, 1996, had come and gone without any serious confrontation. A sigh of relief went up, both among the FBI men on the line—most, I am sure, unaware that they were surrounded—and among scores of the cold, hungry, and dirty militiamen now loading up their utility vehicles, pickups, vans, and horse trailers to move out of Montana.

For once, Connie and I were happy that the monolithic FBI did not move, and thus avoided the spark that might have set off a national conflagration in scores of cities and towns.

But the assignment was not over, and our work for the Bureau entered another phase, in a lasting way more dangerous for us than any we had encountered in the first year we were under cover for the FBI. As the longest siege in American history dragged on, the bored militiamen were replaced by politicians, well-known spokesmen for the patriot movement, and, ominously, some dangerous fanatics the public never knew existed. It was this last group that would send my family into deeper cover and ultimately fleeing for our lives.

The press corps stationed around Jordan also became bored. The story began to fade away and most of the media folks went home.

Except for a couple of hundred feds and local lawmen, a

smattering of newspeople from the mainstream media, and the twenty-one men, women, and children inside the Freemen compound, the big drama had ended in less than a month. But the standoff would continue for many more weeks.

Departing militiamen assured those few fanatical Freemen still hanging out at Cat Creek and at the Freedom Center in Billings that they could return on a minute's notice if shooting began. They departed with some of the more radical of their leaders, clearly disappointed that the new revolution would not start in Montana.

Connie and I never went back into Cat Creek, but instead were directed to focus our efforts on the Freedom Center in Billings. The center, located in the main house on Rudy Stanko's cattle feedlot and farm, was on Duck Creek Road, ten miles out of town. Scores of penned-up cattle were kept there in small lots and force-fed to fatten them up for slaughter.

Regardless of the high-sounding name, the Freedom Center was not a typical think tank. The most distinguishing feature of the place was the perpetual, pervasive odor of cow manure and urine. The smell invaded every room of the center. Neighbors who complained of the stench were reminded that cattle feedlots "smelled like money."

Connie and I would spend much of May and early June 1996 rushing home from our visits to the center to shower off the cloying aroma of fattening cattle. It ruined our appetite for beef in any form.

While a standoff between the score of Freemen and women with children inside the compound went on near Jordan, Schweitzer and Petersen were conducting their own mini-standoff inside the Yellowstone County jail at Billings.

The Freemen leaders refused to acknowledge the authority of their jailers to fingerprint or photograph them. Schweitzer went on a hunger strike, and for a time was transferred to a federal facility in Missouri where his health could be monitored around the clock. He finally gave up his fast and was returned to the Billings jail to take up other forms of protest.

Each time Schweitzer and Petersen were brought into the courtroom of Federal Magistrate Richard Anderson, they created some sort of ruckus, always denying that the federal court had jurisdiction over them since they were sovereign white males.

Stuart Waterhouse, the militiaman who had earlier told a San Antonio CBS affiliate that militias were prepared to attack federal agents all across the United States, came to Montana and slipped into the Freemen compound. He was later arrested when he walked off the 960-acre Clark wheat farm. He joined the two Freemen leaders in the Billings jail and was held without bail as an accessory after the fact. Waterhouse would be the first of ten people participating in some phase of the standoff to be charged for abetting the Freemen. Similar charges were prepared against the family members of the Montana Freemen if they aided in any phase of the standoff.

The Freemen still holed up inside Justus Township defiantly refused to negotiate with any of the Bureau's own team, and outsiders were allowed to enter negotiations for the first time in Bureau history.

The government agreed to let former Green Beret James "Bo" Gritz, a leading antigovernment spokesman, negotiate with the Clarks, Skurdal, and Jacobi, who were still inside the compound. Gritz had successfully negotiated the end of the twelve-day Ruby Ridge standoff, in which Randy Weaver's wife and son and one U.S. marshal had died. But after several days Gritz gave up in disgust over the irrational demands of the Freemen.

Karl Ohs, a Montana legislator, tried to find a suitable team of nonfederal officials to reopen talks. In mid-May, Ohs induced the Freemen to allow two FBI negotiators, accompanied by Colorado state Senator Charles Duke, to begin discussing an end to the standoff. The Freemen would not speak directly to the FBI's men, but would talk through Senator Duke. Duke shuttled between the two groups with their messages.

Then, on May 16, Duke took two agents to a cattle guard at the fence line on the Clark farm. Soon four Freemen came out and the two sides met face-to-face for the first time. The standoff was now in its seventh week. Finally, a table and chairs were hauled out to the site and the two groups met again the following day.

Duke later told newspeople the talks were going well. He identified the Freemen at the conference as Edwin Clark, Dale

Jacobi, Rodney Skurdal, and Russell Landers, a North Carolina Freeman who had earlier used bogus checks to purchase vehicles and supplies in his state for delivery to Montana.

These initial talks continued as the standoff went into its eighth week, and the meeting site was improved with a tent to shield the negotiators from the spring rains drenching the area.

Soaked and miserable news media representatives filmed the sessions from hundreds of yards away, but the subjects under discussion were not revealed. Senator Duke would say only that thirty to forty issues remained on the table.

As the talks continued, a woman, identified variously as Gloria or Tammy Ward and her eight- and ten-year-old daughters, were seen attending one of the sessions. The FBI urgently wanted the women and children to leave the compound. The bitter memory of the eighty people, including women and children, who died at Waco when the Branch Davidian compound was destroyed hung over the negotiations at Jordan every day.

After a week of talks moderated by Duke, the negotiations again broke down. Skurdal was seen through the telephoto lens of a news camera wildly waving his arms in the air. The agents and Duke left quickly.

Shortly after, heavily armed Freemen took up positions at several points around the farm. The Bureau had used forty-two third-party negotiators, including well-known right-wing spokesmen, state representatives, family members, and local officials. The Freemen would not budge.

On May 23, the Freemen raised an American flag, flying the banner upside down in the international symbol of distress. The negotiations were terminated, and Senator Duke told the news media, "They've got a pretty comfy life in there now. They have color TV and cable . . . and plenty to eat and plenty to drink. Time is now to start tightening the noose a little bit."

When I saw this comment aired on a Billings television station I could not help but sarcastically mention to Connie, "Yeah, but the Freemen have the noose."

Senator Duke, who had been identified as a sympathetic voice to right-wing patriot views, was himself frustrated with the Freemen's recalcitrant position. He accused them of breaking an earlier agreement to let the children out of Justus Township.

Meanwhile, local officials and citizens of Jordan and the surrounding farms and ranches were getting upset with the long, fruitless negotiations. Petitions were circulated in the community demanding that the FBI stop talking and take action.

At that point the Bureau pulled in three large trucks with generators and informed local ranchers they were planning to cut electricity to the Clark farm. The generators would provide electric power to surrounding homesteads for the duration.

On May 29, after a Fox-TV news crew defied the FBI's ban on media approaching the Freemen, the Bureau ordered the media-hill operation closed down, and forced news crews out of camera range of the farm. District Judge James M. Burns issued an order for the press to clear off the hill immediately.

A local utility company fired up the first generator for a test to provide alternative electricity to the thirty homes that would be cut off when the lines to the Clark ranch were severed. On June 4, power was finally cut to Justus Township. Despite a warning from local authorities that this ploy would do no good because the ranch was equipped with gasoline generators, that night the compound was dark for the first time.

The news media also discovered that the Bureau had brought in three APVs—armored personnel vehicles. It looked as though a confrontation was about to begin.

The day after the lights went off in Justus Township, the Wards, including the two young girls, left the compound. A sister of Gloria Ward had been allowed inside to talk the family into surrendering. No federal charges were pending against Elwin Ward or his wife. However, the girls' father from Gloria's previous marriage was seeking custody of the daughters. A federal judge in Utah immediately took the children from Gloria and gave custody to their father.

During the months of May and June, Connie and I had been routinely dropping in on the Freemen's Billings operations at the Freedom Center.

We made regular reports on events going on at that location, but the Bureau was so engrossed in its action—or lack of action—in the Jordan area that our reports largely went unnoticed.

The Bureau was satisfied that it had the Freemen operation bottled up either at the Clark wheat farm or in the Yellowstone County jail. The FBI could not have been more wrong.

The center on the feedlot near Billings was humming with activity.

On June 8, Montana's 150 senators and representatives were notified by mail that they faced liens on their personal property unless the state convened a special grand jury to investigate the federal government's action. The liens would be filed in ten days, the warning said. The warning was signed by Daniel Petersen, LeRoy Schweitzer, and Richard Clark. All three Freemen leaders were locked down in maximum security in the Billings jail.

Officials were stunned. How could the Freemen be conducting business as usual from maximum security?

Petersen and Schweitzer had been arrested on March 25, and Richard Clark had given himself up to authorities on March 30. Clark had been off the ranch when the arrests and subsequent standoff began.

Authorities were shocked that such a sweeping and audacious action could be taken by the Freemen. They assumed the Freemen operation was practically finished and its main leaders safely put out of action. Once again, the Freemen had made "ass-you-me" out of the government's assumptions.

The new warning to Montana's assemblymen read: "The legislators have ten days to start the inquiry into what authority the federal government has to send 'an armed body of men' to the Freemen compound."

One of the primary instruments of the federal fraud scheme for which the Freemen were indicted had always been the filing of bogus liens against public officials and private citizens who crossed them. Even though the liens were completely extralegal, those property owners had to go to significant expense to have them removed. It was one of the most dreaded forms of harassment against their neighbors—other than threats to hang them—used by the Freemen for years. And the bogus lien scheme was a vital part of the financial-terrorism training course the Freemen sold to the estimated fifteen hundred militants from other states attending their seminars.

Now they brazenly continued their financial terrorism against officials in Montana, despite being locked up or under armed siege.

After ignoring our reports for weeks, the Bureau suddenly wanted Connie and me to find out how this outrage could occur. It took us less than an hour to learn that Freemen operating out of the Freedom Center in Billings were getting detailed instructions from Schweitzer at the Yellowstone County jail.

The regular visits by sympathizers to the jail were a cover for continuing terrorist activities.

Discovering how the Freemen issued the threat to file the bogus liens was only one of the pieces of intelligence to come from the new headquarters for Freemen activities, now located just outside Billings.

During most of May 1996, a whole host of radical white supremacists, neo-Nazis, and other fanatical followers of various Christian Identity or Aryan Nations organizations had passed through the Billings center.

Randy Parsons volunteered to run the information center. He is a self-described constitutionalist and Freeman of character. His work for the Freemen was purely an act of love, because he comes from a wealthy Montana ranching family and certainly had no need to participate in the Freemen's fraud schemes. Parsons is a tall, flashy guy with a big mouth. I had first met him at Winnett when I was tending bar at the Kozy Korner. He came in one day and announced in a loud voice, "I am a Freeman of character!"

That day there were two or three pretty tough ranchers sitting at the other end of the bar who just happened to have had a few beers too many and no love for the Freemen. It was a chore for me to keep these cattlemen from hauling Parsons out of the place for a good beating.

Parsons had been given the job of keeping the Freedom Center operating, and he depended on volunteers from the ranks of the

Freemen to fill in. But since these volunteers came and went as they pleased, Parsons was usually working around the clock.

The center on Duck Creek Road was actually better equipped to carry out the clandestine activities of the Freemen than the cabin at Roundup had been. The living room in the main house was converted into a computer room and telecommunications center. Regular short-wave radio programs were broadcast from this center. Parsons did a sort of insider's news update, and whatever hate luminary was visiting the center at any given time would broadcast a commentary.

The Freedom Center, like all the facilities supporting the Freemen cause, was an armed camp. Parsons's side arm of choice was a .40 caliber Baby Eagle automatic.

On one of our first visits, Connie was treated to a demonstration by the son of one of the Freemen holed up inside Justus Township. He was proudly showing off his newest toy—a military assassin-style sniper rifle.

The only other regular denizen working around the place was a character who couldn't have cared less about Freemen philosophy. He was an old retired hippie who tended the livestock on Rudy Stanko's feedlots. He helped to keep the stench in the house muted somewhat by chain-smoking marijuana. Unfortunately for Connie, she was relegated to hours of listening to this old cowboy's tales of his hippie life in the 1960s.

We were welcomed at the center by Parsons, since he would take any manpower he could get. The forty-year-old Freemen follower now had the burden of carrying out LeRoy Schweitzer's orders from his jail cell, in addition to operating the information center. When he saw me, he embraced me in a big bear hug and said, "I'm glad you're still alive."

The out-of-state militia groups continued to maintain regular contact with the center by facsimile machine or Internet.

But more frightening were the mysterious individuals who began to gravitate to the center while the long standoff at Jordan played itself out. It seems the very dregs from every radical right-wing militant organization in the United States showed up to offer their services.

A trio arrived one day, claiming they represented an armed and militant cell in New York. These men would not name their organization and identified themselves as Impression One, Impression Two, and Impression Three. These New Yorkers were unlike any of the rugged outdoor types in the militia units.

They dressed in suits, ties, and overcoats, and looked more like movie mobsters than militiamen. I thought that they were so out of character they might possibly be agents from some obscure federal security apparatus. But it took only a few minutes of listening to their anti-Jewish, antiblack rhetoric and their repeated references to bombing New York targets to realize these were definitely not feds.

Impressions One, Two, and Three stayed overnight at the Freedom Center, gathering information on contacts they wanted to make with the more militant leaders of cells in other states. Parsons had access to extensive contact lists because of his job as administrator of the Freedom Center in the absence of the jailed Freemen leaders. I overheard the New York trio telling Parsons that they were en route to Hayden Lake for meetings with the leaders of the Aryan Nations.

They disappeared as quietly as they had come, and I was unable to provide the FBI with any real identity of the men, except their physical descriptions. The car they were driving was a rental.

Connie and I attended dozens more meetings at the Freedom Center. It became an intelligence mother lode for identifying additional white-supremacist groups, and was actually more fruitful in many ways than the cabin at Roundup had been.

We saw some of the most deadly characters we had met to date pass through the center during the weeks of the standoff. Each time a new fanatic came through, we alerted the FBI.

It was in the course of this latest suboperation that a strange encounter took place with one of the most dangerous groups I have ever stumbled across in my career as a civilian undercover operative—before, during, or since the Freemen operation.

Nothing or no one we had met so far was to have a more chilling impact on me than the character who came to the Freedom Center at Stanko's feedlot in late May 1996.

⋆ CHAPTER 35 ⋆

A particularly boastful white supremacist arrived at the Freedom Center during the height of the standoff negotiations at Justus Township. I'll call him Tarantula Eyes because I still dream of his fixed stare. The man identified himself as the leader of a large phantom cell operating from a mountainous area of North Carolina.

Anyone meeting him would have assumed this well-groomed man to be a retired executive with a sophisticated, slightly Southern accent. He had a disarming, friendly smile at first greeting, but soon lapsed into a stony observation of whomever he met—almost to the point of making uncomfortable the subject of his attention. In only minutes he had a way of making the person he talked to feel like a fly trapped in a web under close scrutiny by a spider.

At five feet, eleven inches and about one hundred ninety pounds, Tarantula Eyes was not physically menacing until he began his probing cross-examination. Then his piercing blue-green eyes seemed to glaze over and lose their color, fading to white. I engaged his stare the first time I had a conversation with him and realized that, while those eyes were boring into my soul, I could not see past some filmy curtain. His very light complexion also seemed to lose pigmentation, leaving the odd impression that I was talking to a transparent image, almost a ghostly being. I had the uncomfortable feeling that my every word, even my mind, was being processed.

Claiming to be a former high-ranking U.S. Navy officer, now in his late sixties or early seventies, this man wore a large signet ring with the letter *P* incorporated into the shape of a cross. Soon after meeting him I asked Tarantula Eyes if the ring had any significance. He looked surprised that I did not recognize the symbol.

"It's the ring worn only by a priest in the Phineas brotherhood," he told me menacingly.

I had never heard of such an organization, but I soon learned it was one of the most super-secret of the clandestine phantom cells operating in America.

Tarantula Eyes settled into a room in the basement at the Freedom Center for the duration of the siege going on miles away. He pretended he wanted to be a peace negotiator, but confided in me that his real aim was to get inside Justus Township to encourage the Freemen to stand up and become martyrs to the cause. At the time, there were dozens of people with similar intentions passing through Billings on the way to Jordan. Many claimed they wanted to serve as negotiators, but most said they were going to get inside to join the standoff.

Of course, I notified the Bureau at Jordan of anyone I thought might have a chance of actually talking their way in, or who seemed like a serious threat.

Tarantula Eyes could have qualified in either or both categories. I don't know if he was armed, but he never let his briefcase get farther than inches from his hand.

He told me a story of his power for evil that will probably haunt me the rest of my life. I had no way to verify the tale, but over the week or more I spent with him, I was certain it was true, especially after I learned more about the Priests of Phineas.

The way he told the story, he had exacted a horrible retribution against an associate who had died owing him $40,000. When Tarantula Eyes demanded payment from the dead man's son, the younger man told him to go to hell. The unholy priest claimed he just calmly walked away as if the bad debt would be forgotten.

However, several days later the young man, who was a pilot, boarded his plane for a hop to Florida. He ran into a bit of turbulent air and the plane was rocked about. The pilot noticed something loose in the passenger area behind him and turned to see the corpse of a young black woman.

Apparently the pilot was into enough of his own problems with the law that he could not just call the authorities. So he continued on to his destination.

When he arrived in Florida he was met by police.

Tarantula Eyes had tipped them off. According to his story the man was arrested, duly prosecuted, and was spending the rest of his life in prison.

"I dropped him a note sometime later saying, 'Your life would have been a whole lot simpler if you had paid your debts,'" the Phineas leader related, with the only hint of a smile I ever saw on his face.

He finished his frightening parable in a matter-of-fact voice that left little doubt it was true, and said he was heading for Jordan to volunteer himself as a negotiator.

I left the Billings center later in the day and called Canady at the FBI command post at Garfield County Fairgrounds to give him the man's name.

While I was waiting for Canady to come to the phone, I could hear two men talking in the room over the open line of the receiver lying on the desk. I recognized the voice of Tarantula Eyes, loudly explaining to one of the agents why he should be allowed into Justus Township to negotiate.

Agent Canady came on the line.

"I called to tell you you've got trouble coming, but it sounds like he's already there," I said. I gave him the man's name. Apparently, Canady was standing only a few feet from Tarantula Eyes while I made my telephone report on why the Bureau should be wary of him.

The Bureau declined his offer. When Tarantula Eyes returned later that night to the Freedom Center, the FBI's refusal to allow him to serve as a negotiator led to a tirade against the government.

In his anger he told me the "goddamn FBI bureaucrats" had no idea who they were dealing with and that he had very high connections in Congress. He said a day of reckoning was coming soon and the FBI, as well as others, were marked for this and all their insults.

Tarantula Eyes assumed the air of a leader around the Freedom Center for several weeks, even though he had no previous connection with the Freemen of Montana. During the considerable time I spent with him, both at the center and in meetings away from the center, I learned enough about this Phineas brotherhood to convince me it is a deadly organization.

Members of the mysterious Priests of Phineas, according to what I was told, may be found operating in any number of militia organizations, usually in the role of chaplain. Often the other members of the militia do not know of the Phineas connection.

Tarantula Eyes also claimed to have his own militia organization, which he called the North Point Teams. The teams, he said, were headquartered on an isolated encampment in the foothills of the Great Smoky Mountains in the northwestern part of North Carolina. But he said Priests of Phineas were well established within other groups all over the country, including the Aryan Republican Army of the Midwest and small fighting cells in several Western and Southern states.

One of the reasons Tarantula Eyes was in the Montana area at this time was to visit allied units operating in Idaho, Washington, and Oregon. He claimed he was putting together closer ties of the phantom cells of the militias, and working with the Aryan Nations leaders out of Hayden Lake to tighten the network of the really dedicated— which I took to mean fanatical—groups around the country.

He named many of the leaders in the radical patriot organizations with whom he had already established links. I knew some of these leaders from their visits to the Freemen cabin at Roundup, and had met several others at the recent gathering in Cat Creek.

He said the Priests of Phineas had successfully infiltrated regular military units, local and state police forces, and a number of other strategic organizations of government. He even claimed to have penetrated the FBI.

The priesthood group is highly fanatical, espousing deadly beliefs even beyond the wildest tenets of the Christian Identity religious movement, which is the bedrock of the white supremacists and Aryan brotherhoods.

Tarantula Eyes told me that a number of his fellow members were already in prison for various hate crimes, from bombings and arson to murder. The Priests of Phineas especially hate black and women's rights groups, and he boasted of the successful bombings of abortion clinics and black churches involved in political causes.

In order to become a priest in the Phineas brotherhood, a member must perform an act similar to the one described in the biblical story from which the name is derived.

The name for the brotherhood comes from chapter 25 of the Book of Numbers in the Old Testament. An Israelite priest named Phinehas saved the children of God from plague by driving a spear through the hearts of a wayward member of the tribe and a Midianite woman, who were fornicating. According to the modern-day followers, the woman was black—Tarantula Eyes claimed the name Midianite was a code word for midnight.

Phinehas was a son of the prophet Aaron, and the first to slay the followers of Baal and practicers of whoredom.

God was so pleased with Phinehas's zeal, according to Tarantula Eyes, that he "gave a permanent covenant of 'everlasting priesthood' . . . he shall have it and his seed, everlasting, even the covenant of an everlasting priesthood . . ."

The man's eyes lit up as he told the story. He said Phinehas's rage was so great that he drove the single spear through both the white man's back and the black woman's intestines with one mighty thrust.

"He ran that javelin right through them both while they were copulating," according to Tarantula Eyes' rendition. As a result, God had promised a small group of priests that they would always bear the responsibility for cleansing the races by killing those who mixed races. The modern Priests of Phineas organization was the heir to that covenant.

The mysterious present-day priest was vague about the other membership requirements in the brotherhood, but told me I would make an ideal candidate. He suggested that when my work was done in Montana I should come to North Carolina and join the training program. Tarantula Eyes said his group was well funded and that I would want for nothing. A house, car, and all living expenses would be provided during my training period. But he cautioned that joining the Priests of Phineas was a lifetime commitment—the only way to leave the organization was by death. Even members in prison continued their work, recruiting and training inmates.

He emphasized that in order to attain priesthood, apparently the highest order in the Phineas brotherhood, a member had to commit the act of Phinehas—in other words, to prove his worthiness by killing a woman or a man who indulged in race mixing, homosexuality, or another offense from their list of mortal sins.

I had no question that the Priests of Phineas's list of mortal sins would be expanded to include the act of the Israelite Caleb—spying. The thought sent shivers down my spine, since in that regard I was as guilty as sin. I reported everything I could learn about these priests to the FBI.

It would not be long before the Bureau would have ample reason to add a growing list of crimes to this American terrorist organization. When Connie and I told the Bureau about Tarantula Eyes, a special debriefing was set up at the Billings headquarters to cover every detail we had learned about this hate group.

Back in April 1996, a task force of FBI agents and local and state authorities in Washington, Idaho, and Oregon had been organized, following a series of violent bank robberies and bombings of newspaper offices and abortion clinics in the Northwest. The terrorists left messages with Bible quotations at each of their attack scenes, signed with the capital letter *P* superimposed on a cross. The men, dressed in combat fatigues and ski masks, would set off bombs at a location removed by several blocks from the bank they then raided with military precision. They also exploded bombs at the end of each bank heist to cover their getaway by panicking their victims.

"There is no group taking particular responsibility for this," said Burdena G. Paenelli, special agent-in-charge of the FBI's Seattle region, in a news conference after one of the assaults.

Once more the Bureau denied there was any connection between the radical supremacist groups beginning to openly terrorize the country.

Similar denials of connections were routinely issued by the Bureau for the score of armed bank robberies and bombings conducted by members of an organization the Bureau called the

Midwestern Bank Bandits. These robbers also left biblical quotations saying the assaults were in the name of Yahweh against the usurers.

Usurers is the word most commonly used by the white-supremacist hate groups to describe Jewish bankers whom they claim are running this country through the Zionist Occupation Government.

★　★　★

The Freedom Center became a veritable beehive of activity as the siege at Jordan wore on. Wooten, who had put together the communications network for the visiting militia units at the Cat Creek ranch, came to the Billings center and offered to help out with the tremendous volume of mail, telephone calls, and personal visits. He and Parsons did not hit it off. I didn't think the more sophisticated freelance newsman could stand many of the homespun ways of the Freemen and their followers, and sure enough, Wooten soon had his fill of it and left.

Connie and I helped out around the center as much as possible, secretly stuffing our pockets and her notebook full of intelligence for the Bureau in exchange for our minor efforts.

At one point late in June I was astounded to overhear one side of a late-night telephone conversation.

Someone called the center and began talking to Randy Parsons. From the conversation I soon realized it was Skurdal on the other end.

But how could he be calling? The siege was still on and the FBI had long since cut all the telephone lines. Nevertheless, the caller was giving a detailed picture of what was going on inside Justus Township.

Apparently, the holed-up Freemen were in much worse shape than the FBI suspected. Supplies were low and they wanted more men to come in. Many of the people inside, particularly the women and children, wanted out.

The call—like all calls coming into the Freedom Center—was being taped by a recorder attached to the phone.

The conversation lasted nearly an hour. From listening to Parsons's end I could tell the leaders took turns talking to him—Dale Jacobi got on the phone, and so did the Clarks.

The more he heard, the more agitated Parsons became. At one point he pulled out his pistol and spun around in my direction. I tensed and placed my hand on my Glock. Had one of the Freemen inside Justus Township told him something about me?

But it turned out he was just nervous and playing with his gun. I relaxed when I saw he was holding the Baby Eagle by the barrel and waving it in the air.

When the conversation ended, Parsons was excited. "It was Rodney Skurdal, inside the Clark compound," he said, elated. The man had been up for forty-eight hours straight trying to deal with the avalanche of work in the center. But this call was like a shot of speed—he was wide-awake and dancing around the communications room. "We have to get some supplies to them!" he shouted.

They were running low on certain foods and, most important to them, they were "going nuts" for cigarettes.

I would later come to believe that Skurdal's absolute addiction to nicotine was a deciding factor in ending the siege. If that was the case, Skurdal will probably really have fits when he finds out many prisons are beginning to ban smoking among the inmates.

When Parsons calmed down I asked, "How the hell are they calling out?"

"They don't know. They had cell phones, but they didn't work, too far from a cell tower," the Freedom Center operator answered. "A kid was playing with a cell phone inside and all of a sudden it worked."

This made me excited, too. I was hardly able to contain myself. I had to have that tape.

"This is wonderful!" I shouted. "We must get the message out to everyone."

Parsons probably never would have relinquished the tape, except that he was nearly delirious from exhaustion. My ploy that I should get it reproduced for all the world to hear the voice of one of our leaders worked. Parsons handed over the one and only copy of the tape.

I rushed home with this newest intelligence prize and thought immediately about calling Canady at FBI standoff headquarters in Jordan. But it was past midnight and I didn't see how I could get anything done at that hour, anyway. In the predawn hours of the next morning I called for Canady at the Jordan command post.

"What have you got now?" The agent was drowsy and almost surly at being bothered so early in the morning.

I told him I had a cassette recording of a conversation between the Freemen leaders inside the compound and the Billings Freedom Center.

"Geez, God, we've got to have it!" a suddenly wide-awake and interested Canady yelled over the phone. "Are you sure?"

"They're talking again, from inside the compound," I told the incredulous FBI agent. "All of a sudden their cell phone is working."

"No fucking way!" the agent shouted. Then silence on the phone. "My God, we've just put up a cell tower to improve our own communications. Get me a copy of that tape—now."

The Bureau had unwittingly broken down its own wall of silence and provided the foes a new link to the outside.

Before I could call headquarters in Billings, my cell phone rang. By now it was well past dawn. I thought it was Canady calling back with more instructions on how to get the tape copied.

But it was Tarantula Eyes. He had been sleeping in the basement at the Freedom Center and was awakened by Parsons jumping around and shouting about the call from Skurdal.

I had already left with the tape by the time the mysterious Phineas priest found out about it. But now he was outraged that I had taken the tape from the Freedom Center. He wanted it back immediately.

I promised to return the tape and set up a meeting with Tarantula Eyes and Parsons at a twenty-four-hour restaurant. But I told him it would take me an hour to get there.

"Thirty minutes," Tarantula Eyes snapped, and slammed down the phone.

First I called the FBI headquarters in the Western Savings Building and explained the urgency of getting the tape duplicated in what amounted to a matter of minutes.

The Bureau assigned the job to a young agent named Dan, who was stuck on the overnight shift. Canady had already called him to say I would be bringing in a tape to be copied on their high-speed duplicator.

"You've got fifteen minutes. Meet me at the Artspace coffee shop," I told the young agent. I started to give him directions to our regular rendezvous location, but he said he knew it already.

Connie drove me through every blinking red and yellow light between our apartment and the coffee shop. The young agent sprinted in, grabbed the tape, and ran the block and a half to the FBI office. He made a copy and was back in minutes.

Still, I was late for the appointment. But I ambled into the restaurant as casually as strolling in the woods. Just as I handed the tape over to Tarantula Eyes, I noticed it had not been rewound.

I explained, "I was so excited to hear from Skurdal that I made one quick duplicate and dropped it in the mail to our unit in Arizona. They've been real anxious for any word. I'll call them and tell them to burn the tape. No harm done."

Tarantula Eyes just scowled at me, took the original tape, and left.

CHAPTER 36

The standoff between the Freemen of Montana and the United States government finally ended without bloodshed on June 13, 1996. Connie and I had been working under cover for the FBI for fourteen months. The four Freemen leaders first targeted by the Bureau were now in custody, along with seventeen other Freemen and supporters participating in the eighty-one-day siege at Justus Township.

Not a shot had been fired, not a drop of blood shed, but a huge amount of the national treasury had been spent. The media heralded the siege as the longest in the nation's history, almost as if setting a new sports record to be broken at some ominous date in the future. *Time* magazine ranked the Freemen saga as among the ten "most intriguing" stories of 1996 in its big "Man-of-the-Year" world-events wrap-up issue.

For the peaceful citizens of eastern Montana, the terror had lasted a lot longer than a year. The final surrender at Justus Township was an anticlimax to almost three years of terrorism in Jordan, Winnett, and Roundup. A measure cannot be taken of the human toll in suffering: fear, intimidation, threats, and financial harassment have no yardstick. Estimates of the government's expenditure for manpower, equipment, and supplies to conduct the siege run as high as $50 million in taxpayer costs.

It should not have been this way. I am afraid that, because of the timidity of federal law enforcement in making early arrests when felonies were being committed openly, such groups—and there are many like the Freemen—are emboldened to carry on their terrorist schemes. Renewed financial terrorism, learned from the Freemen, continues to be waged against local officials in several states.

Still, the FBI and other law enforcement agencies are thwarted by the powerful gun lobby and Congress in efforts to get the new tools and legislation needed to combat modern, high-tech terrorism in America.

Soon after the tents surrounding Justus Township were folded, the media abandoned the story of the restless uprising in America's heartland. There just wasn't enough sizzle to keep the ratings high.

If the television reporters were waiting for a pyrotechnical grand finale like the fiery end of the Branch Davidian standoff at Waco, it was not to be. There was barely a whimper as a dozen or so Freemen walked out of the compound, loaded into two vans, and drove off in dust swirls. All this at the fuzzy far limits of the cameras' maximum telephoto range.

Two days before, the Bureau had transported Edwin Clark, a key member of the antigovernment group, to Billings for a conference in jail with LeRoy Schweitzer. Clark, whose father, Ralph, and uncle Emmett remained behind the armed barricades while he went to inform the Freemen chief the compound could be held no longer, was guaranteed safe passage by FBI agents, who escorted him on the flight to Billings.

Clark had also been accompanied to Billings by lawyers from a right-wing legal foundation. Three lawyers went inside the Yellowstone County jail and talked in privacy with the Freemen's chief justice, who had been locked up since his capture on March 25. The three lawyers from the CAUSE Foundation—a Black Mountain, North Carolina, group—were involved in the final negotiations to end the siege.

On June 12, the last child, a sixteen-year-old girl, left the compound, becoming the tenth person to voluntarily walk out of Justus Township since the standoff began.

At midday on June 13, the few remaining newspeople who had weathered the eighty-one-day siege were startled to see a caravan of vans and a rental truck pull up to the perimeter of the Clark property.

Meanwhile, in Billings, U.S. Attorney Sherry Matteucci held another press conference, saying only, "I do think we are closer than we have ever been to resolving this without violence."

By sunset all the members of the Freemen standoff calmly walked to the vans, leaving behind their arms, and—with television cameras filming the surrender through telephoto lenses—loaded into the vehicles. At 10 P.M. news bulletins announced that "all sixteen had voluntarily turned themselves over to authorities without incident."

Two wives of Freemen were not arrested, but fourteen others were loaded on two vans and escorted in an armed convoy to the Yellowstone County jail. There they joined the Freemen leaders arrested months earlier.

Back at Justus Township, the rental truck was loaded with computers, arms, file cabinets, short-wave radios and other telecommunications equipment, and hundreds of pounds of documents.

Montana Senator Karl Ohs, who had worked earlier as a negotiator, was given supervisory custody of the mountain of evidence, and assured the Freemen it would not be mishandled or tampered with by government attorneys.

This assurance had been the last sticking point to a peaceful surrender. Of course, the FBI had full access to the thousands of pages of documents—all of which were to be copied. The Justice Department later revealed it had scanned 241,287 documents onto computer CDs.

Connie and I knew that within these documents was the indisputable evidence of the existence of America's new network of domestic terrorist organizations and the identities of many of its members and sympathizers.

After the arrests, the FBI announced that the Freemen were forced to surrender by a shortage of food, diminishing water supplies, and only enough fuel to operate their electricity generator for two hours each day. The announcement did not mention that the Freemen were out of cigarettes.

So the longest siege in the history of the United States was indeed ended. And there had been no bloodshed. To many in the Bureau and in the government, the operation had been a public relations success.

Even President Clinton breathed a photo-op sigh of relief. He thanked the law enforcement officers for a peaceful conclusion.

"We'll all say a little prayer of gratitude tonight for this peaceful resolution of a difficult situation," President Clinton told the White House press corps.

Connie and I had been key participants as undercover civilian operatives. So we should have been celebrating, too. But we only said a prayer of thanks that the main event had ended. From our point of view, it was certainly no occasion to celebrate.

The armed standoff might have been over, but another standoff was shaping up in the courtrooms of Billings. At the first arraignment hearing for the Freemen, the courtroom of U.S. Magistrate Richard Anderson was turned into a circus.

Nine screaming Freemen interrupted the judge throughout the proceedings.

Freemen supporter Steven Charles Hance shouted at the federal judge, "You're going down, son."

All the newly arrested defendants were denied bail and joined the Freemen already being held in the Yellowstone County jail.

Sealed indictments were opened, charging a dozen of the Freemen with multiple felony counts. The charges included "conspiracy to defraud the United States, frauds and swindles, bank fraud, interference with commerce by threat or violence, carrying firearms during crimes of violence, unlawful transport of firearms, being a fugitive from justice, possessing firearms and affecting interstate commerce, and interstate shipment of firearms." In addition, the four Freemen leaders were charged with threatening the life of a federal official.

The four leaders of the Freemen movement who ran the operation at the cabin in Roundup before moving to Justus Township had the most federal felony charges filed against them. The formal indictment charged LeRoy M. Schweitzer, age 58, of Belgrade, Montana, with forty-five felony counts. Daniel E. Petersen Jr., 53, of Winnett, was charged with forty-nine counts. Rodney O. Skurdal, 44, of Roundup, was indicted on forty-three counts. The 55-year-old Canadian citizen, Dale M. Jacobi, who lists a residence in Thompson Falls, Montana, was charged with fifty-one counts.

Others indicted, their ages, hometown of record, and the number of charges against them included:

★ Emmett B. Clark, 67, of Brusett, thirty-seven counts;
★ Richard Emmett Clark, 48, of Grass Range, thirty-seven counts;
★ William L. Stanton, 66, of Brusett, thirty-seven counts;
★ Ebert W. Stanton, 23, of Brusett, thirty-seven counts;
★ John P. McGuire, 58, of Sonoma, California, forty-one counts;
★ Ralph E. Clark, 65, of Brusett, thirty-seven counts;
★ Cherlyn B. Petersen, 51, of Winnett, thirty-seven counts; and
★ Agnes B. Stanton, 53, of Brusett, thirty-five counts.

Additional indictments were returned against Russell D. Landers, 45, and his wife, Dana Dudley Landers, 47, of Four Oaks, North Carolina.

In November 1996, these indictments were consolidated and new indictments charging forty counts of conspiracy, bank and mail fraud, wire fraud, false claims, threats to federal officers, and weapons offenses were returned by a federal grand jury in Billings.

Eight other defendants were charged as accessories after the fact for their part in the Justus Township standoff. Those charged for preventing the FBI from issuing lawful warrants against the Montana Freemen were:

★ Steven C. Hance, 47, and his sons, John R. Hance, 20, and James E. Hance, 24, of Charlotte, North Carolina;
★ Jon Barry Nelson, 40, of Kansas;
★ Elwin Ward, 55, of Salt Lake City, Utah;
★ Stuart D. Waterhouse, 37, of Texas and Osage, Arkansas;
★ Edwin F. Clark, 45, and his son, Casey M. Clark, 21, of Brusett.

Edwin Clark was indicted on an additional bank fraud charge, and Ward was charged with making a false claim. Waterhouse and the Hances were indicted on additional illegal weapons charges.

Two others were charged in earlier indictments and were not included in the revised indictments. They were Lavon T. Hanson,

45, of Opheim, Montana; and Cornelius J. Veldhuizen, 59, of Wood-stock, Minnesota. Both were charged with bank and mail fraud. Veldhuizen was also charged with assisting federal fugitives to avoid arrest.

"These charges are extremely complex, involving interrelated activities and charges," U.S. Attorney Matteucci told reporters. "They can now be prosecuted properly with the cooperative effort of these state and federal investigative agencies." She cited the Montana Department of Justice's Criminal Investigation Bureau and the Internal Revenue Service's Criminal Investigation Division for joining the FBI in developing the complicated cases.

Shortly after the indictments were opened, Agent Canady told Connie and me that we would have to testify. As the case was being developed we waited without further word from the U.S. prosecutor's office.

Judge Anderson appointed attorneys for all the defendants, but they denounced the court and refused to cooperate with their court-appointed counsel.

At every appearance throughout the legal process, the Freemen would disrupt court proceedings, until finally the judge ordered the defendants removed from the courtroom. The proceedings were videotaped and shown live via closed-circuit television in a holding area so the Freemen could witness what was going on in the court-room without disrupting the process.

Nothing would be routine in this case. The Freemen even refused to follow normal booking procedures. They would not stand still for mug shots, allow themselves to be fingerprinted, or even give their names to the jailers.

Because of their refusal to cooperate, the Freemen were denied all visitation and telephone privileges and, thus, were finally isolated from the outside world. They were held in their cells twenty-three hours a day without contact with other inmates at central eating facilities, with only one hour outside the cells for exercise.

More than six months after the arrests, most of the defendants remained jailed in Billings without bail, and the primary leaders continued to refuse to allow themselves to be booked or fingerprinted.

★ ★ ★

Now all the accused Freemen, not just the leaders, were jailed. There could be no possible reason for further delay in Connie's and my final payday from the Bureau.

I waited a day or two, hoping to hear from Tommie Canady that the "check was in the mail," or at least to get an invitation to come by the office and settle on an amount of final payment.

No check came in the mail, and no call came from the FBI office in Billings. Finally, a week after the siege ended, I phoned Agent Canady. He was not available and he did not return my call.

Connie and I wanted to leave Montana. Although the Freemen leadership was in jail, there were still more than one hundred other known Freemen and sympathizers in eastern Montana, including a fairly sizable group right in Billings.

We finally forced the issue and called Canady to tell him we were coming into the FBI office at the Western Federal Savings Building in downtown Billings.

When we drove up, we saw several agents standing around talking in the parking lot. Canady and his chief aide were among them.

Protocol would dictate that we wait to be invited to join the group, but by this time we were so angry we just pushed right into the conversation. Dirty looks were exchanged by all.

Canady motioned for Connie to get back into the car while he, his aide, and I talked. She was in no mood to be ordered around at that point because only the day before our pickup had been repossessed by goons from the finance company.

We gave a quick verbal report about the latest activities at the Freedom Center and talked briefly about the complicated Freemen trials. The agent said the Bureau had already copied most of the documents seized at Justus Township. We read later that the government lawyers were claiming it would take months to copy the "mountain" of material as an excuse to delay the proceedings. The first motion to delay was granted from June until October, an adequate time for the preparation of the case—and plenty of time to make sure the visiting national media left town and forgot the Freemen.

Connie indirectly opened the discussion about the Bureau's tardiness in getting our final payment, pointing out that we had now lost our transportation, too.

Canady again responded, "You've got a lawyer, don't you?"

Then Connie lowered the boom.

"I'm tired of all this crap," she snapped at the agents. "You've got the Freemen now, and I don't care anymore."

The agent just said okay.

"So when do we get our paycheck?" I asked.

"I told you before, after the trials," Canady answered.

This was the first time I had heard this excuse. Originally payment was due at the end of our first sixty days under cover. Then it was after the arrest of the Freemen leaders. Now it was after the trial!

I think the agent saw the storm coming in Connie's expression, because he quickly added, "I'll put in a little something for you now."

Canady's assistant chimed in, "How much do you think?"

Just to get a rise out of the agents, I said, "About $200,000."

Canady exploded. "We didn't agree to that!"

"Look, Tom," I said, "we need to get out of here. There are Freemen and militia members everywhere."

"I told you, after the trials," the agent insisted.

"That's not what you said before," I argued.

Our handler just glared at us.

Canady's aide mumbled something about new rules and said, "It's even getting hard for agents to get their own expenses paid."

Hearing the Bureau poor-mouthing was too much to tolerate. Mustering all my self-control, I placed my hand on Connie's arm and said, "Let's get out of here."

So we left empty-handed and returned to our apartment with vague promises about getting "some money" after the trials were over, which could be years in the future. Not even the "little something" promised by Canady was forthcoming.

Over the next two weeks one excuse followed another, until finally an angry Canady admitted the FBI had no intention of paying us the full amount of our "bonus."

"You don't think we'd agree to pay you $25,000 for two months' work, do you?"

I reminded him of his assurances, the handshakes, the promises to pay Connie the same rate. Connie became so enraged at what was now clearly becoming a betrayal that she said she could not deal with it anymore. She just wanted to take our children and run.

We couldn't flee town on a motorcycle, as we had from one narcotics bust gone awry years before. We had to get a settlement from the Bureau to move a whole family. We had furniture and a lifetime of the personal things a family collects.

Despite the new delay, I still believed the Bureau might sort this out. In all my years under cover for various government agencies, I had never run into such a blatant double-cross by any law enforcement group, especially the FBI.

I swallowed my anger and decided the best course was just to move my family out of harm's way. So we called again to plead for at least enough cash to get the family out of town. Connie even suggested that if the Bureau was going to take much more time to sort out this matter, we should voluntarily go into the federal witness protection program. Canady just laughed at her suggestion.

On June 24, 1996, we picked up our last cash payment of $2,000. I guess as far as Canady was concerned, that was the end of our undercover assignment, although he never gave us notification in writing, as our agreements stipulated.

Connie was so angry that I had to keep her from calling Jim Cleaver. I was sure I could work something out with Canady. After all, this was the Federal Bureau of Investigation of the United States. Despite its being a bit bureaucratic, I still held the agency in the highest esteem.

I met with Tommie alone at the Artspace coffee shop. I suggested that a partial payment now would get us safely out of town and, thus, out of his hair while he sorted out the details of the final payment.

"You didn't get them, we did," he said.

"What are you talking about now?" I was exasperated with what sounded like yet another ploy.

"The Bureau made the arrests, you didn't," the agent responded.

I was stunned by his cool, illogical excuse.

"What about the part that we'd get paid no matter if we got them or not?" I said.

"Nobody ever said that," Canady replied.

Then he said, "We've already paid you something like $16,000."

I pointed out that a good portion of the earlier payments had been to cover actual expenses incurred on behalf of the operation.

"Are you planning to include our expenses?" I asked.

"Absolutely, of course I am," said Canady.

I argued that we had a deal—whether he liked to admit it or not—to pay our expenses, plus $25,000 on top for two months, and that he had extended that agreement to Connie when she joined the operation and went under cover.

"We were actually inside the cabin at Roundup from late March 1995 until late August," I said, steadily staring the agent in the eyes. "Then we went back inside, physically at Cat Creek from April 1996, and at the Freedom Center until after the arrests in June."

I told him if we added it all up we were due well over $100,000.

"That's nonsense," he snarled. "That's what you wanted. Nobody ever agreed to it."

"Even if not, nobody ever disagreed, either. You just let us hang out there with our lives at risk, thinking we had a deal." I was becoming too angry to negotiate calmly.

"And what about your confirmation of the figure we stated?" I asked. "Your exact words were, 'That's far less than even one day of a siege would cost.' How the hell would I know what a day of a siege would cost the Bureau?"

FBI Agent Tommie Canady, only months from retirement, rose and walked stiffly from the coffee shop. This was late in July 1996. I was never again to meet in person with our handler.

I went back to the apartment and talked to Connie about the conversation. We spent a couple of days trying to calm down—we were furious and hurt by the betrayal. In the more than one year we had worked directly under Canady, we had shared a lot more with him than civilian operatives usually share with their handlers. We thought Tommie was more than an employer in the dirty business of domestic espionage. We thought he was also a friend.

We had gathered intelligence on one of the most costly frauds in the history of America and spent months with one of the most vicious criminal elements in the country. Throughout the year we received the highest praise for the value of our intelligence from every level of the Bureau.

Now, all of a sudden, we realized we were totally on our own— no cover, no backup, no money to get out of town, no chance of even getting our family into the witness protection program. Even the biggest thugs and most murderous gangsters turned by the Bureau are given that option.

By August 1996, we were broke. I began hocking personal items for cash. I ultimately hocked most of my gun collection, our major appliances, and other valuables. My 1990 pickup had been repossessed, so we didn't even have wheels to flee in the night.

We thought it could not get any worse, but again we were wrong. At least up until then, the Freemen inside and outside the Yellowstone County jail still had no clue that the FBI had agents inside the Freemen operation.

⋆　⋆　⋆

One evening Connie was watching a televised report of an appearance of the Freemen before a federal magistrate. I was puttering around in the kitchen when my wife let out a scream.

I rushed into the living room to catch the last part of a broadcast. A U.S. assistant district attorney was being interviewed about the day's court session.

The U.S. attorney's office had told the federal judge that wiretap information had been obtained based on affidavits from undercover agents the FBI had had inside the Freemen stronghold at Roundup back in mid-1995. The government had blown our cover in that thoughtless press conference. Ultimately, the government would have to turn over these tapes to defense attorneys on a motion for discovery of evidence.

The federal defender's office was demanding the tapes be produced immediately. The Justice Department was trying to get a court extension of time to reproduce the tapes, which we knew had already been reproduced. The government attorney said there were 675 hours of intercepted wire and oral communications gained through wiretaps between July 27, 1995, and June 13, 1996.

Connie and I had been the source of the Bureau's obtaining a wiretap order, and had signed affidavits in June 1995 on which the order was granted. The affidavits had already been turned over to the Freemen's defense lawyers in the mounds of documents released by the Justice Department.

The Freemen, still in jail and refusing to cooperate with their counsel, had been given access to these affidavits, but so far, because of the mountain of paperwork and their refusal to participate in the American judicial system, they apparently had not yet come across the names of Dale and Connie Jakes.

Now it was only a matter of time until our identities were revealed. I had a sick feeling in the pit of my stomach. All I could think about was Tarantula Eyes and his story of placing the corpse of a murdered black girl in the passenger compartment of some innocent guy's airplane.

I called Canady at his office the next day and asked what the hell he was doing revealing that the Bureau had agents inside the Freemen operation.

"My God, what have you done? You didn't even warn us this was coming!" I said. "We were promised when we signed the affidavits they would not be used until we were safely out of harm's way."

Canady claimed he did not realize the U.S. attorney's office planned to reveal the existence of the affidavits.

I said fine, and asked him what he was going to do about it. "You're going to have everybody after us now," I said.

"Much of this evidence is so singular it can't point to anyone but you," the agent conceded. "Just be alert, be cautious. Stay at home."

Angered by the FBI's nonchalance and the Bureau's continued failure to fulfill its financial obligations, we decided to approach Montana Senator Max Baucus. The senator had been active in working with Washington and local Montana officials early in the standoff to make sure there was not another bloodbath. He had personally gone to Jordan during the first days to try to calm the waters.

We were referred to an aide in Senator Baucus's Billings office who took our complaint about the FBI's reneging on our payment. We signed a secrecy agreement, and the senator's office soon launched an investigation on our behalf. But the aide cautioned us that the process could take a long time.

A few days later we received a letter from Senator Baucus which read: "Thank you for contacting my office concerning payment for your confidential services.

"I have asked my Billings office to investigate this matter and they will be responding to you as soon as they have more information."

The letter was signed in a big, bold scrawl, Max Baucus.

Connie and I also went to the U.S. attorney's office and complained that the premature leak of our affidavit had put us at great risk. A federal civil attorney in the office sympathized and, after hearing our story, said we definitely had a civil case for recovery from the Bureau. The lawyer also said such a civil case would take considerable time and money. We had neither.

Several days later I got a call from Agent Canady. His voice was calm, but I could tell he was extremely angry.

"Dale," he said slowly. "No matter what you do, it's not going to change anything. And if you keep this up, you'll never work the undercover trade again."

This was one of the last conversations I was to have with our FBI handler. After this veiled threat, Canady would have other agents in the Billings office call and, on one occasion, drop by our safe-house apartment on which the Bureau had long since ceased making rent payments.

★ CHAPTER 37 ★

A few days after the conversation with Agent Canady, Connie and I were watching the Summer Olympics on television. Domestic terrorism was about to explode once again in the faces of Americans. Along with our fellow citizens and much of the world, we were rocked by the explosion in Centennial Olympic Park. This latest act of terrorism in America, coming immediately after the horrifying loss of lives on TWA Flight 800, was doubly hard for my family to watch.

We had been so close to the violence threatened by the Freemen and the more fanatical elements in the militia movement that these tragic events seemed like part of our own nightmare. Although no clues had linked the TWA explosion to any terrorist group—foreign or domestic—the Bureau's spokesman repeatedly referred to a terrorist bomb or missile as two of the three possible causes for the disaster.

There was no doubt in anyone's mind that the bombing at the Olympic Games was an act of domestic terrorism. The news media suddenly showed interest, recounting all the hate crimes of recent months, including the militia bombings and robberies and the Klan-like arsons against black churches.

On August 24, 1996, the front page of the *New York Times* finally warned the country of what Connie and I had known for so long, and what the Federal Bureau of Investigation still refused to acknowledge. The headline read:

TERRORISM NOW GOING HOMESPUN
AS BOMBINGS IN THE U.S. SPREAD

I had heard cynical newsmen say, "It ain't so unless the *New York Times* says it's so." And now the *Times* was saying it was so.

The article pulled together small stories from over several months that told of incidents committed all across the country by different militia groups that Connie and I had encountered in our fourteen months under cover for the FBI. For us, it was like reading a home-town paper, but the story was about the new nationwide phenome-non of American terrorism.

And still the government just didn't get it.

In Congress, the president's request for stronger antiterrorism measures was talked to death. After a summit with White House and congressional leaders, GOP officials beholden to the National Rifle Association decided what was needed was another task-force study on terrorism issues in general.

House Majority Leader Dick Armey said, "I understand the sense of urgency the whole nation feels. But it's always prudent to take things in an orderly fashion."

That's approximately what the government had been telling the citizens of Garfield, Petroleum, and Musselshell Counties during their three nightmare years of terrorism at the hands of the Freemen.

The gun lobby wanted removed from the antiterrorism legisla-tion any control of explosives through the introduction of tracers, called taggants, into powder and other explosive chemicals.

I had worked around black powder and other explosives all my life and knew that taggants were harmless and in no way affected the efficacy of legitimate gunpowders.

The American Civil Liberties Union got in the act and wanted to block any expansion of law enforcement wiretap capabilities. Con-nie and I were fully aware of the problems the Bureau and other lawmen had in keeping up with highly mobile and sophisticated criminals using modern computers and cellular phones.

The Bureau, the ATF, and local and state criminal investigators are hamstrung by thirty-year-old technology and techniques while being forced to do battle with multinational narcocriminals with jet fleets and globe-spanning banking systems. Our federal agents and local police now face well-armed domestic terrorists who are linked by sophisticated, advanced communications networks. Lawmen are not only outgunned, but now they are also outcommunicated.

As angry as we were about the Bureau's delay in delivering our promised pay, we were more alarmed at what was happening to law enforcement in our country. Even with the hardship and potential danger to my family caused by the delay of payment, right or wrong, I maintained my faith in the Federal Bureau of Investigation. The Bureau, as monolithic as it has become, is still America's first line of defense and best hope for the protection of the orderly, law-abiding society we all cherish. I had to believe that eventually the Bureau would do the right thing—after all, if the FBI fails America, what institution of law enforcement can we trust?

That is not to say that we weren't mad as hell. We were—and I think with good and ample reason.

During the coming days, as we scrambled to figure out a way to get our family out of Billings, Connie and I spent a lot of time trying to understand how our situation had gotten out of hand. For the first time since we fled the drug operation in California in the late 1980s, we confronted our own motives for choosing to spend so much of our lives as undercover operatives.

Why had we voluntarily chosen to go back into that life of extreme depravity and often real physical danger? Under the circumstances, would we do it all again? After experiencing the bureaucratic snafu and broken promises, did we still care?

Pondering these questions, Connie and I conducted our own personal debriefing about the Freemen undercover operation.

The bottom line was, we did still care; we would accept our responsibility and do it again, even knowing the consequences.

A long time ago, I heard something that has always stuck with me: Evil triumphs when good men do nothing. Throughout our undercover careers, both Connie and I were motivated by this belief.

And certainly that adage was proven true when we encountered the terrorism of the Freemen against the good people of Winnett. Fortunately or unfortunately, we happened to be in the direct path of an incredible series of evil events unfolding at that place, at that time. And we happened to be the only people with the unique qualifications to do something about it.

As private citizens we had the responsibility to act, to the best of our ability. Because of our personal circumstances we could not have been effective without the financial support promised by the Bureau to dedicate full time to the operation. As former career undercover operatives, we had a right to expect to be paid for our services by the Bureau. So while the financial considerations might have been secondary, they were essential to our being able to participate.

Our personal postoperation debriefing was a time of soul-searching and ambivalence.

To some degree we could empathize with the disillusioned men and women we had met inside the ranks of the militias—certainly not the hatemongers, but those real victims of the shattered American dream. Nevertheless, those who had allowed themselves to be duped by their fanatical leaders were, and are, just plain wrong.

As we had done so often in the past, we turned to the Bible to try to understand our role and responsibility in this troubling incident.

The Book of Romans had given us guidance during this particular operation. As ancient as the teaching in the verses is, the message we found there—particularly in Romans 13:3 and 13:7—seemed to us like reading a how-to manual for this case.

One admonition in particular stood out, as we read it again together that night:

> For rulers are not a terror to good works, but to the evil.
> Do that which is good, and thou shalt have praise . . .
> Render therefore to all their dues; tribute to whom tribute is due; custom to whom custom; fear to whom fear; honour to whom honour . . .

It doesn't take a Bible scholar to understand the clear meaning of this passage. If a person really believes the Good Book, clearly civil governments are ordained of God, even if run by men who aren't necessarily good or wise in their administration. Our government, with all its warts, is still the best yet devised, and absolutely necessary to restrain the criminal elements of human society. The Bible says specifically that Christians must be law-abiding citizens of the government under which they live. That means paying tribute (taxes), obeying the custom (the laws of the land), rendering fear (support for those appointed to carry out the public duty), and giving honor (allegiance) to those we elect.

That's not to say as citizens we can't use the established system to fight for lower taxes, change the laws, protest abuse of power, and, ultimately, if our appointed or elected leaders act like bums, kick them out.

These verses of Romans, along with our strong belief in the U.S. Constitution and the Bill of Rights, gave us the strength we needed at one of the darkest moments we experienced in the operation.

The Freemen operation could easily have made us as cynical as some of the militiamen we had been working against.

But our reading of the Bible is unlike the same book misquoted by the false prophets calling themselves Freemen and all the other supremacists and racists of America's hate movements.

Many of the militias springing up around the country are misled by these fanatics.

Connie and I talked about this last job almost as a calling. The Christian God we knew in our lives had sustained us throughout this ordeal. And we had a strong feeling that the God who guided the original Founders to declare "one Nation, under God" was directly involved, too.

"The God I know would not want the teachings of the Bible so perverted," Connie said.

"Nor would God's servants—that includes our fed bosses and us—stand for this criminal activity without some response," I added.

In our continuing review of the operation, we also felt ambivalent over the money situation.

We reckoned that perhaps we should have gotten out early in the operation at the first hint that the agent running our operation could not or would not deliver on the financial commitment. But if we had just split, the people of Winnett and the other small towns in the area would have continued to live under a cloud of terror. Even months after we went inside the Freemen operation, and with our best efforts to bring the case to a close with the arrest of the terrorist leaders, the bureaucratic delays were insufferable.

Once we were inside there seemed no good way to turn back. It is not my nature or Connie's to walk away from a job unfinished. Perhaps our dogged determination is driven by a little too much pride, or a bit of patriotic overzealousness on our part.

Just as we had a modicum of empathy for some of the rank and file members of the militias, misguided though they might be, we also understood the extreme pressure under which many of the field agents of the bureaus have to work.

"These agencies have an impossible task," Connie pointed out during our introspection on the operation. We talked about funding reductions and manpower shortages faced by the federal law enforcement agencies.

At the same time budgets are being cut, sophisticated new crimes are on the rise, and every stripe of criminal is coming out of the woodwork. The Freemen were just the latest example of a unique type of criminal using biblical and patriotic rhetoric to cover antisocial conduct.

Connie said the most worrisome thing she had encountered during the operation was the stark contrast between the agents on this job compared to those G-men we had known in the past.

"They [the FBI agents] are so frustrated and confused that they are to the point of believing they are at war with the American people," she lamented. "It becomes a vicious cycle. The people sense this in the conduct of the agents and they begin to mistrust them, too."

Even while demanding that such agencies as the FBI, DEA, and ATF return to their historic roles as public servants, the public—ourselves included—must continue to support law enforcement at the federal, state, and local levels, or only chaos will result.

After taking stock of our situation, we cried a little together, prayed a lot over it, and put the experience into our bag of memories, satisfied that we had been right and justified to get involved again and to see the operation through to the end.

Connie and I had one other important belief that sustained us in those times. God wants his children to put feet to their prayers; and considering that our situation was probably approaching its highest level of danger of the whole operation, we did just that.

While we resolved to continue every effort to hold the Bureau accountable for the payday promised by its representative Agent Canady, we had to do whatever was necessary to protect our family.

★　★　★

Daily existence became an exercise in tactical living. We had always kept a low profile wherever we lived, but now, with exposure to the scores of Freemen members and sympathizers possible at any time, we really ducked our heads.

Billings is not a very large place, only a little more than a hundred thousand people. But it is as good a small city as a person could find to hide out in. Since half the town is built up on a high mesa and the rest along the valley of the Yellowstone River, there are really two communities. So we developed a pattern of not developing a pattern. We wouldn't shop for groceries in the same store for weeks on end. We bought gasoline for the old clunker we were driving at different stations, too.

Our children had to play, but we made sure that one or the other of us could see them at all times. There was a park across from our apartment complex, and from our window we could keep an eye on them. We never let the kids go to the apartment pool, which was out of sight, unless one of us could accompany them.

We set up double-blind mail drops. We already had our unlisted apartment phone billed to names twice-removed from us. Our cell phone, which was our lifeline—the children had to have a cell phone with them at all times—was in yet another name.

Our few close friends in town, some of whom Connie had known since childhood, knew little about us except that we were doing something for the government.

Finally, toward the end, we had to go to a select few friends and tell them about our situation. There were some lawmen—federal agency guys (non-FBI) and state officers, too—in other parts of the country that could be counted on, but I hesitated to call upon them until it was clearly a matter of life or death.

I still had no indication we were under suspicion by the Freemen, but I decided to run out a test line.

A big rally was planned to raise a defense fund for the jailed Freemen. I called the Freedom Center on Duck Creek Road and volunteered to help. After explaining to Parsons that I had been out of town on business for a few weeks, the center operator welcomed me back and gave no hint that I had been made.

We regretted our offer to help with the rally almost immediately, but having volunteered we had to follow through. I was assigned to pick up an old flatbed truck to be used for a stage and to rig up the sound system.

I made sure the truck was late to the rally, held in Pioneer Park in north Billings on a Saturday. A neo-Nazi skinhead band and a tiny cluster of Freemen supporters were waiting in the park when we arrived.

I also made sure the sound system was inoperable.

Whenever a curious group of citizens drifted over, the band would strike up some horrid, heavy-metal hate tune. The strangers would hear one lyric or take one look at the group and say, "Ugh, it's them," and leave.

The rally was a complete flop. Hardly anyone showed up and no funds were raised.

In the weeks since the standoff ended I had grown a beard and long hair, which I wore in a ponytail. The Freemen I had worked with over the past months had always known me as clean-shaven so, except for those who knew me best, I passed unnoticed.

Following the scene in the park, a woman crusader for the right-wing cause who had been staying at the Freedom Center invited Connie and me to dinner at a local restaurant. I'll call her the Blue Orchid, since her real name sounds like a flower. But she is no flower. She tried to recruit us as part of her traveling team, which was going around the country in an effort to organize the more radical hate groups into a cohesive strike force.

Blue Orchid told us that under the banner of Christian Identity the more dedicated groups—including the Klan, the Priests of Phineas, the Aryan Republican Army, skinheads, the militias' phantom cells, and other neo-Nazi groups—were beginning to unite. The Freemen standoff in Montana had been the catalyst that finally convinced these organizations they needed a more cohesive structure.

"They will maintain their secret identities," Blue Orchid told us. "But we will provide a system to coordinate efforts the next time we are confronted by the jackboots."

Connie and I pretended to be interested in her job offer, but reported Blue Orchid to the Bureau immediately. We were told the FBI was aware of her groups' activities and that the Bureau had been watching her for some months.

"She's a very dangerous person," a Bureau man warned me in a telephone conversation. "We know all about her. I'd suggest you stay clear of her and her associates."

By midsummer 1996, we had exhausted all our savings and hocked everything of value—even the kids' video movies and Connie's treasured stereo entertainment center. Since we could not commit to a job at a single, traceable location in Billings, all our planning had to be long distance. I even turned down a job managing a furniture store after Connie and I debated the risks versus the need for income. I would have loved the work and the normalcy but, needless to say, our physical safety won the argument.

While my telephone contacts were still fairly good within the right-wing groups, I continued to stumble onto bits of troubling information. In this business rumors are often more valuable than official statements, which are most likely to be calculated to deceive or divert investigators. But then, that's sort of like mainstream politics, too.

So, although we clearly had been cut off from our employment with the Bureau, I still had to get new information to law enforcement officials who could do something about it.

Unfortunately, that responsibility rests with the Bureau, and Canady had made it clear he had nothing to say to us.

I was beginning to believe that Connie's earlier half-joke about our handling agent never getting authorization to employ us at the fee schedule we had agreed upon might be true. Because of my years of good experience working on assignments with the Bureau, I simply could not take that possibility seriously. And I knew

Canady wasn't running a rogue operation, because too many other high-level officials were involved. But perhaps he had become overzealous and let his promises overreach his authority. Even if that were the case, it made no difference to us. Canady was the Bureau's designated rep, and the Bureau would ultimately be obligated to fulfill his commitments.

However, we soon learned, to our amazement, that we were not the only victims of the Billings FBI office's welshing. In conversations around town and in the several communities affected by the standoff, we began to hear complaints that the Bureau was late paying the bills it had amassed.

Rental agencies and car dealerships had not been paid for the fleets, equipment, and services they provided the FBI from March through June 1996. We heard about restaurants, cafes, mom-and-pop motels, and small stores where FBI chits went unredeemed. Private contractors who had dozed roads, small utility companies who tailored service, and dozens of others who contributed goods and services to the Bureau had not been paid for their efforts.

I joked to Connie that one way to minimize the outrageous cost of the siege was for the Bureau to simply ignore the bills. But in our case the breach of agreement was more than just a financial problem. If we could not find the means to get out of town, it would very possibly become a life-threatening problem.

We were now existing on our wits and a prayer, and looking for any way to get out of Billings. In September, I was shopping at a supermarket when I heard a man behind me call my name. I spun around to face a Freeman I had not seen since the siege ended. After a quick study of his face I breathed a sigh of relief that he showed no malice.

We chatted about the situation at the Yellowstone County jail, where the arrested Freemen were still raising havoc with the justice system. Then he told me that jailing the leaders of the Freemen movement would change nothing. There were plenty of others to take their place in other groups.

"The fight's going to be taken right to their front door now," the man boasted. "New York City is going up in November."

I tried to get more details without sounding like a cop administering the third degree, but learned only that he had talked to an interstate truck driver from western Montana recently. The driver, a radical-militia-group soldier, had been in a meeting on one of his cross-country runs and been told that a group was planning a major bombing incident in the Big Apple. It seems the word along the line was that the "true believers" were fed up with the inaction by the moderates in the militias. The hard-liners were splitting off from those units unwilling to declare war.

What better way to announce their presence than by a big demonstration attack in the one place where the media and the world would get the message loudest and clearest—New York City.

I didn't have any way of verifying the story, but with the prospect of lives at stake, I had to get word to the Bureau.

At about that time, FBI agent Robinson, who had been Canady's aide during our operation, paid a suspicious call to our apartment. He had a check for $63, which he said was for some unpaid expense item we had turned in months before.

Connie sarcastically asked him, "What about the $145,000 you owe us?" He blushed and said he knew nothing about that.

Clearly, Robinson had been sent on a fishing expedition to determine what we planned to do about our complaint. And he was not comfortable with the assignment. But I had to get word about the New York City rumor to the Bureau, just in the event there was any truth to it at all.

I said, "Well, let me give you a little going-away present," and I told the agent everything I had heard about the threatened New York City bombing. Of course, it didn't happen in November 1996, as my source had warned. Maybe it was a deliberate plant, but the Bureau needed to know that the radical militia groups were now talking about moving up their terrorism a few notches from the rural areas of the South, Northwest, and Midwest to the commercial center of America.

Almost immediately after the visit from the agent, I had a telephone conversation with another contact in the Freemen community. My main motive for staying in touch with the radicals I knew around Billings was to keep an ear to the rail in case a freight train was headed down the tracks toward me and my family. So, I made periodic calls to former acquaintances.

This time I picked up some specific intelligence involving members of the Priests of Phineas, the frightening terrorist cell described to me by Tarantula Eyes.

There had been another bombing of a Planned Parenthood facility, followed by another bank robbery in Spokane, Washington, in July. My source told me that a whole series of such attacks was planned for the Northwest as part of a major fund-raising drive to finance a nationwide organizational effort by various hate groups. Also during the spring and summer, the Midwest had been ravaged by more than a score of especially brutal armed bank robberies, which authorities had described as politically motivated.

My source told me that the Priests of Phineas were definitely running the show, and that a terrorist cell of at least five members was operating out of the Hayden Lake, Idaho, safe haven run by the Aryan Nations.

I could get this new information to the FBI at Spokane, because I had a longtime trusted associate with the Spokane police department from my undercover narco days fifteen years before. I knew they had formed a local-federal task force to bird-dog the case since a series of bank robberies and the bombing of a Spokane newspaper office the previous April.

I contacted the Spokane officer, who was no longer working under cover, and he referred me to a Spokane-based FBI agent named Mark Thundercloud. I called the agent and was warmly and gratefully received. Thundercloud actually called me on a cell phone as he tromped around in the ruins of the latest terrorist bombing in Spokane. I told him everything I knew about the Priests of Phineas—basically the same information I had given the Billings office during the Freemen siege—plus the specifics I had picked up about the current wave of terrorism.

Several weeks later, on October 9, the Bureau and local lawmen swooped in on three men parked at a Yakima, Washington, convenience store. The men were arrested for the robberies and bombings. Although the terrorists would not cooperate with authorities, the task force did verify their links to the Phineas brotherhood. The three—Charles Barbee, Robert Berry, and Jay Merrell—were charged and later indicted for armed bank robberies and bombings.

At the time of the arrest in Yakima, lawmen seized enough military-type weaponry and explosives to arm a dozen more terrorists. According to my source, the manpower to use these weapons was in place, and the loss of the arms and explosives was no setback, since there were plenty more on the black market where that cache came from.

This bit of intelligence would be the last I was able to glean from my sources in Montana because the information gate was suddenly—and frighteningly—slammed in our faces late in September.

My tripwires picked up a hint that we might be under suspicion by some of the Freemen who remained at large in eastern Montana. A week after the information was passed about the Spokane case, my alarm bells went off. There was that faint smell of singed hair an experienced CI senses when he or she is standing too close to the fire.

A Freeman who had been a confidant for some time was suddenly cool in his conversation, but still wanted to know how he could locate me. He said he had some papers I might be interested in seeing, but would only bring them over to my house. I made an excuse and declined his offer.

A day or so later, Connie and I were coming back from our mail drop when we spotted two Freemen in a pickup approaching from the opposite direction. They recognized us, but we pretended not to notice them. After we passed, I turned to look through the back window. They had made a rubber-burning U-turn a block behind us and were coming up fast.

I told Connie to lose them, and she maneuvered our old clunker expertly and rapidly. She might as well have been driving one of James Bond's customized numbers. Connie was always an expert driver and especially adept at losing a tail. I think her aggressive driving skills are a combination of steel nerves laced with an utter delight for crushing trash cans in narrow alleys. At any rate, she easily lost the Freemen in the pickup.

But it was now definitely time to go, whether we had the cash to move our family or not. I got into high gear, bit the bullet, and called on some very close and confidential friends.

We left Billings at four in the morning, pulling a twelve-foot U-Haul trailer with everything movable we had left in the world. Our friends drove an escort in front and behind us for nearly a hundred miles as we headed west.

On one of our many brief stopovers as we fled across the Rockies, I called back to Billings and was told that inquiries had been made about our whereabouts. Our hidden life and cover in Billings had been partially blown, through no fault of our own. Because of the financial circumstances forced by the Bureau's nonpayment, an unavoidable link to us—the pawn shops—led to our exposure. We were told that some unidentified men were inquiring about buying some of the possessions we had hocked to survive. The inquisitors were demanding they be given our address so they could clear their purchase of our things in person.

✳ ✳ ✳

We had a major role in bagging the bad guys.

And one of our greatest rewards for going under cover against the Freemen is knowing that our friends in Winnett, Montana, can go to bed in peace each night. But our government's refusal to follow through on financial promises or help relocate our family has left us abandoned, turning slowly in the wind, at great daily risk.

It didn't use to be this way in America—and certainly not in our previous dealings with the Federal Bureau of Investigation.

Watching a televised press conference of the FBI fiasco over the handling of the hero of the Olympic Park bombing, Connie and I had strong reason to sympathize with Richard Jewell. We, too, had had our almost heroic image of the Bureau badly tarnished.

And that is a really sad and maybe even tragic situation for Americans. I am afraid the Bureau and other federal law enforcement agencies will soon need us—freelance civilian undercover agents or just plain citizens—more than ever.

As surely as my family is sitting in the mountains with an eye always on the narrow road leading up to our hideaway, a new war has begun. The law enforcement agencies are going to need a great many civilian eyes and ears if they are to have any chance of winning this one.

Connie and I and the kids are doing just fine right now.

We are survivors, and while we are temporarily on the run under cover again, this time we are working for the most clearly understandable of all motives—to stay alive. We are determined to get the paycheck due us from the Federal Bureau of Investigation so we can disappear and start over again somewhere in the United States.

We want to come in from the cold, one last time. And this time, I have promised Connie, it will be forever.

Maybe.

★ AFTERWORD ★

The armed confrontation between the Freemen of Montana and the United States was not the end of the conflict between the ideologies of white supremacy and democracy. The arrest of the Freemen near Jordan, Montana, was not even the end of that chapter in this tragic saga. A complicated and expensive ordeal in the federal courts will snarl the legal system for years to come. As the Montana Freemen leaders and a handful of their followers waited in jail without bond for their trials in federal court, other similar separatist groups continued a virtual war against the American way of life and system of government.

On November 16, 1996, the 960-acre ranch that was infamously known as Justus Township was sold at public auction for $150,000. American taxpayers had technically spent as much as $50 million to retake this tiny piece of real estate from a band of insurrectionists.

The twenty-four Freemen arrested during the eighty-one-day standoff at Brusett, Montana, were brought, chained and defiant, into a federal courtroom in Billings on February 28, 1997, to begin the long process of the criminal prosecution on scores of felony charges. The day marked the fourth anniversary of the ATF raid on the Branch Davidian compound in Waco that left four federal agents dead.

The usual decorous atmosphere of federal court proceedings was continually disrupted by shouting Freemen who refused to acknowledge the authority of the United States to try them. This tone of anarchy was set earlier when the first Freeman arrested in the standoff was tried and convicted by a U.S. District Court jury in Raleigh, North Carolina.

On February 19, 1997, Freeman Russell Dean Landers and a Freemen sympathizer, James Vincent Wells, both of North Carolina, were found guilty of bank fraud, mail fraud, conspiracy, and intimidation of federal agents. Landers and Wells were convicted of cashing hundreds of thousands of dollars in worthless Freemen warrants.

Some of the proceeds were used to purchase a Chevrolet Suburban and a luxury recreational vehicle, which they delivered to the Freemen of Montana. Testimony at the trial revealed the vehicles were part of a battle fleet to be used to kidnap government officials in Montana. Landers faces 31 years in federal prison and fines of $1.5 million. Wells, who was convicted of additional charges not involving the Freemen, faces 104 years in prison and fines of $4.25 million.

At the height of their power, the Freemen and their supporters and sympathizers in the more radical militias never exceeded a tiny percent of the Montana population. Connie and I still find it astounding that such a small group could cause such chaos. We found the vast majority of Montanans to be truly patriotic, churchgoing, and family-oriented Americans.

I read a report estimating that more than 300,000 Americans are actively engaged in or affiliated with the various so-called patriotic militias, and that between 3,000 and 10,000 belong to the deadly phantom cells, whose members will bomb, burn, and kill for their perverted ideology.

The intelligence we gathered while under cover for the FBI revealed that militias are well organized and operating in at least forty-six states. Even if many of these members are not racists or antigovernment militants, they still pose a threat to Americans and our democratic way of life by providing financial aid, comfort, and even sanctuary to their more dangerous cohorts.

A review of only a few of the incidents occurring during the first two months of 1997 provides a frightening picture of the scope of the problem:

Two bomb blasts an hour apart on January 16, 1997, injured seven people at an Atlanta family-planning clinic. A few weeks later, on February 21, two powerful bombs exploded, injuring five people at an Atlanta gay and lesbian nightclub. In both these bombings the second explosive device was set to kill or maim law enforcement agents and rescuers responding to the first bombs. A group calling itself the Army of God claimed credit for these bombings.

In January 1997, ten of the original twelve members of the Arizona Viper Militia pleaded guilty to reduced charges stemming from their arrest in July 1996 in a plot to blow up federal buildings in the Phoenix area.

Also in January, federal juries in Missouri sentenced fifteen members of an antigovernment group to prison terms ranging from two to seven years, for filing bogus liens against public officials. Leaders of the group were trained by the Montana Freemen.

In early February, pipe bombs were sent to federal employees in San Diego.

On February 15, two gunmen with ties to white-supremacist groups opened fire on an Ohio highway patrolman and sheriff's deputy after a routine traffic violation stop. Fortunately, the officers escaped injury in the running gun battle that ensued. A nationwide all-points bulletin was issued for the men and their suspected accomplices. Authorities said quick arrests were unlikely because the men probably were being harbored in the network of hate groups.

On February 18, the leader of a white-supremacist cell admitted in a federal court in Pittsburgh that his organization was engaged in armed bank robberies to fund domestic terrorism. Five members of that Pennsylvania unit were charged with seven of twenty-two Midwest bank robberies attributed to the Aryan Republican Army.

During the opening session of the 1997 Texas legislature, Governor George W. Bush declared a state of emergency because of the hundreds of false liens filed by groups in the state against public and private property. Texas Attorney General Dan Morales had called for legislation to crack down on separatist groups using phony court judgments, fraudulent warrants, and bogus liens to disrupt the legal and banking system in the state. A number of other state legislatures were considering similar new laws to cope with rapidly spreading financial terrorism.

In May 1997, a six-day siege between Texas lawmen and a right-wing separatist group calling itself the Republic of Texas ended in the arrest of faction leader Richard McLaren and five of his followers. More than a hundred lawmen, led by the Texas Rangers, surrounded the terrorists in a remote compound at Fort Davis after the group shot up a neighbor's home and kidnapped the man and his wife. The couple had protested the Republic's years of paper terrorism and threats of violence against citizens in the resort community. One armed insurrectionist was killed. Another, with ties to the Freemen movement, escaped. Indictments alleging $1.8 billion in bank and mail fraud, resulting from schemes like those designed by the Montana Freemen, were returned against the Republic of Texas members arrested at the siege and in a network spread across the state.

Early in 1997, the Federal Bureau of Investigation acknowledged that the rapidly growing number of cases of domestic terrorism had prompted the assignment of more agents to its counterterrorism units. The Bureau quietly created a new section to deal exclusively with the growing phenomenon of American terrorist activities.

The pivotal role of the Montana Freemen in coordinating various antigovernment forces was revealed in a copyrighted report in the *Dallas Morning News* on January 11, 1997. An investigative reporter, Thomas G. Watts, linked federal and state criminal cases in twenty-three states to the Freemen of Montana.

Connie and I find no joy in the accuracy of the intelligence we provided the Bureau that warned of a nationwide conspiracy. As Americans who love our country, we are heartsick at what is occurring. There can be no pleasure for us in saying to a skeptical bureaucracy, "We told you so."

Frustrated as we are with the FBI's early handling of the Freemen case and the ongoing dispute over our pay, we still recognize the urgency for a coordinated national strategy to combat this crisis.

A vital first step will have to be the acknowledgment at the highest levels of government—in the White House, the Justice Department, and Congress—that a real and present danger actually exists. The Federal Bureau of Investigation—the nation's preeminent law enforcement body—must be overhauled to gain the support of the American people. After so many problems and mistakes, the Bureau faces the difficult task of earning back the trust once accorded it.

But as it has been throughout America's history, the real solution to our nation's problems must come from the people. We believe Americans will have to take back their communities from the hate groups and from the government bureaucracies.

The maintenance of our democracy can and will be accomplished not by force of arms, but by a renewal of the American spirit in the countryside and communities and cities everywhere—one church, one voting precinct, one school, one city hall at a time. And it is going to take an active and invigorated program of support and cooperation with our local law enforcement agencies at the city, county, state, and national levels.

Some citizens are already challenging hate groups operating in their towns through the formation of fight-back organizations. In dozens of towns and cities where hate crimes are prevalent, ordinary citizens have bravely banded together to say they won't tolerate bigotry, hate, and intimidation in their communities. Dozens of hate-watch groups have been created on the Internet to alert the public about the activities of the more radical organizations.

The United States of America was founded on faith in God and the belief that every person has a voice and an active, vital part in the whole community. We are a nation of people who base our way of life on the moral teachings of the Bible. Americans have and are still willing to stand up for what is right—not only collectively as a community, but also individually in our own personal lives. We have the freedom to make a difference.

Members of the militias, who expressed no sympathy even as they saw the bloody and broken bodies of children and women being pulled from the bombed federal building in Oklahoma City, are not going to suddenly have an epiphany. From our personal association with the hate groups, we are certain that a well-organized, linked, and deadly conspiracy is out there waiting to strike.

The validity of the intelligence we gathered at the cabin in Roundup and in our subsequent undercover work for the FBI was chillingly affirmed when the Klanwatch Project of the Southern Poverty Law Center issued its 1997 report on hate groups in America. The data gathered by the center for law enforcement agencies, entitled "Two Years After: The Patriot Movement Since Oklahoma City," warned of a rapid increase in more violent militias. Klanwatch said at least 858 so-called patriot groups were active in all fifty states. Of the 380 armed militias identified, the report noted that 101 were linked to white-supremacist and anti-Semitic organizations, and had developed a highly sophisticated nationwide intelligence network. It also warned that 112 common-law courts were operating in thirty-four states, waging a war of paper terrorism through the use of phony financial claims and bogus instruments.

The report concluded, "The patriot movement is firmly entrenched in this country. A winnowing process has taken place since Oklahoma City. While casual adherents have abandoned the cause, new groups have been formed to take their place. What remains are true believers who are isolated from the political mainstream and committed to an extreme antigovernment agenda."

Only an active, aware citizenry can stop them.

Also from our personal experience, we are positive that the right people in the federal government are aware of the danger. But they are either cowed by political expediency or too smug to challenge the status quo until the bombs start bursting. Only the people can change the complacency of our elected and appointed leaders.

As surely as America has now learned the term *American terrorism*, we will be hearing more from these false prophets and traitor patriots again and again in the future. Every American, regardless of race, creed, or color, is a potential victim of the paranoid members of the separatists and white-supremacist movement. Unless the ordinary citizen recognizes the danger and assumes his or her responsibility, the nation will surely face an escalation of American terrorism as we move toward the millennium year 2000.

★ APPENDIX ★

FREE [man] NEWSLETTER

"for those who have eyes to see and ears to hear"

May 1995
Vol.1
Issue 1

Non domestic mailing location
C/O 245 Johnny's Coal Road
Roundup Montana state, U.S. of A.
["without the United States"]
Ph. [406] 323-2214
Fax. [406] 323-3454

Editor comments

This is our first attempt at putting the research of the "Law" both **God's and man's,** compiled by various "freeman characters" over the past several years, together, in the form of a newsletter. The main objective being to inform the American People of the "HIDDEN TRUTH," so they may develop an understanding of the solution to the problems facing our country today. We feel that everyone knows that there are a million problems within the so called government, thus this letter will not dwell on the problem unless we have a solution "in law."

The "Freeman" characters contributing to the articles in this newsletter are not lawyers, however, they do offer free assistance to anyone who wishes to study and learn the truth for themselves. Because of the complexity and the amount of research materials required to teach the laws and codes, instruction is only offered in house, on a one on one basis with private parties. Please call or write for further information.

This first issue will be an introduction of a general nature, to the research work by several "Freeman" characters who over the past several years have uncovered massive fraud in our so called government. Future issues will attempt to concentrate on one or two particular subjects or problems and remedies.

Your comments and suggestions are invited.

Publication Dates

Monthly, at this time. Response may require additional publications.

Subscription Motto

To none will we deny, delay, or sell justice, or right. [Yet, a man is worthy of his hire.]
This newsletter will be totally funded on voluntary contributions.

Greetings

It is a little known fact that both governments and lawyers use words of art, capitalization, and punctuation to change the meaning and/or intent of mans laws ,codes, and/or statutes. In this letter we will show how this has been done in the Montana Code Annotated [M.C.A.] , to hide the truth in the law from the masses. For the readers from other States, we are sure that diligent research will prove that this same unlawful practice has been in existence for some time.

At this time we will cover some definitions which will be used in this and future issues of our newsletter.

What is a "Freeman"	[1] one who enjoys liberty; or who is not subject to the will of another.
	[2] one who enjoys or is entitled to a franchise or peculiar privilege [Noah Webster dictionary 1828] (peculiar - Gods peculiar treasure - Holy Scriptures Ex.19:5)
	[1] A person in the possession and enjoyment of all the civil and political rights accorded to the people under a free government. (Blacks Law 5th. Edit.)
	[1] One born free, one who has been freed from slavery.
	[2] In the feudal period, a freeholder, as distinguished from a villein. (Ballentines Law Dict. 3rd. edit.)
What is a villein	[1] A tenant of the lowest order in the feudal period.
	[2] Possessed by the lord of the manner, the same as one of a flock. (Ballentines Law Dict. 3rd. edit.)

Pages 328 and 329: *The Freemen newsletter, sent periodically to a mailing list of several thousand supporters and sympathizers throughout the United States.*

. What is a **lawful man**	[1] <u>**A freeman**</u>
	[2] A Man who can make oath and testify as a witness.
	[3] A man who has not been outlawed or attained.
	(Ballentines Law Dict. 3rd. edit.)
Antecedent	[1] Going before in time prior.
	[2] In grammar the noun to which a relative or other substitute refers.
	[3] Anterior
	[4] Preceding; as, an event antecedent to the deluge.
	(Noah Webster 1828)
Common Law	[1] In its broadest aspect the <u>common law</u> may be said to be the general Anglo-American system of legal concepts and the traditional techniques which <u>forms the basis of the law of the states which have adopted it</u>.
	[2] The common law of England, in its broadest significance is the basic component of the common law as adopted by the American courts.
	(Ballentines Law Dict. 3rd. edit.)
Public servant	[1] All municipal officers and employees are public servants for the purpose of determining the offense of obstructing a public servant as provided in M.C.A. 45-7-302 & 7-1-4138
Servant	[1] A person that attends another for the purpose of performing menial offices for him, or who is employed by another for such office or for other labor and is subject to his command.
	(Noah Webster 1828)
Compiler's comments	[1] A person or group of persons who perform the task of arranging statutes and codes in an order designed to facilitate their use i.e. delete obsolete and/or add new laws <u>authorized by the legislature</u>.(M.C.A. 1991 preface).
Code [i.e. <u>MCA codes</u>]	[1] **A secret to be revealed to a select few, <u>i.e. lawyers, judges, and politicians</u>.**

Our research of the C.D. ROM disk of the M.C.A. for March 1994 of the State of Montana and the M.C.A. code books, as well as the 1884, 1889, and the 1972 constitutions of Montana, Magna Charta, the constitution of the United States of America and the Uniform Commercial Code has led these writers to an understanding of these "codes" and the discovery of the willful, deliberate, deceitful and criminal acts, by certain lawyers, politicians, and public officers or public servants, of changing the wording, deleting words, inserting words, or deleting entire sections without legislative authority.

Due to time and space constraints we will cite only a few of the many examples that we have discovered: M.C.A. Sec. 46-6-411 official comment (by compiler's) " No change in the law except an <u>apparent error</u> R.C.M. 1947 Sec. 94-6025 was corrected by changing the word <u>unlawful to lawful</u>.

This change was done based on the <u>opinion of the compilers</u> without legislative sanction.

Another amazing discovery in the preface to the M.C.A. 1991 volume 1 page ii editorial changes. [1] punctuation; more tha. 125,000 commas were deleted "with no change in meaning but with clarity enhanced." [3] Grammatical construction: " There were only three types of corrections that were made often under this category; making a pronoun agree with its antecedent in number, gender, and person; changing **nor to or** and changing a verb to agree in number with the subject of a sentence. Again these changes were made by our public officers (hirelings) without any legislative sanction.

In brief, the lawmaking power (entrusted by the American national citizens to the legislative sector of government) is being conferred (unconstitutionally) upon executive appointees (hirelings). Exercise of this power has produced the clearinghouse "planning network" that is now over the entire U.S. of A., to force all independent units of local government under the dictatorship of the <u>United Nations New World Order.</u>

Keep in mind that the constitution for the United States of America shackled the federal government to the functions listed in the Constitution and reserved all other powers to the Sovereign states and the powers not specifically given to the States were reserved for the People.

Please duplicate and pass this letter on to a friend

Stay tuned.

Rodney O. Skurdal
Non Domestic Mailing Location
c/o 245 Johnny's Coal Road
Roundup, Montana state, U.S. of A.
["**without** the United States"]
"Non Domestic/Non Negotiable"

office of the sheriff
Attn. G. Paul Smith
Musselshell county office of the sheriff
Roundup, Montana state, U.S. of A.
["**without** the United States"]
"Non Domestic/Non Negotiable"   30 April, 1995
TO: G. Paul Smith, office of the sheriff, office of clerk, in care of Musselshell county court
         commissioners; and other private interested parties
United States of America   )
Montana state [organic]   ) ss. Common Law Affidavit
Musselshell county de jure   )
Re: <u>Common Law Affidavit by Rodney O. Skurdal in relation to actions committed by purported sheriff
         G. Paul Smith, i.e., "perjury of his public oath of office"</u>
G. Paul Smith; **"You asked for it, you got it"**
         G. Paul Smith, I had wrote up a twenty-four page letter, but I do not believe that you would read such, so I
have attempted to shorten it without addressing the many issues that I could have presented. Hopefully you will at
least read this letter and exhibits.
         In reference to your phone call on the 27<u>th</u> day of April, 1995, this letter is to refresh your memory in
regards to your official duties pursuant to your contract [i.e., **your** public oath of office] with 'We the People', i.e., in
relation to the parties of the contract.
         To start off with, I will attempt to refresh your memory to the first time we had our first face to face
contact, whereby your purported deputy Rusty Graff presented this Sovereign a 'traffic [commerce] ticket' some
time back; whereby you stated to this Sovereign, Rodney O. Skurdal, that; **'If I had a contract with you, I would
not honor it anyway.'** This was your first open admission of the common Law crime of **"perjury"** committed
before this Sovereign. G. Paul Smith, your **'public oath of office'** is in fact and in Law, a **'contract'** to **"<u>We the
People</u>"** of the Posterity. Principal vs. agent, i.e., Master vs. servant, i.e., People vs. public officers, by your own
by-laws UCC/MCA 30-1-103.
         The next important time that I recall, is in relation to the alleged/purported 'contempt' charges whereby I
was compelled to be a 'inmate in your house of prostitution', i.e., your own by-laws MCA 45-2-101 (29) and denied
many issues to show cause as to why I should not be held in 'contempt' of court by purported Robert E. Mihalovich
as witnesses by you, G. Paul Smith; whereby after your willful theft of a one hundred credit units, i.e., a purported
'one hundred dollar federal reserve note', whereby I demanded a true, correct and certified copy of your purported
booking sheet, whereby, you, G. Paul Smith, again threatened this Sovereign with the statement, via, your knowing,
willful and intentional **'perjury of your public oath of office'**, something to the effect, **"<u>Get the hell out of here
or I'll will</u> <u>trump</u> <u>up more charges against you and throw you back into jail</u>"**. Even with your answers to the
"Request for Admissions", in the federal case, you openly and willfully admitted to your actions of perjury of your
public oath of office.
         Per said phone call, you stated that you, G. Paul Smith, <u>did not need a 'performance bond' to hold office
as sheriff</u>, which is contrary to your public oath of office and your own by-laws, i.e., MCA statutes. See
exhibits/attachments 1 (affidavit) & 2 (your public oath of office). It comes down to this G. Paul Smith, no [fidelity]
bond, no lawful authority to hold office of the sheriff in Law. The following is from the de facto private copyrighted
MCA CD ROM, March 1994 disk, whereby <u>your own public oath of office</u> mandates a fidelity [bond], to wit:
". . . I will discharge the duties of my office <u>with fidelity</u>."
         [Article III, Section 3, constitution of the state of Montana, 1972.]
1994 MCA -- Special Session Edition   Section 3. Oath of office. Members of the legislature and all executive,
ministerial and judicial officers, shall take and subscribe the following oath or affirmation, before they enter upon
the duties of their offices: "I do solemnly swear (or affirm) that I will support, protect and defend the constitution of

Pages 330–332: *Three pages excerpted from a thirty-page bogus law-
suit filed against a sheriff in eastern Montana. Hundreds of such
harassing lawsuits were filed against local, state, and federal officials
in eastern Montana by the Freemen, and in dozens of other states by*

Musselshell county court
common law venue, Supreme Court
country of Montana

United States of America   )
Montana state { organic }   ) ss.   **Common Law Affidavit by Rodney O. Skurdal**
Musselshell county de jure)   **Criminal Declaration in Law; "Ex Parte"**

TO: office of county court clerk, in care of Musselshell county commissioners, Roundup, Montana state, United States of America; clerk of the 14th judicial district court, Musselshell county-court, Roundup, Montana state, United States of America; Attorney General of the state of Montana, Department of Justice, 215 North Sanders, Helena, Montana state, United States of America; Roundup Record and Tribune, 24 Main Street, Roundup, Montana state, United States of America; and the Billings Gazette, 401 North Broadway, Billings, Montana state, United States of America.

    I, Rodney O. Skurdal, a 'freeman character' and 'freeholder' in and for Musselshell county, Montana state, United States of America ["**without** the United States"], duly expatriated from within the [de facto] United States, by this special appearance, do hereby write this **Common Law Affidavit, Declaration in Law, in "good faith"**, by my Unalienable Right under my common law venue as secured by Article V, Section 26, of our Constitution of Montana, under our "republican form of government", Article IV, Section 4, of our national Constitution, with the protection against all second class 'citizens of the United States' [14th 'persons', 'subjects' and 'citizens of the United States'], via the 11th Amendment.

    This **Common Law Affidavit, Declaration in Law, being made in "good faith"**, is to again bring forth the corruption being committed against the good and lawful People in and for Musselshell county, which will put forth prima facie evidence that all of the county offices are vacated, except for the office of county treasurer.

    This is my second attempt to correct the **injustice** committed by our county officials/officers, in their knowing, willful and intentional acts of perjury of their public oaths of office, and an attempt to inform the general public that we, the so-called criminals, i.e., 'freemen characters', are being persecuted in our attempt to compel our 'public officers' to specific performance pursuant to their public oaths of office and their own by-laws, i.e., MCA statutes/codes/regulations/public policy or what ever you may wish to call them.

WARNING: A word of warning to any honorable news papers, that if you print this truth, our public officers will prosecute you for **"criminal syndicalism"**, for printing the truth for once, and some other off the wall criminal charges for giving aid and comfort to us alleged criminals, i.e., **"freemen characters"**, for printing the truth.

    I made an attempt about two years ago to bring this to the attention of our so-called 'honorable' district court judge Roy C. Rodeghiero, pursuant to the by-laws/statutes of the non registered private de facto corporation state of Montana, at MCA 2-9-513, whereby this sovereign, Rodney O. Skurdal, was told, before several witnesses and as a true and correct certified copy of said transcript, that Roy C. Rodeghiero, stated something to the effect, 'I will decide what laws will be enforced in my court.' By the statute, MCA 2-9-513, it was his, Roy C. Rodeghiero, duty to order the offices **"vacated"**, which he refused to do.

    In Law and by their own by-laws, MCA statutes, each and every state, county, city and/or town officer and/or official **"must"** be **privately bonded**, in order to hold any public office or they are acting without lawful authority, and any acts committed by them while occupying said office, would be acts of fraud and perjury of their public oaths of office. **"Ignorance of the law is no excuse!!!"**

    I have been to the county clerk and recorders office, Jane E. Mang, several times in the past three years, even with witnesses, so that she could never say that I was making this all up, demanding true and correct certified copies of the county officials public oaths of office and their **"Bond's"**, pursuant to the statutes herein contained.

    I have been repeatedly told by Jane E. Mang, and, yes, sometimes, by her deputy clerks, that they [clerk & recorder] **must** have all county officers/officials bonds recorded with that office, i.e., clerk & recorder.

    When I brought to her attention MCA 7-4-2619 (14) in the past, that the office of the clerk and recorder **"must"** have a book entitled **"Official Bonds"**, Jane E. Mang stated that she had no such book nor has the county commissioners furnished her with such a book.

Exhibit I

Page 1 of 14: Bond's   [bond.doc.C:\cdrom\bond]

militants trained at Freemen seminars. The lawsuits and phony liens against property have clogged the dockets of courts in twenty-two states in a reign of paper terrorism that is causing many states to change their laws.

This is only one issue, 'bonds', of the many, that we freemen characters have found, whereby, our public officers have violated their public oaths of office and/or statutes.}

"We Must obey God rather than men." Acts 5:29. Holy Scriptures; see 1st Kings, Chapter 18.

This Common Law Affidavit, Declaration in Law {Ex Parte}, of necessity, in Law, is true, correct and certain, being made in "good faith", and pursuant to MCA, Rules of Evidence, Rule "202 (b) (1) and (11) {notice the notary public seal, ". . . and of notary public."}, (d) "When mandatory", (1) of the common Law"; {see your own by-laws/statutes, MCA, Title 26, chapter 1, part 10; 26-1-1005, ". . . having a seal in such foreign country."; and "Again, you have heard it was decreed to the ancients, that you shall not perjure yourselves, but give up your vow to the Lord. But I tell you in short, Do not vow at all: not by heaven, for that is the throne of God; nor by the earth, because that is His footstool; nor by Jerusalem, for that is the city of the great King. Neither vow by your head, because you are not able to make a single hair white or black, But let your language be "Yes, yes; No, no; for whatever exceeds these proceeds from evil. "Matthew 5:33-37, Holy Scriptures, Ferrar Fenton. Title 28, U.S.C., § 1746 (1), {"without the United States"} "Non Negotiable."

teste meipso this 13th day of March, in the year of our Almighty Yahweh, through our Redeemer, "Yahshua"/"Emmanuel", 1995, A.D..

Notarial Acknowledgment:

Rodney O. Skurdal, "Coram Ipso Rege"
in care of 245 Johhny's Coal Road
Roundup, Montana state, United States of America
{"without the United States"} Non-domestic to the United States;
Non-resident to the state of Montana

Daniel E. Petersen, "Freeman character"
Attested and Acknowledged the above is true and correct in Law,
teste meipso this 13th day of March, 1995, A.D..

notary public Seal:

Rodney O. Skurdal, duly appointed, commissioned, empowered and privately bonded I, Rodney O. Skurdal, a de jure notary public in our country of Montana in the county aforesaid, hereby attest and acknowledge the freeman characters known to me as Rodney O. Skurdal and Daniel E. Petersen, did sign before me on this 13th day of March, Nineteen Hundred Ninety Five, A.D., this instrument entitled "Common Law Affidavit, Declaration In Law, Ex Parte", filed for record in our Musselshell county court in common law venue, original and exclusive jurisdiction.

Fees: _____ , Oath: _____ , Affidavit: _____1.00_____ ,
Postage: _____ , Mileage: _____ , Misc.: _____ .

"Blessed are those persecuted for righteousness' sake, for their is the kingdom of heaven."
"Blessed are you when men revile you and persecute you and utter all kinds of evil against you falsely on my account. Rejoice and be glad, for your reward is great in heaven, for so men persecute the prophets who were before you." Matthew 5:10-12.

Chain of Command
1. Almighty God, pursuant to His Holy Scriptures, creator of all good and evil;
2. Adam, i.e., White race of Man/Israel, God's chosen People;
3. We the People |Adam| of the Posterity, obedient to the Laws of Almighty God, a.k.a., our 'Common Law';
4. Constitution(s), [1] States' then, [2] National, with limited powers;
5. 'republican form of government', i.e., 'of the people'-'by the people'-for the people';
    a) legislative, executive & judicial offices; <u>pursuant to the Word of All Mighty God, i.e., "God, Son and Holly Ghost"</u>.
6. which created public offices filled by our 'public officials/servants'; either appointed or by election;
7. 14th Amendment, creation of second class of citizens,; and at the bottom of the chain,
8. corporations, persons, subjects and citizens of the United States, subject to its jurisdiction.

De jure county government
"America", i.e., 'United States of America', is the new Land of 'milk and honey', the new 'Zion', as contained in the Bible, [q.v.] in which Israel/Adam will never move from and its cities will not have walls around them, and the Land which Almighty God promised Israel.

God made <u>two covenants with Abraham</u>, or rather, one with Abram and the other with the same man after Almighty God changed his name to Abraham.

The first of these Covenants is in Genesis 17:1-8, the second in Genesis 22:16-18, whereby God states "By Myself have I sworn, ...", making this declaration of the covenant maker, "<u>unconditional</u>": "And the angel of the Lord called unto Abraham the second time and said, By myself have I sworn, <u>saith the Lord</u>, for because thou hast done this thing, and hast not withheld thy son, thine only son: that in Blessing I will bless thee, and in multiplying I will multiply thy seed as the stars of the heaven, and as the sand which is upon the sea shore; and thy <u>seed shall possess the gate of his enemies; and in thy seed shall all nations of the earth be blessed; because thou hast obeyed my voice</u>."

Matthew 22:32 states: "<u>I am the God of Abraham, and the God of Isaac, and the God of Jacob</u>"; notice that He is not a God onto the other races, but only that of Israel, the White Race, "Adam", for the Word of God was only given to Israel; "He showed His word ... His statutes and His judgments unto Israel. *He hath not dealt so with any nation: and as for His judgments, they have not known them.*" Ps. 147:19-20. "O children of Israel ... You only have I known of all the families of the earth." Amos 3:1-2. "... you shall be My own possession among all peoples; for all the earth is mine, and you shall be to Me a Kingdom of Priests and a Holy Nation. These are the words which you shall speak to the children of Israel." Exodus 19:5-6.

Emmanuel |Matthew 1:23 & Isaiah 7:14|, i.e., 'Jesus', repeatedly stated that He was "<u>only sent to the lost sheep of the House of Israel</u>", Matt. 15:24, Matt. 10:5-6, Ezek. 3:5. He did not come to save the other races nor the jews, a.k.a., Canaanites [*], the descendants of *Cain*, who were fathered by Satan: "They (jews) answered him, "Abraham is our father." "Emmanuel" (a.k.a., Jesus; Isaiah 7:14; Matt: 1:23.) said to them; "if you were of Abraham's children, you would do what Abraham did, but now you seek to kill me, ...You did what your father did. ... If God was your father , you would love me, . . . <u>You are of your father the devil</u>, and your will is to do your father's desires. <u>He was a murderer from the beginning, and has nothing to do with the truth, because there is no truth in him.</u>" John 8:39-47. Notice how Emmanuel let the 'jews' know who their father was, the devil, Satan; Cain and his descendants, who were fathered by Satan, and notice that the jews father was a murderer and a lier from the beginning, none other than 'Cain', killing the First Born of Adam, "Abel".

'*' "<u>Canaanites</u>", a.k.a., 'jews'; Notice what Emmanuel says to a Canaanite woman and what Emmanuel calls her in the following:

"And Jesus went away from there and withdrew to the district of Tyre and Sidon. And behold, a <u>Canaanite</u> woman from that region came out and cried, "Have mercy on me O Lord, Son of David; my daughter is severely possessed by a demon." But he did not answer her a word. And his disciples came and begged him, saying, "<u>Send her away</u>, for she is crying after us." He answered, "<u>I was sent only to the lost sheep of the house of Israel</u>." But she came and knelt before him, saying, "Lord, help me." And He answered, "It is not fair to take the

Page 1

Pages 333–335: Excerpts from the teaching text used in one of the training courses on white supremacy conducted by LeRoy Schweitzer during the Freemen seminars at Roundup and later at Justus Township.

two forms of government on the face of this earth; good vs. evil; white vs. black; **clean** vs. dirty; **light** vs. darkness; **Righteousness** vs. wicked; **Lawful** vs. unlawful; **right** vs. wrong; **God's Laws** vs. man made laws, etc., etc.; a.k.a./i.e., "**God** vs. Satan." Once you have applied for these benefits, via your 'application forms', i.e., 'social security card, drivers license, marriage license, etc., from your '**new gods**', [congress] you have voluntary become their new "**slaves**", to "**tax**" at their will; for you are no longer "**Free**", i.e, a 'freeman'.

Quasi-contracts/adhesion contracts **?**

Those who run to their public servants [Baal], asking for more **hand outs** at the costs of their fellow mans labor; "**You shall not steal.**" Exodus 20:15; see also verse 17, supra.; for has not **Almighty God [Emmanuel]** stated that **those who do not work, shall not eat,** II Thessalonians 3:10. **Is not the laborer worthy of his hire [just compensation],** Luke 10:7, etc., etc., etc., etc. ..., all under the purported new Baal's **humanism laws, 'those who take and keep on taking without working; a.k.a., "welfare'".**

What did 'Jesus', "Emmanuel", say about taxes on Israel?

""**What do you think, Simon? From whom do the kings of the earth take toll or tribute? From their sons or others[*]?**" And when he said, "**From others**," Jesus said to him, "**Then the sons are free.**" Matt. 17:25-26. [*] 'others', was used in this particular KJV Bible, yet some Bibles states 'strangers' or 'aliens', meaning those of the other races and/or from other lands 'residing' in our Land. If we the white race are God's chosen People, **formed from the earth,** and our Lord, God, stated that "**the earth is mine**" [q.v.], why are we paying taxes on "**His land**". Does not the Bible state that Almighty God gave us the new land of Zion, 'the land of milk and honey', that we would never move again, that has a border to the north and to the south by land, with a sea to the east and to the west, our "United States of America" [q.v.]. Why are you allowing "**your**" public 'servants' to tax His Land that He gave us, "We the People"/Adam/white race, "Citizens of Montana", pursuant to our "Preamble". Why have you thrown away your inheritance[**] from Almighty God, your land and i.e., your 'body', **for the earth [land] is mine, saith the Lord** [q.v.], and were we not "formed" from the dust of the earth/land? [**]inheritance see Article V, Section 26, of our Constitution of Montana, 1889.

We all know that there are three distinct and separate forms of government in this Great Nation called "**America**", i.e., the "United States of America"; each having a 'supreme court', by common knowledge and practice.

| 1| National | 2| state | 3| county |

In our "**republican form of government**" ['republican' **means** "**three**"] as contained within our National Constitution, **Article IV, Section 4,** i.e., it is a "**trinity** form of government", if you will, pursuant to the Word of Almighty God;

[1]God	[2]Son	[3]Holy Spirit"
[1]of the [white] People	[2]by the [white] People	[3]for the [white] People
[1]Judicial	[2]Executive	[3]Legislative
	[county governments= most being three voting districts/three grand divisions]	
[1]voting/district 1	[2]voting/district 2	[3]voting/district 3
[1]commissioner one	[2]commissioner two	[3]commissioner three
[1]supreme court justice 1	[2]supreme court justice 2	[3]supreme court justice 3
[1]district judge 1	[2]district judge 2	[3]district judge 3

The main problem is that 'We the People' [most] have abandon our de jure/God's county government, a.k.a. "church", contrary to the word of Almighty God, Amos 5:14-15, and that of our Constitution of Montana, Article V, Section 26 and of Article XX, Section 6; to wit: "Upon a change from Territorial to State government the seals in use by the supreme court and the Territorial district courts in and for the several counties respectively, shall pass to and become, until otherwise provided by law, the seals respectively of the supreme court and of the district courts of the State in such counties."

Most counties have three [some more] precincts, i.e., townships, whereby one county commissioner is either appointed or elected by the people of that precinct and/or township, sometimes called voting 'districts', i.e., 'probate/district courts', a/k/a the "three grand divisions". Each county commissioner of said precinct, i.e., township, are in fact a "supreme court justice" for said precinct, i.e., township and a probate/district judge for said precinct and/or township.

In addition to one county commissioner for each township/precinct, each township must have at least two justices of the peace pursuant to Article VIII, Section 20; "There shall be elected in each organized township of

"No white person born within the limits of the United States and subject to their jurisdiction...owes his status of Citizenship to the recent amendments to the Federal Constitution". Van Valkenburg v. Brown, 43 Cal. Sup Ct. 43.

A Citizen is not a "resident" of the corporation state of Montana, but is in fact a de jure Citizen in Montana state. The California Supreme Court has made a determination that the 14th Amendment was not intended to include, nor did it include the White People born within any of the several States of the union of States. Van Valkenburg v. Brown, (1872) 43 Cal. 43. This decision was rendered right after the alleged enactment of the 14th Amendment, this decision was upheld by the United States Supreme Court in the Slaughter House Cases, 83 U.S. (16 Wall.) 36, 21 L.Ed. 394; U.S. v. Susan B. Anthony, 24 Fed. 829. "It is quite clear, then, that there is a citizenship of the U.S. and a citizenship of a State, which are distinct from each other and which depend upon different characteristics or circumstances in the individual." Slaughter House Cases, 83 U.S. (16 Wall.) 36, 21 L.Ed. 394.

Title 42, United States Code, § 1981. "All persons within the jurisdiction of the United States are entitled to the same right in every state or territory to make and enforce contracts, to sue, to be parties, to give evidence, and to the full and equal benefit of all laws and proceedings for the security of persons and property as is enjoyed by white citizens, and must be subject to like punishment, pains, penalties, taxes, licenses, and exactions of every kind, and to no other."; and, Title 42, United States Code, § 1982. "All citizens of the United States have the same right, in every state and territory, as is enjoyed by white citizens thereof to inherit, purchase, lease, sell, hold, and convey real and personal property." Notice again the exclusion of the 'White Race/Citizens'; implying that the "white citizen" is not a 'person' nor a 'citizen of the United States'.

"'White person' as used in the constitution and statutes, has a signification, which ex vi termini excludes black, yellow, and all other colors. It is used in its generic sense, as including the Caucasian race and necessarily excludes all o 'ers." People v. Hall, 4 Cal. 399, 404; "The word 'white' as used in the United States naturalization laws, applied to the race referred as the "Caucasian race"." Takuji Yamashita, 70 P. 482, 483, 30 Wash. 234; "'Citizen' as used in Article I, Section 23, of the constitution, refers only to those who participated in the formation of the government or have a right to participate in its administration; and these include only white male citizens of the United States of the age of 21 years and white males of foreign birth of like age who have declared their intention under the acts of congress to become Citizens of the United States and have resided in this State six months. Thomasson v. State, 15 Ind. 449; "It is quite clear, then, that there is a citizenship of the United States and a citizenship of a State, which are distinct from each other and which depend upon different characteristics or circumstances of the individual." Slaughter house Cases, 19 How. 393, 418 [emph. add./mine]; "At the time of the adoption of the Preamble, the phrase "We the People" was known and understood to mean the People of the white Race and none other. The Preamble emanated from and for the people so designated by the words 'to ourselves and for our posterity'." Dred Scott v. Sanford, 19 How. 60 U.S. 393 [emph. add./mine]; ". . . But the language of the laws above quoted, shows that citizenship at the time was perfectly understood to be confined to the white race, and that they alone constituted the sovereignty in the government." Dred Scott v. Sanford, supra.

The day before the passage of the purported 14th Amendment, congress passed 15 United States Statute at Large, Ch. 249-250, pages 223-224, Sect 1, R.S. 1999; allowing the White Race/People/Citizens to expatriated from becoming subject to the new created second class of people under the 14th Amendment, in order to remain a de jure 'C'itizen of a sovereign State/People instead of becoming a second class 'citizen of the United States' subject to its jurisdiction. Title 18, USC § 1281, as supported by Briehl v. Dulles, 248 F 2d. 561, pp. 583, at footnote 21, [1957].

There is a clear distinction between United States and State citizenship, U.S., citizenship does not entitle citizen of the privileges and immunities of the Citizen of the State. K. Tashiro v. Jordan, 256 P. 545, 201 Cal. 239, 53 A.L.R. 1279, affirmed 49 S.Ct. 47, 278 U.S. 123, 73 L.Ed. 214, 14 C.J.S. Sec 2, p.1131, n. 75. In fact Black's Law Dictionary, 5th Addition, agrees with the distinction between different classes of citizenship: "privileges and immunities clause." "There are two Privileges and Immunities Clauses in the federal Constitution and Amendments, the first being found in Art. IV, and the second in the 14th Amendment, Sec. 1, second sentence, clause 1. The provision in Art. IV, Sec. 2, states that "The Citizens of each State shall be entitled to all Privileges and Immunities of Citizens in the several States," while the 14th Amendment provides that "No State shall make or enforce any law which shall abridge the privileges or immunities of citizens of the United States." pages 1078-1079. Note the lack of